The New England Cook Book

The Latest and the Best Methods for Economy and Luxury at Home

Collector's Edition
of the 1905 Classic,
with a New Foreword
by Annie B. Copps

Charleston   London

History
PRESS

Published by The History Press
Charleston, SC 29403
www.historypress.net

Copyright © (new material) 2007 by Annie B. Copps
All rights reserved

Originally published 1905 by Chas. E. Brown Publishers
The History Press edition 2007

Manufactured in the United Kingdom

ISBN 978.1.59629.400.4

Library of Congress CIP data applied for.

Foreword

There is always so much to glean from history. In the case of this fascinating cookbook written in 1905, the meticulous observations and instructions of Marion Harland, Miss M. Parloa, Mrs. D.A. Lincoln and Thomas J. Murrey, among other contributors, are both an entertaining collection of recipes (which quickly become stories in themselves) and a fascinating slice of life from just over one hundred years ago. Egg yolks are "yelks," there is not one, but two "mock turtle" recipes that require the scalding and cleaning of a calf's head (don't ask about the tongue) and everything is cooked over fire—live, wood-burning fire.

The original foreword from the cookbook comments on the difficulties of previous generations, declaring, "In no department of industry has the last century brought greater changes than in the department of housekeeping," and it is written from a perspective of how lucky the modern world is to have so many advancements. Imagine what Marion Harland and the other contributors would think of microwaves, trash compactors and vacuum sealers—let alone TV dinners, canned diet shakes and protein bars.

Yes, it is easy to poke fun, but this charming cookbook is also a bit of time travel, and it is a fun game to piece together a story from the words left to us. To follow one of the hundreds of recipes (which were clearly written with great care and affection for the reader) is an adventure in social observation. In referring to the use of a whole calf's head as an ingredient, the authors do so casually, in the same way a recipe today would call for one pound of ground meat. It is a mental journey to consider a young woman in 1905, in all her layers of skirting and foundation garments, going to market and lugging home a whole head of any large animal. Where would she store it? Refrigeration was not the six-foot-tall, double-sided stainless fridge of today.

As a food writer and editor of the twenty-first century, I deal with recipes that are written with as much attention to detail as possible—measurements, temperatures, equipment, timing, etc. must be clearly explained, and all recipes are tested repeatedly before they go to print. In *The New England Cook Book*, I love the ease and assumed knowledge of the instructions. Most recipes are a paragraph long and in most cases appear without specific measurement, instruction or cooking times. In general, the recipes rely on an assumption of the cook's knowledge.

We are indeed what we eat, and perhaps what our ancestors have eaten (and how they ate it). Savor this book as social history and as a glimpse at the timeline of how we and our cuisine have evolved.

Annie B. Copps
Senior Food Editor
Yankee magazine

NEW ENGLAND COOK BOOK

Marion Harland   Miss. M. Parloa

Mrs. D. A. Lincoln   Thomas J. Murrey

AND MANY OTHER AUTHORITIES

—

PRICE $2.00

THE NEW ENGLAND COOK BOOK

THE LATEST AND THE BEST
METHODS FOR
ECONOMY AND LUXURY AT HOME

CONTAINING

NEARLY A THOUSAND OF THE BEST UP-TO-DATE
RECEIPTS FOR EVERY CONCEIVABLE NEED
IN KITCHEN AND OTHER DEPART-
MENTS OF HOUSEKEEPING

CHAS. E. BROWN PUBLISHING COMPANY
PUBLISHERS
47 WINTER STREET, BOSTON

Oh! better no doubt is a dinner of herbs,

When season'd by love, which no rancor disturbs,

And sweeten'd by all that is sweetest in life

Than turbot, bisque, ortolans, eaten in strife!

But if out of humor, and hungry, alone

A man should sit down to dinner, each one

Of the dishes of which the cook chooses to spoil

With a horrible mixture of garlic and oil,

The chances are ten against one, I must own,

He gets up as ill-tempered as when he sat down.

OWEN MEREDITH.

TABLE OF CONTENTS.

GENERAL INDEX.

FOREWORD.

IN no department of industry has the last century
brought greater changes than in the department of
housekeeping. Then, the housekeeper was at the
head of, and the principal worker in, a manufacturing
plant in which was made nearly everything used by the
family. The housewife made with her own hands the
candles for lighting and the soap for cleaning. The
flax was taken as it came from the field and the wool as
it came from the sheep, and all the processes of spin-
ning, weaving, knitting, bleaching, dyeing and making
the cloth into clothes for all the members of the family,
and the linen for the table or bed, were carried on by
the women of the household. Then the housekeeper
took the grain as it came from the field and the fruit as
it came from the vine and tree, and attended to all the
steps by which it was converted into food.

To-day all this is changed. While food has still to
undergo some measure of preparation within the household, and while there are still a sufficiency of duties for
the housekeeper, the work has been greatly simplified
and made easier by the invention of many labor-saving
devices, appliances and processes.

In a civilized community the position of housekeeper
will always be first in importance to the well-being of
the family, and the duties of the housekeeper are coming more and more to be the spending of a definite
amount of money for a great variety of ready-prepared

articles, the most successful housekeeper being the one
who can spend the money to the greatest advantage.

Competition is daily becoming more strenuous and
the claims of manufacturers and dealers more pictur-
esque. The unscrupulous will adulterate their goods
and sell an inferior article for the sake of the larger
profit, and it is of the greatest importance to the housekeeper to know what are standard goods and where
they can be obtained. The housekeeper who is led to
spend money for inferior goods, or to deal with irre-
sponsible concerns, lowers the standard of living of the
whole family.

For this reason the publishers of THE NEW ENGLAND
COOK BOOK have introduced a department of " Supplies, Furnishings, etc.," which is a feature never before
attempted. We have investigated the claims of manufacturers of and dealers in goods that are used by the
housewife or the members of the family, and, having
satisfied ourselves as to the excellence of the goods
offered and the reliability of the manufacturers and
dealers, we have allowed them to state in their own way
their claims for recognition.

We can assure the readers of THE NEW ENGLAND
COOK BOOK that the articles here described are of the
highest quality as to material and manufacture, that the
individuals and firms here represented are of unques-
tioned reliability, and that the use of the goods here
described, or the patronage of the houses referred to,
will insure the certainty of getting the very best that the
market affords.

I.—THE ART OF COOKING.

THERE is a *science* and there is an *art* of cooking. The science tells what should be done and why; the art takes hold and does the thing, without, in most cases, knowing any reason why certain methods produce certain results. The one is theoretical, the other practical; the one deals with principles, the other with performances.

The science of cookery proceeds on the basis that man needs certain elements of repair and growth for the various tissues of his body, that these elements exist in nature in various forms, and that the mission of the cook is so to prepare these suitable substances that man may receive them in their most enjoyable and assimilable forms, and thus have his waste repaired and his growth provided for. This basis is solid. On it the whole culinary system is founded. But, from the merely utilitarian idea of repairing waste and supplying force, cookery rises to the supreme height of exquisitely delighting the taste while doing its most important work of feeding the body. Indeed, the art of cooking well, and of serving well-cooked victuals well, is "a fine art " in the best sense of the term. There are *artistes* in this line. Meals may be served artistically. They may become a delight to the most refined natures and a real benefaction to both body and soul.

The great aim of all cooking is to retain all the valuable elements of the food, and to put them into such forms as shall awake desire, stimulate digestion, and secure to the eater, in the readiest and most pleasing way, all the nutriment these viands afford. For instance, in cooking meats it is desirable to retain all the natural juices. To this end, when meat is to be boiled it should be plunged into hot water, which at once renders the outer part measurably impenetra-

ble, ana so confines the juices. On the other hand, if the
juices are to be drawn out for the production of soup, it
must be placed in cold water, and gradually warmed and
slowly boiled, so as to allow the exudation of the juices.
On the same principle, broiling and roasting, by quickly closing the surface of the meat, retain the juices as well as the
odors, and make the meat both juicy and savory. The re-
tention of the fatty substances renders such preparations
somewhat less digestible, however, than boiled food or lean
meat.

High art in cookery, as elsewhere, demands high rates of
expenditure. Instructions on that grade alone would not
meet the want of American homes. But high aims in this
department are equally commendable with high aims elsewhere. So important a factor in domestic economy as cooking cannot be ignored and should not be treated lightly.
Good food, well cooked and well served, goes far to make
home happy and its inmates healthy.

The chemical aspect of food and cooking may be left to
the chemist and the physiologist. They will perfect the
scientific aspects of the case. But the *art* of cooking, which
teaches just how and when to do the right things, is for us
to learn and to practice day by day. Such is the relation of
stomach and brain on the one side, and of stomach and
cook on the other side, that the cook becomes the sov-
ereign, to whom many a brain mightier than his own
bows in servile allegiance.

What cookery was practiced in the garden of Eden history does not tell. Vegetarians insist that permission to
eat animal food was not given until after the flood (Genesis
xi, 3, 4), when, by indulgence, man's appetites had become
abnormal. If vegetable food only were used in Eden, and
that mainly of the nature of fruits, but little cooking was
needed, and the simplest forms would suffice amply.

SOUPS

BLANK PAGE FOR ADDITIONAL RECIPES

GENERAL INDEX.

GENERAL INDEX.

GENERAL INDEX.

GENERAL INDEX.

GENERAL INDEX.

GENERAL INDEX.

THE NEW ENGLAND
COOK BOOK

II.—SOUP STOCK, SOUPS, ETC.

GENERAL SUGGESTIONS ON SOUP STOCK AND SOUP MEAT, HOW TO PREPARE THEM, HOW TO ENRICH THEM, THICKENING SOUP, COLORING SOUP, FLAVORING SOUP, ETC. THIRTY-FIVE RECIPES FOR SOUPS AND INCIDENTAL PREPARATIONS.

THE first and great essential to making good soup is *stock*, or good, fresh meat. To make stock, take the liquor left after boiling fresh meat, bones large or small, the large ones being cracked, that the marrow may be extracted, trimmings of meat, bones, and meat left over from a roast or broil, put any or all of these in a large pot or soup-kettle with water enough to cover them. Let them simmer slowly over a steady fire, keep the kettle covered, stir frequently, pour in now and then a cup of cold water, and skim off the scum. If it is fresh meat or bones, commence with cold water; if cooked, with warm water. Bones are as useful as meat in making stock, as they furnish gelatine. A quart of water is usually enough for a pound of meat. Six to eight hours will make stock fit for use. Let it stand over night, then skim off the fat, put the stock into an earthen jar, and it is ready for use.

Fresh meat should be freed from all superfluous skin and fat, which make a soup greasy, rather than rich.

The glutinous substance contained in the bones renders it important that they should be boiled with the meat, as they add to the strength and thickness of the soup. The meat, however, should be cut off the bone and divided into small pieces. Place in cold water over a gentle fire and boil by the long and slow process, that the essence of the meat may

35

be drawn out thoroughly. When it comes to the boiling point, throw in a little salt to assist the scum to rise; then skim carefully to prevent its becoming turbid. When no more scum accumulates, and the meat is softened so as to readily separate with the use of the fork, it should be strained, the vegetables put it, the seasoning done, and the necessary amount of hot water added if too much has boiled away.

All soup meats are better boiled the day before using, so as to allow the grease to chill over night, when it can readily be removed before putting over the fire again.

The following thickening is almost indispensable to all good soups: A tablespoonful or more of flour mixed to a smooth paste with a little water, and enriched with a teaspoonful of butter, or good beef drippings well stirred in. If it be necessary to add water to a soup, always use boiling water, as cold water injures the flavor. If making a rich soup that requires catsup or wine, let either be added just before the soup is taken from the fire.

Soup may be colored yellow by the use of grated carrots; red with the juice of tomatoes; green with the juice of powdered spinach; brown with carefully scorched flour, kept ready for use. Onions are thought by many to be a necessity in all soups—that their flavor must lurk somewhere, either defined or undefined. Their flavor may be much improved if fried until nicely browned in hot butter before being added to the soup. Potatoes should never be boiled with soup, because they add nothing to its flavor and are themselves injured by the long cooking. They should be boiled separately, and then added.

A most desirable quality in soup is that no one flavor predominate over the others, but, that by a careful blending of the different ingredients it shall contain and harmonize all flavors. Soups and broths should always be strained. It makes them more relishable as well as inviting to the eye. A slight acid, like lemon or tomato, gives a peculiar relish to some soups, as do many of the palatable condiments prepared by such manufacturers as **Skilton & Foote Co., D. & L. Slade Co.,** and several others, for this especial purpose. With such helps and a sufficient quantity of *stock* on hand, a choice, rich soup of any variety may be gotten up in thirty minutes.

RECIPES.

Beef Soup.—Boil a shin of beef, or a piece off the shoulder, slowly and thoroughly, the day before desiring to use it; skim well the next day and thin the jelly, if necessary, with water; add a little brandy, a grated carrot, two tablespoonfuls of butter rubbed smooth in brown flour, a little vermicelli, and spices to taste. Two or three eggs may be boiled hard, mashed smooth, and placed in the tureen before turning in the soup.

Beef Soup, No. 2.—Boil a shin of beef of moderate size, crack the bone, remove the tough outside skin, wash, and place in a kettle to boil with six or eight quarts of water. Let it boil about four hours, until it becomes perfectly tender, then take it out of the liquid. Add salt, one pint of tomatoes, two onions cut in small pieces, two turnips cut in quarters, one grated carrot, one large tablespoonful of sugar, a little sweet marjoram and thyme rubbed fine, one red pepper cut in very small pieces, also a celery top or a small quantity of bruised celery seed. This soup may be thickened according to taste either with vermicelli, macaroni, noodles, or drop dumplings.

For an incidental side dish, take the soup meat that has been cut from the bones, chop fine while warm, season with salt and pepper, add one teacup of soup saved out before putting in the vegetables. Pack in a dish, and slice down for tea or lunch when cold.

Beef Soup with Okra.—Cut a round steak in small pieces and fry in three tablespoonfuls of butter, together with one sliced onion, until very brown; put into a soup kettle with four quarts of cold water, and boil slowly an hour; add salt, pepper, and one pint of sliced okra, and simmer three and one-half hours longer. Strain before serving.

Corned Beef Soup.—When the liquor in which corned beef and vegetables have been boiled is cold, remove all the grease that has risen and hardened on the top, and add tomatoes and tomato catsup and boil half an hour—thus making an excellent tomato soup; or add to it rice, or sago, or pearl barley, or turn it into a vegetable soup by boiling in the liquor any vegetables that are fancied. Several varieties of soups may have this stock for a basis and be agreeable to the taste.

Ox-tail Soup.—Chop the ox-tail into small pieces; set on the fire with a tablespoonful of butter, and stir until brown, and then pour off the fat; add broth to taste, and boil gently until the pieces of tail are well cooked. Season with pepper, salt, and three or four tomatoes; boil fifteen minutes and then serve. This soup can be made with water, instead of the stock broth, in which case season with carrot, onion, turnip, and parsley.

Mutton Broth.—After the steaks have been cut from the leg, the lower part is just adapted for a soup. The neck-piece is also very nice. Boil the meat very gently in cold water, adding a turnip, a carrot, and a spoonful of rice. All the fat should be removed. Toward the last, add a little minced parsley. Dumplings are an excellent addition.

Vegetable Soup.—Take two pounds of shin of beef and two pounds of knuckle of veal; remove all the fat and break the bones and take out the marrow ; put into a pot with five pints of water ; add a teaspoonful of salt, and then cover and let it come to a boil quickly ; remove the scum that rises, and set where it will simmer for five hours ; one hour before serving, add two young carrots, scraped and cut in slices, half a head of celery, and a small onion cut into squares ; in half an hour add one turnip sliced, and in fifteen minutes one cauliflower broken in small pieces.

Bean Soup.—Soak one and a half pints of beans in cold water over night. In the morning drain off the water, wash the beans in fresh water, and put into soup-kettle with four quarts of good beef stock, from which all the fat has been removed. Set it where it will boil slowly but steadily for three hours at the least. Two hours before it is needed for use, slice in an onion and a carrot. Some think it improved by adding a little tomato. If the beans are not liked whole, strain through a colander and send to the table hot.

Black Bean Soup.—Three pounds soup bone, one quart black beans, soaked over night and drained ; one onion, chopped fine ; juice of one lemon. Pepper, salt, and Durkee's Challenge Sauce to taste. Boil the soup bone, beans, and onions together six hours ; strain, and add seasoning. Slice lemon and put on top when served.

Tomato Soup.—Take a knuckle of veal, a bony piece of beef, a neck of mutton, or almost any piece of meat you may happen to have ; set it over the fire in a small quantity of water, cover it closely, and boil very gently, to extract the juices of the meat. When nearly done, add a quantity of peeled tomatoes, and stew till the tomatoes are done ; add salt and pepper to your taste. This is a very cheap, healthful, and easily made soup.

Tomato Soup, No. 2.—Take one quart of tomatoes. When boiling, add one teaspoonful of soda, two pulverized soda crackers, one pint of hot water, one pint of milk, salt, and pepper; strain through a colander and serve hot.

Green Pea Soup.—Boil the empty pods of a half-peck of green peas in one gallon of water one hour; strain them out; add four pounds of beef cut into small pieces, and boil slowly for an hour and a half longer. Half an hour before serving add the shelled peas, and twenty minutes later half a cup of rice flour, salt, pepper, and a little chopped parsley. After adding the rice flour stir frequently so as to prevent scorching.

Dried Split Pea Soup.—One gallon of water, one quart of soaked split peas, half a pound of salt pork, one pound of beef. Put over the fire, seasoning with salt and pepper, celery salt, salpicant, curry powder, marjoram, or savory; let it boil slowly for two hours, or until the quantity of liquor does not exceed two quarts. Pour into a colander and press the peas through with a spoon. Fry two or three slices of stale bread in butter till brown, scatter them in the soup after it is placed in the tureen.

Corn Soup.—Cut the corn from the cob, and to a pint of corn allow one quart of hot water; boil an hour and press through a colander; put into a saucepan an ounce of butter and a tablespoonful of flour, being careful to stir well to prevent it being lumpy; then add the corn pulp, a little cayenne pepper, salt, a pint of boiling milk, and half a pint of cream.

Onion Soup.—Slice ten medium-sized onions and fry brown in butter with a tablespoonful and a half of flour; put into a saucepan, and stir in slowly four or five pints of milk and water (about one-third water); season to taste, and add a teacupful of grated potato; set in a kettle of boiling water, and cook ten minutes; add a cup of sweet cream and serve quickly.

Mock-turtle Soup.—Scald a calf's head and wash it clean; boil it in a large pot of water for half an hour, cut all the skin off, and take the tongue out. Take the broth made of a knuckle of veal, put in the tongue and skin, with one onion, half-ounce of cloves, half-ounce of mace, half a nutmeg, all kinds of sweet herbs chopped fine, and three anchovies. Stew till tender; then take out the meat, and cut it in pieces two inches square; cut the tongue, previously skinned, in slices; strain the liquor through a sieve; melt half a pound of butter in a stewpan; put in it half a pound of flour and stir it till smooth—if at all lumpy, strain it; add the liquor, stirring it all the time; then put to the meat the juice of two lemons, or one bottle of Madeira wine, if preferred; season rather highly with pepper, salt, and cayenne pepper; put in a few meat balls and eight eggs boiled hard. Stew gently one hour, and serve in a tureen; if too thick, add more liquor before stewing the last time.

Mock-turtle Soup. No. 2.—Take a calf's head and about two pounds of delicate fat pork. Put both into a soup-kettle, with two onions, sweet herbs, celery, pepper, and mace. Fill the kettle with water, and boil very gently till the meat is tender. Take out the head and the pork, return the bones of the head into the soup; let it stew several hours longer; and, when cold, take off the fat, strain the soup, and thicken; add the juice of a lemon and half a pint of white wine. Cut up the head and pork into pieces; warm them up in the soup, adding some choice meat balls made from finely minced, savory meat. The pork will be found quite an addition to the soup and a substitute for the fat of the turtle.

Gumbo Soup.—Cut up two chickens, two slices of ham, and two onions into dice; flour them, and fry the whole to a light brown; then fill the frying-pan with boiling water, stir it a few minutes, and turn the whole into a saucepan containing three quarts of boiling water; let it boil forty minutes, removing the scum. In the meantime soak three pods of okra in cold water twenty minutes; cut them into thin slices, and add to the other ingredients; let it boil one hour and a half. Add a quart of canned tomatoes and a cupful of boiled rice half an hour before serving.

Southern Gumbo Soup.—Cut up one chicken, and fry it to a light brown, also two slices of bacon; pour on them three quarts of boiling water; add one onion and some sweet herbs tied in a bag; simmer them gently three hours and a half; strain off the liquor, take off the fat, and then put the ham and chicken (cut into small pieces) into the liquor; add half a teacup of sliced okra, also half a teacup of boiled rice. Boil all half an hour, and just before serving add a glass of wine and a dozen oysters with their juice.

Julienne Soup.—Scrape two carrots and two turnips, and cut in pieces an inch long; cut slices lengthwise about one-eighth of an inch thick; then cut again, so as to make square strips; put them in a saucepan, with two ounces of butter, three tablespoonfuls of cabbage chopped fine, and half an onion chopped; set on the fire and stir until half fried; add broth as you wish to make thick or thin; boil until done; salt to taste; skim off the fat, and serve; it takes about two hours to prepare this soup properly. It can be served with rice or barley.

Macaroni or Vermicelli Soup.—Two small carrots, four onions, two turnips, two cloves, one tablespoonful salt, pepper to taste. Herbs—marjoram, parsley, and thyme. Put any cooked or uncooked meat and its bones in enough water to cover them; when they boil, skim them and add the vegetables. Simmer three or four hours, then strain through a colander and put back in the saucepan to reheat.

Boil one-half pound macaroni until quite tender, and place in the soup tureen, and pour the soup over it—the last thing. Vermicelli will need to be soaked a short time only—not to be boiled.

White Soup.—Boil a knuckle of veal for three hours. Add a quarter of a pound of macaroni, and when done, a pint of cream. Season with lemon-peel and mace.

Turkey Soup.—Take the turkey bones and boil three-quarters of an hour in water enough to cover them; add a little summer savory and celery chopped fine. Just before serving, thicken with a little browned flour, and season with pepper, salt, and a small piece of butter.

Chicken Soup.—To the broth in which chickens have been boiled for salad, etc., add one onion and eight or ten tomatoes; season with pepper and salt; add Challenge Sauce or Salpicant, if desired; boil thirty minutes; add two well-beaten eggs just before sending to the table.

Lobster Soup.—To boil a lobster, put it in a fish-kettle and cover it with cold water, cooking it on a quick fire. Remove the small bladder found near the head, and take out a small vein found immediately under the shell all along the back of the lobster, and use the rest. Two lobsters will make soup for six or eight persons, and salad also. All the under shell and small claws are pounded in a mortar to make the soup; when pounded, put it into a pan and set it on the fire with broth or water. The meat is cut in small pieces, to be added afterward. The soup is left on the fire to boil gently for half an hour; then put it in a sieve and press it with a masher to extract the juice. To make it thicker, a small piece of parsnip can be added and mashed with the rest into a pan, so that all the essence is extracted in that way from the lobster. When you have strained it put a little butter with it and add as much broth as is required; put some of the meat in the tureen and pour the soup over it.

Clam Soup.—Wash the clams free from grit; boil them in a pint of water till they will come from the shells easily. Take a small quantity of the liquor, add some milk, thicken it with a little flour, and add the clams. Split crackers are very nice added.

Portable Soup.—Boil a knuckle of veal, also the feet, a shin of beef, a cowheel or any other bones of meat which will produce a stiff jelly, in a large kettle, with as much water as will cover them. Let it stand a long time over the fire before it boils. Skim it most thoroughly, until the broth appears entirely clear. Then fill up the kettle with hot water, and boil it eight hours, or until it has evaporated so as to be somewhat thick. Run it through a hair sieve, set it in a cool place where it will harden very quickly. Skim off every particle of fat, and return it to a saucepan; skim and stir continually, so that it may not scorch, and all the previous labor be lost, until it becomes a very thick syrup. As soon as it can be no longer done in this way, transfer it to a deep jar, and set into a kettle of water, hot, but not boiling, until it jellies very thick. This will keep good many months, if packed dry in tin canisters. This is the concentrated essence of soup, and is a most convenient article of use, either at home in an emergency or in traveling, and especially at sea. To make a pint of soup, cut off a piece as large as a walnut, dissolve it in the boiling water, and it is ready for use.

Fluid Beef.—Among the advanced preparations of the day meat extracts are taking a high place. One of the finest of these preparations is " **Armour's** Fluid Beef." It contains all the nutritive constituents of the beef, and is readily available for soups, sandwiches, beef tea, etc. For medical uses, traveling, picnics, etc., it is very convenient. **To**

use for soups and beef tea, add a teaspoonful to a cup of boiling water and season to taste; or as a sandwich paste, it may be used on toast, with or without butter. Put up in cans of various sizes, from two ounces to one pound, which can be left open without injury to contents.

RECIPES INCIDENTAL TO SOUPS.

Meat Balls for Soup.—Take fresh cooked meat or fowl and chop fine; season with pepper, salt, and herbs, and a little lemon; mix together with an egg; roll in bread-crumbs, and fry in hot lard.

Browned Flour for Soups.—Dredge the bottom of a spider well with flour, and shake it over hot coals, letting it brown gradually, but not burn. Keep it in a dry place, in a tin canister, without wholly closing the lid. It is very convenient to have it already prepared, although when used fresh it is much nicer.

Home-made Noodles—a substitute for Vermicelli.—Wet with the yelks of four eggs as much fine, dry, sifted flour as will make them into a firm but very smooth paste. Roll it out as thin as possible, and cut it into bands of about an inch and a quarter in width. Dust them lightly with flour, and place four of them one upon the other. Cut them in the finest possible strips, separate them with the point of a knife, and spread them on the pie-board so that they may dry a little before they are used. Drop them gradually into the boiling soup, and in five minutes they will be done.

Drop Dumplings.—Take prepared flour, add a little beef drippings or lard, well rubbed through, and moisten to a soft dough. With floured hands pinch off very small pieces and form into balls by rolling in the palm of the hand. In boiling dumplings of any kind, put them in the water one at a time. If they are put in together they will blend with each other.

Clamcakes. — Fried bread crumbs for soups are pre-pared in this way : Cut slices of stale home-made bread half an inch thick, trim off all crust, and cut each slice into squares ; fry these in very hot fat ; drain them on a clean napkin, and add six or eight to each portion of soup. — *Thomas J. Murrey.*

Marrow Dumplings for Soups. — Grate the crust of a breakfast roll, and break the remainder into crumbs ; soak these in cold milk ; drain, and add two ounces of flour ; chop up half a pound of beef-marrow freed from skin and sinews ; beat up the yolks of five eggs ; mix all together thoroughly, if too moist add some of the grated crumbs ; salt and pepper to taste ; form into small round dumplings ; boil them in the soup for half an hour before serving. — *Thomas J. Murrey.*

Potage a la Reine. — Remove the fat from one quart of the water in which a chicken has been boiled. Season highly with salt, pepper and celery-salt, and a little onion if desired, and put on to boil. Mash the yolks of three hard-boiled eggs fine, and mix them with half a cup of bread or cracker crumbs soaked until soft in a little milk. Chop the white meat of the chicken until fine like meal, and stir it into the egg and bread paste. Add one pint of hot cream slowly, and then rub all into the hot chicken liquor. Boil five minutes, add more salt if needed, and if too thick add more cream, or if not thick enough add more fine cracker-dust. It should be like a purée. — THE BOSTON COOK BOOK: *Mrs. D. A. Lincoln. Roberts Brothers, Publishers.*

(Queen Victoria's Favorite Soup

FISH

BLANK PAGE FOR ADDITIONAL RECIPES

III. — FISH, OYSTERS, Etc.

HINTS CONCERNING FISH — HOW TO DRESS, HOW TO BOIL FISH,
HOW TO BAKE FISH, HOW TO BROIL FISH, HOW TO FRY FISH,
ETC. FIFTY-THREE RECIPES FOR COOKING FISH, OYSTERS, ETC.,
AND FOR INCIDENTAL PREPARATIONS.

RECIPES.

Broiled Shad.—Scrape, split, wash, and dry the shad on a
cloth; season with pepper and salt; grease the gridiron
well; as soon as it is hot lay the shad on to broil with the
inside downward. One side being well browned, turn it.
It should broil a quarter of an hour or more, according to
thickness. Butter well and send to table hot.

Baked Shad.—Many people are of the opinion that the
very best method of cooking a shad is to bake it. Stuff it
with bread-crumbs, salt, pepper, butter, and parsley, and
mix this up with beaten yelk of egg; fill the fish with it,
and sew it up or fasten a string around it. Pour over it a
little water and some butter, and bake as you would a fowl.
A shad will require from an hour to an hour and a quarter
to bake.

Halibut Cutlets.—Cut your halibut steaks an inch thick,
wipe them with a dry cloth, and season with salt and cayenne pepper. Have ready a pan of yelk of eggs well
beaten and a dish of grated bread-crumbs. Put some fresh

lard or beef drippings in a frying-pan and hold it over the fire till it boils. Dip your cutlets in the egg, and then in the bread-crumbs. Fry a light brown; serve up hot. Salmon or any large fish may be fried in the same manner.

Baked Cod or Halibut.—Use a piece of fish from the middle of the back, weighing four, five, or six pounds. Lay the fish in very cold salt-and-water for two hours; wipe dry; make deep gashes in both sides at right angles with the back-bone, and rub into these, as well as coat it all over with, a force-meat made of the crumbs, pork, herbs, onion, and seasoning, made to adhere by raw egg. Lay in the baking-pan and pour over it the drawn butter (which should be quite thin), season with the anchovy sauce, lemon juice, pepper, and a pinch of parsley. Bake in a moderate oven nearly an hour—or even more if the piece be large—basting frequently lest it should brown too fast. Add a little butter-and-water when the sauce thickens too much. When the fish is done, remove to a hot dish, and strain the gravy over it. A few capers or chopped green pickles are a pleasant addition to the gravy.

Boiled Halibut.—Take a small halibut, or what you require from a large fish. Put it into the fish-kettle, with the back of the fish undermost; cover it with cold water, in which a handful of salt and a bit of saltpetre the size of a hazel-nut have been dissolved. When it begins to boil skim it carefully, and then let it just simmer till it is done. Four pounds of fish will require half an hour nearly to boil it. Drain it, garnish with horse-radish or parsley. Egg sauce, or plain melted butter, are served with it.

Boiled Rockfish.—After the fish has been nicely cleaned, put it into a pot with water enough to cover it, and throw in salt in the proportion of half a teaspoonful to a pound of fish. Boil it slowly until the meat is tender and easily separates from the bones. A large fish will require an hour to cook. When done, serve on a hot dish, and have a few hard-boiled eggs, cut in thin slices, laid around it and over it. Eat with egg-sauce.

White Fish.—This fish may be broiled, fried, or baked. To bake it, prepare a stuffing of fine bread-crumbs, a little salt pork chopped very fine ; season with sage, parsley, pepper, and salt. Fill the fish with the stuffing, sew it up, sprinkle the outside with salt, pepper, and flour, and bake. In frying white fish, pour off the fat as it accumulates, as it is apt to be too fat when served.

Broiled Salmon.—The steaks from the centre of the fish are best. Sprinkle with salt and pepper, spread on a little butter, and broil over a clear but slow fire.

Smoked Salmon, Broiled.—Take a half pound of smoked salmon and parboil it ten minutes ; lay in cold water for the same length of time ; wipe dry and broil over a clear fire. Add two tablespoonfuls of butter while hot; season with cayenne and the juice of half a lemon; pile in a "log-cabin" square upon a hot plate, and serve with dry toast.

Boiled Salmon.—A piece weighing six pounds should be rubbed with salt, tied carefully in a cloth, and boiled slowly for three-quarters of an hour. It should be eaten with egg or caper sauce. If any remain after dinner, it may be placed in a deep dish, a little salt sprinkled over, and a teacupful of boiling vinegar poured upon it. Cover it closely, and it will make a nice breakfast dish.

Baked Salmon with Cream Sauce.—Butter a sheet of foolscap paper on both sides, and wrap the fish up in it, pinning the ends securely together. Lay in the baking-pan, and pour six or seven spoonfuls of butter-and-water over it. Turn another pan over all, and steam in a moderate oven

4

from three-quarters of an nour to an hour, lifting the cover, from time to time, to baste and assure yourself that the paper is not burning. Meanwhile, have ready in a saucepan a cup of cream, in which you would do well to dissolve a bit of soda a little larger than a pea. This is a wise precaution whenever cream is to be boiled. Heat this in a vessel placed within another of hot water; thicken with a heaping teaspoonful of corn-starch; add a tablespoonful of butter, pepper and salt to taste, a liberal pinch of minced parsley, and when the fish is unwrapped and dished, pour half the dressing slowly over it, sending the rest to table in a boat. If you have no cream, use milk, and add a beaten egg to the thickening.

Salmon Steaks or Cutlets Fried.—Cut slices from the middle of the fish one inch thick; wipe dry, and salt slightly; dip in egg, then in cracker crumbs; fry very quickly in hot butter; drain off every drop of grease, and serve upon a hot dish. Sprinkle green parsley in bunches over it. The French use the best salad-oil in this recipe instead of butter.

Pickled Salmon.—Soak salt salmon twenty-four hours, changing the water frequently; afterward pour boiling water around it, and let it stand fifteen minutes; drain off and then pour on boiling vinegar with cloves and mace added.

Fried Perch.—Scale and clean them perfectly; dry them well, flour and fry them in boiling lard. Serve plenty of fried parsley round them.

Fried Trout.—Wash, drain, and split; roll in flour, season with salt; have some thin slices of salt pork in a pan, and when very hot put in the fish and fry to a nice brown.

Stewed Trout.—Clean and wash the fish with care, and wipe it perfectly dry; put into a stewpan two tablespoonfuls of butter, dredge in as it melts a little flour, grate half a nutmeg, a few blades of mace, a little cayenne, and a tea-spoonful of salt; mix it all together; then lay in the fish, let it brown slightly; pour over some veal gravy, a lemon thinly sliced; stew very slowly for forty minutes; take out the fish, and add two glasses of wine to the gravy. Lay the fish on a hot dish, and pour over it some of the gravy. Serve the rest in a sauce-tureen.

Fried Catfish.—Catfish must be cooked quite fresh—if possible, directly out of the water. The larger ones are generally coarse and strong; the small-sized fish are the best. Wash and clean them, cut off their heads and tails, remove the upper part of the backbone near the shoulders, and score them along the back with deep gashes or incisions. Dredge them with flour, and fry them in plenty of lard, boiling fast when the catfish are put into the pan. Or you may fry them in the drippings or gravy saved from roast beef or veal. They are very nice dipped in a batter of beaten egg and grated bread-crumbs, or they may be done plain, though not in so nice a way, with Indian meal instead of bread-crumbs. Drain off the lard before you dish them. Touch each incision or cut very slightly with a little cayenne before they go to table.

Fried Eels.—After skinning, emptying, and washing them as clean as possible, cut them into short pieces, and dry them well with a soft cloth. Season them with fine salt and cayenne, flour them thickly, and fry them in boiling lard; when nicely browned, drain and dry them, and send to the table with plain melted butter and a lemon, or with fish-sauce. Eels are sometimes dipped into batter and then fried, or into egg and dried bread-crumbs, and served with plenty of crisped parsley

Fish Chowder.—Take a fresh haddock, of three or four pounds, clean it well, and cut in pieces of three inches square. Place in the bottom of your dinner-pot five or six slices of salt pork, fry brown, then add three onions sliced thin, and fry those brown. Remove the kettle from the fire, and place on the onions and pork a layer of fish. Sprinkle over a little pepper and salt, then a layer of pared and sliced potatoes, a layer of fish and potatoes, till the fish is used up. Cover with water, and let it boil for half an hour. Pound six biscuits or crackers fine as meal, and pour into the pot; and, lastly, add a pint of milk; let it scald well, and serve.

New England Chowder.—Take a good haddock, cod, or any other solid fish, cut it in pieces three inches square; put a pound of fat, salt pork, cut into strips, into the pot; set it on hot coals and fry out the grease; take out the pork, but leave the grease in the bottom of the pot, and put in a layer of fish, over that a layer of sliced onions, over that a layer of fish, with slips of the fried pork, then another layer of onions and a few sliced raw potatoes, and so on alternately until your fish is all in; mix some flour with as much water as will fill the pot; season to suit your taste, and boil for half an hour; have ready some pilot bread, soaked in water, and throw them into your chowder five minutes before taking off; serve in a tureen.

Fish-balls.—Two cupfuls cold boiled codfish, fresh or salted. Chop the fish when you have freed it of bones and skin; work in one cupful of mashed potatoes, and moisten with a half cup of drawn butter with an egg beaten in. Season to taste. Have them soft enough to mold, yet firm enough to keep in shape. Roll the balls in flour, and fry quickly to a golden-brown in lard or clean dripping. Take from the fat so soon as they are done; lay in a colander or sieve and shake gently, to free them from every drop of grease. Turn out for moment on white paper to absorb any lingering drops, and serve on a hot dish.

Lobster Chowder. — Meat of one fine lobster, picked out from the shell and cut into bits, one quart of milk, six Boston crackers split and buttered, one even tea-spoonful of salt, one scant quarter-teaspoonful of cayenne, two tablespoonfuls of butter rolled in one of prepared flour, a pinch of soda in the milk. Scald the milk, and stir in seasoning, butter, and flour, cook one minute, add the lobster, and simmer five minutes. Line a tureen with the toasted and buttered crackers, dipping each quickly in boiling water before putting it in place, and pour in the chowder. — *Marion Harland.*

Clam Scallops. — Chop fifty clams fine, and drain off in a colander all the liquor that will come away. Mix this in a bowl with a cupful of crushed cracker, half a cupful of milk, two beaten eggs, a tablespoonful melted butter, half a teaspoonful of salt, a pinch of mace and the same of cayenne pepper. Beat into this the chopped clams and fill with the mixture, clam-shells, or the silver or stone-china shell-shaped dishes sold for this purpose. Bake to a light brown in a quick oven and serve in the shells. Serve with sliced lemon. — *Marion Harland.*

Little Pigs in Blankets. — Season large oysters with salt and pepper. Cut bacon in very thin slices; wrap an oyster in each slice, and fasten with a little wooden skewer. Heat a frying-pan and put in the "little pigs." Cook just long enough to crisp the bacon. Place on slices of toast that have been cut into small pieces and serve immediately. Do not remove the skewers. This is a nice relish for lunch or tea; and, garnished with parsley, is a pretty one. The pan must be very hot before the "pigs" are put in. Great care must be taken that they do not burn.—NEW COOK BOOK: *Miss Maria Parloa. Estes & Lauriat, Publishers.*

Roasted Oysters.—Take oysters in the shell; wash the shells clean, and lay them on hot coals ; when they are done they will begin to open.   Remove the upper shell, and serve the oysters in the lower shell, with a little melted butter poured over each, and season to taste.

Oyster Toast.—Select fifteen plump oysters; mince them, and season with mixed pepper and a pinch of nutmeg ; beat the yelks of four eggs and mix them with half a pint of cream.   Put the whole into a saucepan and set it over the fire to simmer till thick ; stir it well, and do not let it boil, lest it should curdle.   Toast five pieces of bread, and butter them ; when your dish is near the boiling-point, remove it from the fire and pour it over the toast.

Cream Oysters.—Fifty shell oysters, one quart sweet cream ; butter, pepper, and salt to suit taste.   Put the cream and oysters in separate kettles to heat, the oysters in their own liquor, and let them come to a boil ; when sufficiently cooked, skim ; then take them out of the liquid and put them into a dish to keep warm.   Put the cream and liquid together.   Season to taste, and thicken with powdered cracker.   When sufficiently thick, stir in the oysters.

Broiled Oysters.—Drain select oysters in a colander.   Dip them one by one into melted butter, to prevent sticking to the gridiron, and place them on a wire gridiron.   Broil over a clear fire.   When nicely browned on both sides, season with salt, pepper, and plenty of butter, and lay them on hot buttered toast, moistened with a little hot water.   Serve very hot.   Oysters cooked in this way and served on broiled beefsteak are delicious.

Fried Oysters.—Select the largest and finest fresh oysters, put them into a colander and pour over a little water to rinse them ; then place them on a clean towel and dry them. Have ready some grated bread-crumbs seasoned with pepper and salt, and plenty of yelk of egg beaten till very light; and to each egg allow a large teaspoonful of rich cream or of the best fresh butter. Beat the egg and cream together. Dip each oyster first into the egg and cream, and then into the crumbs. Repeat this twice, until the oysters are well coated all over. Have ready boiling, in a frying-pan, an equal mixture of fresh butter and lard. It must very nearly fill the frying-pan, and be boiling fast when the oysters go in, otherwise they will be heavy and greasy. Fry them of a yellow brown on both sides, and serve hot.

Oyster Salad, see Salads.

Spiced or Pickled Oysters.—Put into a porcelain kettle one hundred and fifty large oysters with the liquor; add salt, and simmer till the edges roll or curl; skim them out; add to the liquor one pint of white wine vinegar, one dozen blades mace, three dozen cloves, and three dozen peppercorns; let it come to a boil, and pour over the oysters. Serve with slices of lemon floating in saucer.

Oyster Omelette.—Allow for every six large oysters or twelve small ones one egg; remove the hard part and mince the rest very fine; take the yelks of eight eggs and whites of four, beat till very light, then mix in the oysters; season and beat up thoroughly; put into a skillet a gill of butter, let it melt; when the butter boils, skim it and turn in the omelette; stir until it stiffens; fry light brown; when the under side is brown, turn on to a hot platter. To brown the upper side, hold a red-hot shovel over it.

Scalloped Oysters, No. 1.—Open the shells, setting aside for use the deepest ones. Have ready some melted butter, *not* hot, seasoned with minced parsley and pepper. Roll each oyster in this, letting it drip as little as may be, and lay in the shells, which should be arranged in a baking-pan. Add to each a little lemon juice, sift bread-crumbs over it, and bake in a quick oven until done.   Serve in the shells.

Scalloped Oysters, No. 2.—Cover the bottom of a baking-dish (well buttered) with a layer of crumbs, and wet these with cream, put on spoonful by spoonful.   Pepper and salt, and strew with minute bits of butter.   Next, put in the oysters, with a little of their liquor.   Pepper them, stick bits of butter in among them, and cover with dry crumbs until the oysters are entirely hidden.   Add more pieces of butter, very small, and arrange thickly on top.   Set in the oven, invert a plate over it to keep in the flavor, and bake until the juice bubbles up to the top.   Remove the cover, and brown on the upper grating for two or three minutes.   Serve in the bake-dish.

Oyster Pie.—Line a dish with a puff paste or a rich biscuit paste, and dredge well with flour; drain one quart of oysters; season with pepper, salt, and butter, and pour into the dish; add some of the liquor; dredge with flour, and cover with a top crust, leaving a small opening in the centre.   Bake in a quick oven.

Oyster Patties.—Put one quart of oysters in a saucepan, with liquor enough to cover them, set it on the stove and let them come to a boil; skim well, and stir in two table-spoonfuls of butter, a little pepper, and salt.   Line some patty-pans with puff-paste, fill with oysters, cover with paste, and bake twenty minutes in a hot oven.   The upper crust may be omitted, if desired.

Oyster Macaroni.—Boil macaroni in a cloth to keep it straight.   Put a layer in a dish seasoned with pepper, salt, and butter, then a layer of oysters, until the dish is full. Mix some grated bread with a beaten egg, spread over the top, and bake.

Oyster Sauce, see Sauces.

Boiled Lobster.—If purchased alive, lobsters should be chosen by weight (the heaviest are the best) and their liveliness and briskness of motion. When freshly boiled they are stiff, and their tails turn strongly inward; when the fish appear soft and watery, they are stale. The flesh of the male lobster is generally considered of the finest flavor for eating, but the hen lobster is preferred for sauce and soups, on account of the coral.

To properly boil lobsters, throw them living into a kettle of fast-boiling salt and water, that life may be destroyed in an instant. Let them boil for about half an hour. When done, take them out of the kettle, wipe them clean, and rub the shell with a little salad-oil, which will give a clear red appearance. Crack the large claws without mashing them, and with a sharp knife split the body and tail from end to end. The head, which is never eaten, should also be separated from the body, but laid so near it that the division is almost imperceptible. Dress in any way preferred.

Deviled Lobster.—Procure a live, heavy lobster; put it in a pot of boiling water, with a handful of salt to it. When done and cold, take out all the meat carefully, putting the fat and coral on separate plates; cut the meat in small pieces, rub the coral to a paste; stir the fat in it, with a little salt, cayenne, chopped parsley, essence of anchovies, and salad-oil, or melted butter and lemon juice; cut the back of the lobster-shell in two, lengthwise; wash clean; stir the lobster and sauce well together; fill the shells; sprinkle bread-crumbs and a few bits of butter over the top; set in the oven until the crumbs are brown.

Stewed Lobster.—A middling-sized lobster is best; pick all the meat from the shells and mince it fine; season with a little salt, pepper, and grated nutmeg; add three or four spoonfuls of rich gravy and a small bit of butter. If you

have no gravy, use more butter and two spoonfuls of
vinegar; stew about twenty minutes.

Lobster Salad, see Salads.

Lobster Croquettes, see Croquettes.

Lobster Sauce, see Sauces.

Lobster Patties.—Proceed as in oyster patties, but use the
meat of a cold boiled lobster.

Terrapins.—Put the terrapins into a pot of boiling water,
where they must remain until they are quite dead. You
then divest them of their outer skin and toe-nails; and,
after washing them in warm water, boil them again until
they become quite tender, adding a handful of salt to the
water. Having satisfied yourself of their being perfectly
tender, take off the shells and clean the terrapins very carefully, removing the sandbag and gall without by any means
breaking them. Then cut the meat into small pieces and put
into a saucepan, adding the juice which has been given out
in cutting them up, but *no water*, and season with salt, cayenne, and black pepper to your taste, adding a quarter of
a pound of good butter for each terrapin and a handful of
flour for thickening. After stirring a short time, add four
or five tablespoonfuls of cream, and a half pint of good
Maderia to every four terrapins, and serve hot in a deep
dish. A very little mace may be added and a large tablespoonful of mustard; just before serving, add the yelks of
four hard-boiled eggs. During the stewing, particular
attention must be paid to stirring the preparation frequently;
and terrapins cannot possibly be served too hot.

Mock Terrapin.—Take half a calf's liver, season and fry it
brown; chop it into dice, not too small; flour it thickly,
and add a teaspoonful of mixed mustard, a little cayenne
pepper, two hard-boiled eggs chopped fine, a lump of but-

ter the size of an egg, and a teacupful of water. Let it boil a minute or two. Cold veal will do as well as liver.

Scalloped Crabs.—Put the crabs into a kettle of boiling water, and throw in a handful of salt. Boil from twenty minutes to half an hour. Take them from the water when done and pick out all the meat; be careful not to break the shell. To a pint of meat put a little salt and pepper; taste, and if not enough add more, a little at a time, till suited. Grate in a very little nutmeg, and add one spoonful of cracker or bread crumbs, two eggs well beaten, and two tablespoonfuls of butter (even full); stir all well together; wash the shells clean, and fill each shell full of the mixture; sprinkle crumbs over the top and moisten with butter, then bake until nicely browned on top.

Soft-shell Crabs.—Season with pepper and salt; roll in flour, then in egg, then in bread-crumbs, and fry in hot lard. Serve hot with rich condiments.

Stewed Clams.—Chop the clams and season with pepper and salt; put in a saucepan butter the size of an egg, and when melted add a teaspoonful of flour; add slowly the clam liquor and then the clams, and cook three minutes; then add half a pint of cream, and serve.

Deviled Clams.—Chop fifty clams very fine; take two tomatoes, one onion chopped equally fine, a little parsley, thyme, and sweet marjoram, a little salt, pepper, and bread-crumbs, adding the juice of the clams until the mixture is of the consistency of sausage; put it in the shells with a lump of butter on each; cover with bread-crumbs, and bake one-half hour.

Clam Chowder.—Forty-five clams chopped, one quart of sliced potatoes, one-half pint sliced onions. Cut a few slices salt pork, fry to a crisp, chop fine. Put in kettle a little fat from the pork, a layer of potatoes, clams, onions, a little pepper and salt; another layer of chopped pork, potatoes, etc., until all are in. Pour over all the juice of the clams. Cook three hours, being careful not to burn. Add a teacupful of milk just before serving.

Scallops.—Wipe dry; dip separately into seasoned egg, then into cracker dust, and fry in hot lard.

RECIPES INCIDENTAL TO FISH.

Bread Stuffing for Fish.—Take about half a pound of stale bread and soak in water, and when soft press out the water; add a very little chopped suet, pepper, salt, a large tablespoonful of onion minced and fried, and, if preferred, a little minced parsley; cook a trifle, and after removing from the fire add a beaten egg.

Bread Stuffing, No. 2.—Bread-crumbs with a little chopped parsley and pork, salt, pepper, and butter. Fill up the fish, sew it closely, then bake.

Cleaning a Shad.—Scale and scrape it carefully; split it down the back and remove the contents, reserving the roe or melt. Wash well and cook as desired.

Soaking Salt Fish.—Very salt fish should be soaked several hours in three or four changes of warm water. Place the skin side up, so that salt crystals may fall away from the under or meat side. Wipe carefully and clean, then soak for an hour in very cold water.

Fish in Season.—As a rule, fish are in best condition just before they spawn, and many are so while they are full of roe, as smelts, mackerel, and shad. As soon as spawning is over, they become unfit for food, some of them becoming positively unwholesome. In season, the flesh is firm and it boils white; when it boils to a bluish hue, the fish are not in season, or are stale.

POULTRY

BLANK PAGE FOR ADDITIONAL RECIPES

IV.—POULTRY AND GAME.

GENERAL REMARKS ON POULTRY AND GAME—HOW TO SELECT, PREPARATION FOR BOILING, FOR ROASTING, ETC. THIRTY-ONE RECIPES FOR POULTRY AND GAME.

RECIPES.

Roast Turkey.—A young turkey, weighing not more than eight or nine pounds, is the best. Wash and clean thoroughly, wiping dry, as moisture will spoil the stuffing. Take one small loaf of bread grated fine, rub into it a piece of butter the size of an egg, one small teaspoonful of pepper and one of salt; a sprinkling of sweet marjoram, summer savory, or sage, if liked. Rub all together, and fill the turkey, sewing up so that the stuffing cannot cook out. Always put the giblets under the side of the fowl, so they will not dry up. Rub salt, pepper, and butter on the outside; put into dripping-pan with one teacupful of water, basting often, turning the fowl till brown all over; bake about two hours; take out the giblets and chop fine. After taking out the turkey, put a large tablespoonful of flour into the pan and stir until brown. Put the giblets into a gravy-boat, and pour over them the gravy.

Boiled Turkey.—Stuff the turkey as for roasting. A very nice dressing is made by chopping half a pint of oysters and mixing them with bread-crumbs, butter, pepper, salt, thyme, and wet with milk or water. Baste about the turkey a thin cloth, the inside of which has been dredged with flour, and put it to boil in cold water with a teaspoonful of salt in it. Let a large turkey simmer for three hours; skim while boiling. Serve with oyster sauce, made by adding to a cupful of the liquor in which the turkey was boiled the same quantity of milk and eight oysters chopped fine; season with minced parsley; stir in a spoonful of rice or wheat flour wet with cold milk; a tablespoonful of butter. Boil up once and pour into a tureen.

Boned Turkey.—Boil a large turkey in as little water as possible until the meat falls from the bones; remove all the bones and skin; pick the meat into small pieces, and mix dark and light together; season with pepper and salt; put into a mold and pour over it the liquor, which must be kept warm, and press with a heavy weight.

Roast Chicken.—Having selected your chickens in view of the foregoing hints, proceed, in the matters of cleansing, filling, and preparing for the oven, precisely as directed in the case of roast turkey. As the roasting goes on, baste and turn as may be needful to secure a rich brown all over the fowls. Prepare the gravy as in the former case.

Stewed Chicken.—Clean and cut the chicken into joints; put it in a saucepan with the giblets; stew in just enough water to cover it until tender; season with pepper, salt, and butter; thicken with flour; boil up once and serve with the gravy poured over it.

Broiled Chicken.—Only young, tender chickens are nice broiled. After cleaning and washing them, split down the back, wipe dry, season with salt and pepper, and lay them inside down on a hot gridiron over a bed of bright coals. Broil until nicely browned and well cooked through, watching and turning to prevent burning. If chickens are large, steaming them for one-half hour before placing on the gridiron will better insure their being cooked through.

Chicken Souffle. — Take the white meat of one chicken, remove all skin and sinews, chop very fine. Put the chopped meat in a skillet or stew-pan, add some white sauce, a little chopped parsley; salt and pepper to taste; stir it until it boils; allow it to cool a little; add yolks of three eggs beaten to a froth, and stir well. Turn into a baking-dish or mould which has been well buttered and the bottom covered with fine cracker crumbs. Bake in a very quick oven. Serve with white sauce.

Chicken Patties. — Prepare crusts in the same way as for tarts. Boil the chicken until tender. Chop the meat, but not too fine. Make a gravy out of the water in which the chicken was boiled by adding a half-cupful of flour and two teaspoonfuls of butter to a quart of water. Season with pepper and salt to taste; put the chopped chicken into the gravy, and boil for five minutes, and fill the crusts with it. Don't have the filling too thin. Serve at once.

Potted Pigeon. — Clean the birds and then stuff them with a dressing proportioned in following recipe. Sew them up and truss them; boil them for half an hour with just water enough to cover them; take them out and drain; roll in flour and fry brown in pork fat; make a gravy out of the liquid in which they were boiled, thickened with flour and seasoned to taste; let the pigeons simmer in this gravy for two hours; serve with the gravy.

Poultry Dressing. — Toast eight slices of white bread; place in a deep dish, add butter the size of an egg, cover with hot water to melt butter and make bread of right consistency; add one even teaspoonful of **Bell's Spiced Seasoning** and one even teaspoonful of salt; mix well and stir in one or two raw eggs.

Fricasseed Chickens.—Cut them in pieces, and put in the stewpan with salt and pepper; add a little water, and let them boil half an hour; then thicken the gravy with flour; add butter and a little cream, if you have it. Catsup is an additional relish to the gravy.

Smothered Chicken.—Dress your chickens; wash and let them stand in water half an hour to make them white; cut them open at the back; put into a baking-pan, sprinkle salt and pepper over them, putting a lump of butter here and there; cover tightly with another pan the same size, and bake one hour; baste often with butter.

Fried Chicken.—Prepare the chicken as for stewing; dry it, season with salt and pepper, dredge with flour, and fry brown in hot butter or lard; take it out, drain, and serve with Challenge Sauce, or some other savory condiment, or pour into the gravy left in the frying-pan a cup of milk, thicken with flour, add a little butter, and season with Salpicant; boil once and pour over the chicken, or serve separately.

Chickens Fried with Rice.—Take two or three chickens, cut them up, and half fry them; then boil half a pint of rice in a quart of water, leaving the grains distinct, but not too dry; stir one large tablespoonful of butter in the rice while hot; let five eggs be well beaten into the rice, with a little salt, pepper, and nutmeg, if the last is liked; put the chickens into a deep dish, and cover with the rice; brown in an oven not too hot.

Chicken Pie.—Line the sides of a deep pie-dish with a good puff paste. Have your chicken cooked, as for a fricassee, seasoned with salt and pepper and a little chopped parsley. When they are nearly cooked, lay them in a pie-dish with half a pound of salt pork cut into small squares, and some of the paste also cut into half-inch pieces; pour in a part of the chicken gravy, thicken with a little flour, and cover the dish with the paste cover. Cut a hole the size of a dollar in the cover, and cover it with a piece of dough. When baking, remove this piece occasionally and examine the interior. Brush egg over the top crust of the pie, and bake in a quick oven. Should the pie become dry pour in more of the gravy. Pigeon pie or any other bird pie may be made by the above recipe.

Chicken Pot-pie.—Cut and joint a large chicken. Cover with water, and let it boil gently until tender. Season with salt and pepper, and thicken the gravy with two tablespoonfuls of flour mixed smooth in a piece of butter the size of an egg. Have ready nice, light bread dough; cut with a biscuit-cutter about an inch thick; drop this into the boiling gravy, having previously removed the chicken to a hot platter; cover, and let them boil from one-half to three-quarters of an hour. To ascertain whether they are done, stick them with a fork; if it comes out clean, they are done. Lay them on the platter with the chicken, pour over the gravy, and serve.

Pressed Chicken.—Boil three chickens until the meat comes off the bones; then, removing all bones and skin, chop the meat, but do not chop very fine; add a piece of butter as large as an egg; salt and pepper to season well. Take about a pint of the broth in which the chickens were boiled, into which put one-half a box of **Swampscott Sparkling Gelatine**; when the gelatine has dissolved, put back the chopped chicken and cook until the broth is evenly absorbed. Pour the whole into a mould or pan and press under a weight until cold. When ready, serve with sliced hard-boiled eggs and garnish with parsley, water-cress or sliced lemon. Veal may be treated in a similar manner.

Jellied Chicken. — Cook a chicken in boiling water until tender, remove skin and bones, and season to taste, and place in mould. Place the bones back in the liquid and boil until there is about one quart of liquid left. Add one-quarter box **Swampscott Sparkling Gelatine** and the juice of one lemon; salt and pepper to taste; strain over the chicken and stand in cool place to harden.

Roast Goose and Duck.—A goose should always be par-boiled, as it removes the rank taste and makes it more palatable. Clean, prepare, and roast the same as turkey, only adding to the force-meat a large onion chopped fine. Ducks do not require parboiling (unless very old), otherwise they are cooked the same as geese.

Canvas-back Duck.—Having picked, singed, and drawn it well, wipe it carefully, so as to have it clean without wash-ing. Truss it, leaving the head on, to show its quality. Place it in a moderately hot oven for at least three-quarters of an hour; serve it hot, in its own gravy, on a large chafing-dish. Currant jelly should be on the table.

Roast Pigeons.—Clean, wash, and stuff the same as poultry; lay them in rows in a dripping-pan with a little water. Unless they are very fat, baste with butter until they are half done, afterward with their own gravy.

Roast Snipe.—Clean and truss, but do not stuff. Lay in rows in the dripping-pan, sprinkle with salt, and baste well with butter, then with butter and water. When they begin to brown, cut as many slices of bread as there are birds. Toast quickly, butter, and lay in the dripping-pan, a bird upon each. When the birds are done, serve upon the toast, with the gravy poured over it. The toast should lie under them while cooking at least five minutes, during which time the birds should be basted with melted butter seasoned with pepper. The largest snipe will not require above twenty minutes to roast. Or, dip an oyster in melted butter, then in bread-crumbs, seasoned with pepper and salt, and put in each bird before roasting. Small birds are especially delicious cooked in this way.

Roast Partridges, Pheasants, or Quails.—Pluck, singe, draw, and truss them ; season with salt and pepper; roast for about half an hour in a brisk oven, basting often with butter. When done, place on a dish together with bread-crumbs fried brown and arranged in small heaps. Gravy should be served separately in a tureen.

Quail on Toast.—Clean, wash, slit down the back, sprinkle with salt and pepper, and lay them on a gridiron, the inside down. Broil slowly; when nicely browned, butter well. Serve with cream gravy on toast. Omitting the cream, gravy, and toast, you have the ordinary broiled quail. Pigeons, woodcock, and small birds may be broiled in the same manner, and are delicious and nourishing for invalids.

Fried Rabbit.—After the rabbit has been thoroughly cleaned and washed, put it into boiling water and let it boil for about ten minutes; drain, and when cold, cut it into joints; dip into beaten egg, and then into fine bread-crumbs, seasoned with salt and pepper. When all are ready, fry them in butter over a moderate fire fifteen minutes; thicken the gravy with an ounce of butter and a small teaspoonful of flour. Serve hot.

Roast Rabbit.—Dress nicely and fill with a dressing made of bread-crumbs, a little onion, sage, pepper, and salt, and a small piece of butter; tie a piece of salt pork over it ; put into a dripping-pan with a little water in a quick oven; baste often ; serve with currant jelly.

Broiled Steaks of Venison.—Heat the gridiron, grease it well, lay on the steaks; broil quickly, without scorching, turning them two or three times; season with salt and pepper. Have butter melted in a well-heated platter, into which lay steaks, hot from the gridiron, turning them over several times in the butter, and serve hot with currant jelly on each steak. It is well to set the platter into another containing boiling water.

Game or Poultry in Jelly.—Take a knuckle of veal weighing two pounds; a slice of lean ham; one shallot, minced; a sprig of thyme and one of parsley; six pepper-corns (white) and one teaspoonful of salt, with three pints of cold water. Boil all these together until the liquor is reduced to a pint; strain without squeezing, and set to cool until next day. It should then be a firm jelly. Take off every particle of fat. Then take one package gelatine, soaked in one cupful cold water for three hours; one tablespoonful of sugar; two table-spoonfuls strained lemon juice, and two tablespoonfuls of currant jelly, dissolved in cold water, and strained through a muslin cloth. Pour a quart of *boiling* water over the gelatine, stir for a moment, add the jellied "stock," and when this is dissolved, add sugar, lemon juice, and coloring. Stir until all are mixed and melted together, and strain without shaking or squeezing through a flannel bag until quite clear. Have ready several hard-boiled eggs, and the remains of roast game, roast or boiled poultry, cut in neat, thin slices, and salted slightly. Wet a mold with cold water, and when the jelly begins to harden, pour some in the bottom. Cut the whites of the eggs in pretty shapes—stars, flowers, rings, leaves—with a keen penknife, and arrange these on the lowest stratum of jelly, which should be thin, that the forms may be visible. Add more jelly, and on this lay slices of meat, close together. More jelly, and proceed in this order until the mold is full. Set in a cool place to harden, and then turn out upon a flat dish. A mold with smooth, upright sides, is best for this purpose.

RECIPES INCIDENTAL TO POULTRY, GAME, ETC.

Gravy for Poultry.—Boil the giblets very tender; chop fine; then take the liquor in which they are boiled, thicken with flour; season with salt, pepper, and a little butter; add the giblets and dripping in which the turkey was roasted.

Plain Stuffing.—Take stale bread, cut off all the crust, rub very fine, and pour over it as much melted butter as will make it crumble in your hands; salt and pepper to taste. See also under " Roast Turkey."

Potato Stuffing.—Take two-thirds bread and one-third boiled potatoes grated, butter size of an egg, pepper, salt, one egg; mix thoroughly.

Oyster Stuffing.—By substituting oysters for potatoes in the above, you have oyster filling. See also under " Boiled Turkey."

Stuffing for Boiled Chicken.—One cupful of bread-crumbs, one tablespoonful of butter, one egg, half a teaspoonful of salt, and one tablespoonful of sweet marjoram. Mix well; stuff and sew in.

Capons.—Young male fowls, prepared by early gelding, and then nicely fattened, are the finest delicacies in the poultry line. They may be known by a small head, pale comb, which is short and withered, the neck feathers longer than usual, smooth legs, and soft, short spurs. They are cooked as ordinary chickens.

Keeping Game.—Game is rendered more tender, and its flavor is improved by keeping. If wrapped in a cloth saturated with equal parts of pyroligneous acid and water, it will keep many days. If in danger of tainting, clean, rub well with salt, and plunge into boiling water, letting it run through them for five minutes; then hang in a cold place. If tainted, put them in new milk over night. Always hang them up by the neck.

Duckling Pot Roast. — This is a very good way to cook this very acceptable bird. Put into a shallow crock a thin strip of bacon and a tablespoonful of mixed whole spice. Clean and truss two ducklings, put them in the crock, add hot water or soup-stock enough to come up half-way on the birds. Then add a sprig of celery and two of parsley; place a narrow strip of bacon over each bird; cover close and set the crock in a moderate oven, where the birds will cook slowly two hours. Remove the ducklings, strain the sauce, and reduce it one-third by boiling; add a gill of dark wine; thicken with a dash of brown flour; simmer fifteen minutes; add a teaspoonful of lemon-juice and serve with the duck. A small quantity of the sauce may be boiled down until thick as cream. This is called glaze; it is brushed over the bird before serving. — *Thomas J. Murrey.*

Fillet of Grouse. — Remove the breast and separate into four or six pieces. Disjoint and cook the remainder in boiling salted water to cover, till tender; then remove all the meat and chop it fine. Thicken the broth (which should be reduced to half a cup), season, and moisten the meat. Spread the minced meat on squares of toast; put a layer of currant jelly on each. Rub the fillets with butter and broil them carefully; season with salt, pepper and butter, and lay them on the jelly. — The Peerless Cook Book: *Mrs. D. A. Lincoln. Roberts Brothers, Publishers.*

Potted Fowl Roast. — Put fowl in pot, half covering with boiling water, and boil until tender, letting the water boil away. Add salt and pepper and let fowl brown in the fat. Serve with a gravy.

MEATS

BLANK PAGE FOR ADDITIONAL RECIPES

V. — MEATS.

I. — BEEF.

HOW TO ROAST, BROIL, AND BOIL BEEF.   NINETEEN RECIPES FOR COOKING BEEF.

RECIPES.

Roast Beef.—The best roasting-pieces are the middle ribs and the sirloin. The ends of the ribs should be removed from the flank, and the latter folded under the beef and securely fastened with skewers. Rub a little salt into the fat part; place the meat in the dripping-pan with a pint of stock or water; baste freely, and dredge with flour half an hour before taking the joint from the oven. Should the oven be very hot, place a buttered paper over the meat to prevent it scorching while yet raw. When the paper is used it will need very little basting. Or, turn the rib side up toward the fire for the first twenty minutes. The time it will take in cooking depends upon the thickness of the joint and the length of time the animal has been killed. Skim the fat from the gravy and add a tablespoonful of prepared brown flour to the remainder.

Roast Beef with Yorkshire Pudding.—Take a large rib roast; rub salt and pepper over it, and dredge with flour. Place on a rack in a dripping-pan, with very little water, until it is heated thoroughly; baste frequently. When nicely browned on the upper side, turn and baste. About three-quarters of an hour before it is done, take out the meat, pour off most of the dripping, put the batter for the pudding in the bottom of the pan, allowing the drippings from the beef to drop into it. When the pudding is done, return the meat and finish roasting. Add some hot water to the dripping and thicken with flour for the gravy.

For the batter of this pudding, take half a cup of butter, three cups of flour, three eggs, one cup of milk, and two teaspoonfuls of baking powder.

Beef a la Mode.—Take a round of fresh beef, extract the bone, and take away the fat. For a round weighing ten pounds, make a seasoning or stuffing as follows: Half a pound of beef suet; half a pound of grated bread-crumbs; the crumbled yelks of three hard-boiled eggs; a little bundle of sweet marjoram, the leaves chopped; another of sweet basil; four onions minced small; a large tablespoonful of mixed mace and nutmeg powdered. Season lightly with salt and cayenne. Stuff this mixture into the place from whence you took out the bone. Make a number of deep cuts about the meat, and stuff them also. Skewer the meat into a favorable shape, and secure its form by tying it round with tape. Put it into a tin bakepan, and pour over it a pint of port wine. Put on the lid, and bake the beef slowly for five or six hours, or till it is thoroughly done. If the meat is to be eaten hot, skim all the fat from the gravy, into which, after it is taken off the fire, stir in the beaten yelks of two eggs. Minced oysters may be substituted for onions.

Spiced Beef.—Boil a shin of beef weighing ten or twelve pounds, until the meat falls readily from the bones. Pick the meat to pieces, and mash the gristle very fine, rejecting all parts that are too hard to mash. Set away the liquor in which the beef has boiled till it is cold; then take off all the fat. Boil the liquor down to a pint and a half. Roll a dozen crackers very fine, and add them to the meat. Then return the meat to the liquor, and heat it all. Add salt and pepper to taste, half a teaspoonful of cloves, half a teaspoonful of cinnamon, half a teaspoonful or parsley chopped fine, and a little powdered nutmeg. Let it boil up once, and put into a mold or deep dish, with a weight adjusted to press it down. When it is entirely cold, cut into thin slices.

Savory Beef.—Take a shin of beef from the hind-quarter, saw it into four pieces, put it into a pot, and boil it until the meat and gristle drop from the bones ; chop the meat very fine, put it in a dish, and season it with a little salt, pepper, clove, and sage, to your taste ; pour in the liquor in which the meat was boiled, and place it away to harden. Cut in slices and eat cold.

Minced Beef.—Cut cold roast beef into thin slices ; put some of the gravy into a stewpan, a bit of butter rolled in flour, pepper and salt, and boil it up Add a little catsup, and put in the minced slices, and heat them through, but do not let it boil. Put small slices of toast in the dish, and cover with the meat.

Deviled Beef.—Take slices of cold roast beef, lay them on hot coals, and broil ; season with pepper and salt, and serve while hot, with a small lump of butter on each piece.

Curried Beef.—Take about two ounces of butter and place them in a saucepan with two small onions cut up into slices, and let them fry till they are of a light brown ; then add a tablespoonful and a half of curry powder, and mix it up well. Now cut up the beef into pieces about an inch square ; pour in from a quarter to a third of a pint of milk, and let it simmer for thirty minutes ; then take it off and place it in a dish with a little lemon juice. While cooking stir constantly, to prevent burning. Send it to table with a wall of mashed potatoes or rice around it.

Beef Hash.—Chop fine cold steak or roast beef, and cook in a little water ; add cream or milk, and thicken with flour ; season to taste, and pour over thin slices of toast.

Beef Stew.—Cut cold beef into small pieces, and put into cold water; add one tomato, a little onion, chopped fine; pepper and salt, and cook slowly; thicken with butter and flour, and pour over toast.

Boiled Corned Beef.—Put four or five pounds of lean corned meat into a pot with plenty of water. The water should be hot. The same care should be taken in skimming as for fresh meat. Allow half an hour for every pound of meat after it has begun to boil. The excellence of corned beef depends very much upon its being boiled gently and long. If it is to be eaten cold, lay it, when boiled, into a coarse earthen dish or pan, and over it a clean board about the size of the meat; upon this put a heavy weight. Salt meat is much improved by pressing.

Stewed Shin of Beef.—Wash, and set it on to stew in sufficient cold water to keep it just covered until done. When it boils, take off the scum, and put an ounce and a quarter of salt to the gallon of water. It is usual to add a few cloves and some black pepper, slightly bruised and tied up loosely in a fold of muslin, two or more onions, a root of celery, a bunch of savory herbs, four or five carrots, and as many turnips, either whole or sliced; if to be served with the meat, the last two will require a little more than the ordinary time of boiling, but otherwise they may be simmered with the meat from the beginning. Give the beef from four to five hours' gentle stewing, and serve it with part of its own liquor thickened and flavored, or quite plain.

Boiled Tongue.—Soak the tongue over night, then boil four or five hours. Peel off the outer skin and return it to the water in which it was boiled to cool. This will render it juicy and tender.

Baked Heart.—Wash carefully and stuff nicely; roast or bake and serve with gravy, which should be thickened with some of the stuffing. It is very nice hashed, with a little port wine added.

Broiled Beefsteak.—Have the choice steaks cut three-quarters of an inch thick; grease the gridiron and have it well heated. Put the steak over a hot, clear fire. When the steak is colored, turn it over, which must be done without sticking a fork into it and thus letting out the juice. It should be quite rare or pink in the centre, but not raw. When cooked sufficiently, lay on a hot platter and season with pepper and salt; spread over the top some small bits of butter, and serve immediately. Salt extracts the juices of meats in cooking. Steaks ought not to be salted until they have been broiled.

Beefsteak with Onions.—Take a nice rumpsteak, and pound it with a rolling-pin until it is quite tender; flour and season; put it into a frying-pan with hot lard and fry it. When well browned on both sides, take it up and dredge with flour. Have about two dozen onions ready boiled; strain them in a colander and put them in a frying-pan, seasoning with pepper and salt; dredge in a little flour, and add a small lump of butter; place the pan over the fire and stir the onions frequently, to prevent their scorching. When they are soft and a little brown, return the steak to the pan, and heat all together. Place the steak on a large dish, pour the onions and gravy over it, and send to the table hot.

Beefsteak and Tomatoes.—Stew a dozen good-sized tomatoes one hour, with salt and pepper. Then put in a pound of tender beefsteak, cut in small pieces, and boil fifteen minutes longer. Lay buttered toast in a deep dish, pour on the steak and tomato, and you have a most relishing and healthful dish.

Stuffed Beefsteak.—Take a rump steak about an inch thick. Make a stuffing of bread and herbs, and spread it over the steak. Roll it up, and with a needle and coarse thread sew it together. Lay it in an iron pot on one or two wooden skewers, and put in water just sufficient to cover it. Let it stew slowly for two hours—longer if the beef is tough; serve it in a dish with the gravy turned over it. To be carved crosswise, in slices, through beef and stuffing.

Beefsteak Pudding.—Prepare a good suet crust, and line a cake tin with it; put in layers of steak, with onions, tomatoes and mushrooms chopped, a seasoning of pepper, salt, and cayenne, and half a teacupful of water before closing it. Bake from an hour and a half to two hours, and serve hot.

II.—VEAL.

CHOOSING VEAL, FOR ROASTING, FOR STEWING; THE HEAD, FEET, KIDNEYS, SWEET-BREADS, ETC.; GENERAL USEFULNESS. TWENTY-ONE RECIPES FOR COOKING VEAL.

VEAL should be fat, finely grained, white, firm, and not overgrown. When large, it is apt to be coarse and tough, and if too young, it lacks flavor and is less wholesome. It is more difficult to keep than any meat except pork, and should never be allowed to acquire the slightest taint before it is dressed.

The fillet, the loin, the shoulder, and the best end of the neck, are the parts preferred for roasting; the breast and knuckle are more usually stewed or boiled. The head and feet of the calf are valuable articles of food, both for the nutriment which the gelatinous parts of them afford, and for the greater variety of modes in which they may be dressed. The kidneys, with the rich fat that surrounds them, and the sweet-breads especially, are well-known delicacies; the liver and the heart also are very good eating; and no meat is so generally useful for rich soups and gravies as veal.

The best veal is from calves not less than four, or more than six weeks old. If younger it is not wholesome. If older its character begins to change materially from the calf's use of grasses and other food.

RECIPES.

Roast Veal.—Take a loin or fillet of veal; make a stuffing as for roast turkey; fill the flat with the stuffing, and sew it firmly to the loin; rub the veal with salt, pepper, and flour, and put it into a pan with a little water. While roasting, baste frequently, letting it cook until thoroughly done. Allow two hours for a roast weighing from six to eight pounds. When done, remove the threads before sending to the table; thicken the gravy with a little flour. Veal should be rather overdone.

Pot-roasted Fillet.—Remove the bone and fill the cavity with a force-meat made of bread-crumbs, a very little salt, pork chopped fine, sage, pepper, salt, and ground cloves. Lay in the pot a layer of slices of salt pork; put in the fillet, fastened with skewers, cover with additional pork, pour over it a pint of good stock, cover down close, and let it cook slowly two or three hours; then take off the cover and let it brown. Serve hot.

Boiled Fillet.—A small and delicately white fillet should be selected for this purpose. Bind it round with tape, after having washed it thoroughly; cover it well with cold water, and bring it gently to a boil; clear off carefully the scum as it rises, and be very cautious not to allow the water to become smoked. Let the meat be *gently simmered* for three hours and a half to four and a half, according to its weight. Send it to table with rich white sauce.

Veal Stew.—Cut four or five pounds of veal into strips; peel a dozen large potatoes, and cut them into slices; place a layer of sliced salt pork with salt, pepper, sage, and onion on the bottom of the pot, then a layer of potatoes, then a layer of the veal nicely seasoned. Use up the veal thus. Over the last layer of veal put a layer of the pork, and over the whole a layer of potatoes. Pour in water till it covers the whole; cover the pot closely; heat it rapidly for a few minutes, and then let it simmer two hours.

Veal Hash.—Take a teacupful of boiling water in a saucepan, stir into it an even teaspoonful of flour wet in a tablespoonful of cold water, and let it boil five minutes; add one-half teaspoonful of black pepper, as much salt, and two tablespoonfuls of butter, and let it keep hot, but not boil. Chop the veal fine and mix with half as much stale bread-crumbs. Put into a pan and pour the gravy over it, then let it simmer ten minutes. Serve this on buttered toast.

Veal Pie.—Line a pudding-dish with good pie crust; into this put a layer of veal cut into small slices from the neck, or other less valuable part; make a second layer of hard-boiled eggs sliced thin; butter and pepper this layer. Add a layer of sliced ham, or salt pork, squeezing a few drops of lemon juice on the ham. Add more veal, as before, with eggs, ham, etc., till the dish is nearly full. Pour over a cupful of stock and cover with a stout crust. Bake in a moderate oven for two hours.

Veal Pot Pie.—Make a crust of a dozen mashed potatoes, two tablespoonfuls of butter, half a teacup of milk or cream, a little salt, and flour enough to stiffen it nicely. Fry half a dozen slices of salt pork, then cut up the veal and boil these together, in but little water, till the veal is almost done. Peel and slice a dozen potatoes quite thin, and roll the dough about half an inch thick and cut it into strips. Now build in your pot a layer of crust, meat, potatoes; then sprinkle with salt and pepper. Then another set of layers, and top off with crust. Pour on the liquor in which the meat was cooked, and let all simmer for half an hour, or until the top crust is cooked. Brown the crust by holding over it a red-hot shovel.

Veal Loaf.—Take a piece of butter the size of an egg, three pounds of raw veal, one heaping teaspoonful of salt, one of pepper, and two raw eggs. Chop the veal fine and mix all together, and put in about two tablespoonfuls of water. Mold this into a loaf, then roll it in eight tablespoonfuls of rolled crackers, and pour over it three tablespoonfuls of melted butter; place in a pan and bake two hours. To be sliced off when cold, and served at luncheon or tea.

Veal with Oysters.—Cut the veal in small, thin slices, place it in layers in a jar with salt, pepper, and oysters. Pour in the liquor of the oysters, set the jar in a kettle of boiling water, and let it stew till the meat becomes very tender.

Veal with Rice.—Pour over a small knuckle of veal rather more than sufficient water to cover it; bring it slowly to a boil; take off all the scum with great care; throw in a tea-spoonful of salt, and when the joint has simmered for about half an hour, throw in from eight to twelve ounces of well-washed rice, and stew the veal gently for an hour and a half longer, or until both the meat and rice are perfectly tender. A seasoning of cayenne and mace in fine powder, with more salt, should it be required, must be added twenty or thirty minutes before they are served. For a superior stew, good veal broth may be substituted for the water.

Veal with Peas.—A quart or more of full-grown green peas, instead of rice, added to the veal, prepared as above, as soon as the scum has been cleared off, will make a most excellent stew. It should be well seasoned with white pepper, and the mace should be omitted.

Cutlets in Cracker.—Pound the cutlet and season, cut the edges into good shape; take one egg, beat it a little, roll the cutlet in it, then cover thoroughly with rolled crackers.

Have a lump of butter and lard mixed hot in your skillet; put in the meat and cook slowly. When nicely browned stir in one spoonful of flour for the gravy; add half a pint of sweet milk, and let it come to a boil. Salt and pepper.

Cutlets, Broiled.—Trim evenly; sprinkle salt and pepper on both sides; dip in melted butter, and place upon the gridiron over a clear fire; baste while broiling with melted butter, turn over three or four times; serve with melted butter, or tomato sauce.

Pressed Veal.—Put four pounds of veal in a pot; cover with water; stew slowly until the meat drops from the bone, then take out and chop fine; let the liquor boil down until there is a cupful; put in a small cupful of butter, a tablespoonful of pepper, a little allspice, and a beaten egg; stir this through the meat; slice a hard-boiled egg; lay in a mold, and press in the meat; when put upon the table garnish with celery tops or parsley.

Minced Veal.—Heat a cupful of well-thickened gravy to a boil; add two tablespoonfuls of cream or rich milk, one tablespoonful of butter, pepper and salt, parsley to taste, a small onion, and three eggs well beaten. When these are stirred in, add the cold minced meat, salted and peppered. Let it heat thoroughly, but not boil.

Veal Scallops.—Mince the meat very small, and set it over the fire; season with grated nutmeg, pepper and salt, and a little cream. Then put it into scallop-shells, and cover with crumbs of bread, over which put bits of butter, and brown at a quick fire. Serve hot, with catsup or mushroom sauce.

Calf's Liver or Heart.—Cut the liver in slices, plunge into boiling water for an instant, wipe dry, season with pepper and salt, dredge with flour, and fry brown in lard. Have it perfectly done. Serve in gravy, made with either milk or water. **Calf's** heart dressed in this way is also very palatable.

Broiled Sweet-breads.—Parboil and blanch the sweet-breads by putting them first into hot water and keeping it at a hard boil for five minutes, then plunging it into ice-cold water somewhat salted. Allow them to lie in this ten minutes, wipe them very dry, and with a sharp knife split in half, lengthwise. Broil over a clear, hot fire, turning whenever they begin to drip. Have ready upon a deep plate melted butter, well salted and peppered, mixed with catsup or Challenge sauce. When the sweet-breads are done to a fine brown lay them in this preparation, turning them over several times ; cover and set them in a warm oven. Serve on fried bread or toast in a chafing-dish, a piece of sweet-bread on each. Pour on the hot butter and send to table.

Stewed Sweet-breads.—Parboil, blanch, and cut into small pieces ; boil fifteen minutes in milk ; stir into this chopped parsley, a little butter, and cornstarch to thicken. Serve hot.

Broiled Kidneys.—Skin the kidneys carefully, but do not slice or split them. Lay for ten minutes in warm (not hot) melted butter, rolling them over and over, that every part may be well basted. Broil on a gridiron over a clear fire, turn ing them every minute. Unless very large, they should be done in about twelve minutes. Sprinkle with salt and pepper, and lay on a hot dish, with butter upon each.

Calf's Tongue.—Of all the tongue preparations, calf's tongue is regarded as best. To pickle them, use for each a quarter pound of salt, one ounce of saltpetre, and a quarter pound of sugar. Rub the tongues daily with this, allowing them to lie in pickle for two weeks, after which they will be ready for smoking or boiling. If used without smoking, they require no soaking, but should simmer several hours till perfectly done, when the skin will peel off readily. If soaking is needed, lay them first in cold water and then in tepid water for two hours each; then boil till done.

III.—MUTTON AND LAMB.

CHOOSING MUTTON AND LAMB, FOR ROASTING, FOR BOILING; CUTLETS, SUITABLE VEGETABLES, ETC.   THIRTEEN RECIPES FOR MUTTON AND LAMB.

THE best mutton is small-boned, plump, finely grained, and short legged; the lean of a dark, rather than of a bright hue, and the fat white and clear; when this is yellow, the meat is rank, and of bad quality. The leg and the loin are the desirable joints; and the preference would probably be given to the latter, but for the superabundance of its fat, which renders it a somewhat wasteful part.

The parts for roasting are the shoulder, saddle, or chine, the loin, and haunch. The leg is best boiled, unless the mutton is young and very tender. The neck is sometimes roasted, but it is more generally boiled; the scrag, or that part of it which joins the head, is seldom used for any other purpose than making broth, and should be taken off before the joint is dressed. Cutlets from the thick end of the loin are commonly preferred, but they are frequently taken from the best end of the neck and from the middle of the leg.

Lamb should be eaten very fresh. In the fore-quarter, the vein in the neck should be blue, otherwise it is stale. In the hind-quarter the fat of the kidney will have a slight odor if not quite fresh. Lamb soon loses its firmness if stale.

New potatoes, asparagus, green peas, and spinach, are the vegetables to be eaten with roast lamb.

RECIPES.

Roast Mutton.—Wash the meat well, sprinkle with pepper and salt, dredge with flour, and put in the dripping-pan, with a little water in the bottom. Baste often with the drippings, skim the gravy well, and thicken with flour.

Boiled Leg of Mutton.—Cut off the shank-bone, trim the knuckle, and wash the mutton; put it into a pot with salt, and cover with boiling water. Allow it to boil a few minutes; skim the surface clean, draw your pot to the side of the fire, and simmer until done. Time, from two to two hours and a half. Do not *try* the leg with a fork to determine whether it is done. You lose the juices of the meat by so doing. Serve with caper sauce, or drawn butter, well seasoned. The liquor from this boiling may be converted into soup with the addition of a ham-bone and a few vegetables boiled together.

Mutton Dressed like Venison.—Skin and bone a loin of mutton, and lay it into a stewpan with a pint of water, a large onion stuck with a dozen cloves, half a pint of port wine, and a spoonful of vinegar; add, when it boils, a little thyme and parsley, and some pepper and salt; let it stew three hours, and turn it often. Make some gravy of the bones, and add it at intervals to the mutton.

Broiled Mutton Chops.—Trim off a portion of the fat, or the whole of it, unless it be liked; heat the gridiron, rub it with a bit of the mutton suet, broil over a brisk fire, and turn often until they are done, which, for the generality of eaters, will be in about eight minutes, if the chops are not more than half an inch thick, which they should not be. Add salt and pepper with melted butter, and serve on a hot plate.

Mutton and Green Peas.—Select a breast of mutton not too fat, cut it into small, square pieces, dredge it with flour, and fry to a fine brown in butter; add pepper and salt, cover it with water, and set it over a slow fire to stew, until the meat is perfectly tender. Take out the meat, skim off all the fat from the gravy, and just before serving add a quart of young peas, previously boiled with the strained gravy, and let the whole boil gently until the peas are entirely done.

Irish Stew.—Blanch three pounds of mutton chops by dip ping them first in boiling water, for two or three minutes, and then into ice-cold water. Place them on the bottom of a clean stewpan, barely covering them with cold water. Bring them slowly to a boil; add one teaspoonful of salt; skim clean; add a little parsley, mace, and a few pepper-corns. Simmer twenty minutes; add a dozen small onions whole, and two tablespoonfuls of flour mixed well with cold water. Let it simmer for an hour; add a dozen potatoes pared and cut to about the size of the onions. Boil till these are done; then dish, placing the chops around the edge of the plate, and pouring the onions and potatoes into the centre. Strain the gravy, add three tablespoonfuls of chopped parsley, and pour over the stew.

Boiled Leg of Lamb.—Choose a ewe leg, as there is more fat on it; saw off the knuckle, trim off the flap, and the thick skin on the back of it; soak in warm water for three hours, then boil gently (time according to size). Serve with oyster sauce. (See Sauces.)

Roast Lamb.—Wash well, season with pepper and salt, put in the dripping-pan with a little water. Baste often with the dripping; skim the gravy well and thicken with flour.

Lamb Stewed in Butter.—Select a nice loin, wash well, and wipe very dry; skewer down the flap, and lay it in a close-shut-ting and thick stewpan, or saucepan, in which three ounces of good butter have been just dissolved, but not allowed to boil; let it simmer slowly over a very gentle fire for two hours and a quarter, and turn it when it is rather more than half done. Lift it out, skim, and pour the gravy over it; send to table with brown gravy, mint sauce, and a salad.

Saddle of Lamb.—This is a dainty joint for a small party. Sprinkle a little salt over it, and set it in the dripping-pan, with a few small pieces of butter on the meat; baste it occasionally with tried-out lamb-fat; dredge a little flour over it a few minutes before taking from the oven. Serve with currant jelly and a few choice early vegetables. Mint-sauce may be served with the joint, but in a very mild form. (See Sauces.)

Broiled Lamb Chops.—Trim off most of the fat; broil over a brisk fire, turning frequently until the chops are nicely browned. Season with pepper and salt, and baste with hot butter. Serve on a buttered dish.

Breaded Lamb Chops.—Grate plenty of stale bread, season with salt and pepper, have ready some well-beaten egg, have a spider with hot lard ready, take the chops one by one, dip into the egg, then into the bread-crumbs; repeat it, as this will be found an improvement; then lay the chops separately into the boiling lard, fry brown, and then turn. To be eaten with currant jelly.

Lamb Steaks, Fried.—Dip each steak into well-beaten egg, cover with bread-crumbs or corn-meal, and fry in butter or new lard. Mashed potatoes and boiled rice are a necessary accompaniment. The gravy may be thickened with flour and butter, adding a little lemon juice; pour this hot upon the steaks, and place the rice in spoonfuls around the dish to garnish it.

IV.—PORK.

PORK REQUIRES CAREFUL CHOOSING ; NEEDS THOROUGH COOK-
ING.   NINETEEN RECIPES FOR COOKING PORK.

PORK, more than any other meat, requires to be chosen with the greatest care. The pig, from its gluttonous habits, is particularly liable to disease, and if killed and eaten when in an unhealthy condition, those who partake of it will probably pay dearly for their indulgence. Dairy-fed pork is the best.

If this meat be not thoroughly well-done, it is disgusting to the sight and poisonous to the stomach. " In the gravy of pork, if there is the least tint of redness," says an eminent medical authority, " it is enough to appall the sharpest appetite. Other meats under-done may be unpleasant, but pork is absolutely uneatable."

RECIPES.

Roast Pig.—A fat pig about three weeks old is best for a roast. Wash it thoroughly inside and out; chop the liver fine with bread-crumbs, onions, parsley, pepper, salt, and potatoes boiled and mashed; make it into a paste with butter and egg. Put this stuffing into the pig and sew it up; put in a baking-pan with a little water and roast over a bright fire, basting well with butter; rub frequently also with a piece of lard tied in a clean rag. When thoroughly done, lay the pig, back up, in a dish, and put a red apple or pickled-mango in its mouth. Make a dressing with some of the stuffing, with a glass of wine and some of the dripping. Serve with the roast pig, and also in a gravy-boat.

Roast Pork.—Choose for roasting, the loin, the leg, the saddle, the fillet, the shoulder, or the spare-rib. The loin of young pork is roasted with the skin on, and this should be scored in regular strips of about a quarter inch wide before the joints are laid to the fire. The skin of the leg also should be cut through in the same manner. This will prevent blistering, and render it more easy to carve. In beginning the roasting the meat should be placed at some distance from the fire, in order that it may be heated through before the skin hardens. The basting should be constant. The cooking must be thorough and the meat well-browned before removed from the fire.

Roast Spare-rib.—Spare-rib should be well rubbed with salt and pepper before it is roasted. If large and thick, it

will require two or three hours to roast; a very thin piece
may be roasted in an hour. Lay the thick end to the fire.
When you put it down to roast, dust on some flour, and
baste with a little butter. The shoulder, loin, and chine are
roasted in the same manner.

Leg of Pork Roasted.—Parboil a leg of pork, take off the
skin, and then roast; baste with butter, and make a savory
powder of finely minced or dried or powdered sage, ground
black pepper, salt, and some bread-crumbs rubbed together
through a colander; add to this a little very finely minced
onion; sprinkle the meat with this when it is almost done;
put a half pint of gravy into the dish.

Baked Pork Tenderloins.—Split the tenderloin lengthwise
nearly through; stuff with a filling of bread-crumbs, pepper, salt, and sweet marjoram. Tie a string around it, to
keep the filling in, and bake in a hot oven for half an hour,
basting well as the cooking proceeds.

Pork Cutlets.—Cut them about half an inch thick from a
delicate loin of pork, trim into neat form, and take off part
of the fat, or the whole of it when it is not liked; dredge a
little pepper or cayenne upon them, and broil (or fry) over
a clear and moderate fire from fifteen to eighteen minutes,
sprinkle a little fine salt upon them just before they are
dished. They may be dipped into egg and then into bread-
crumbs mixed with minced sage, then finished in the usual
way. When fried, flour them well, and season with salt and
pepper. Serve with gravy made in the pan.

Boiled Ham.—The soaking which must be given to a ham
before it is boiled depends both on the manner in which it
has been cured and on its age. If highly salted, hard, and
old, a day and night, or even longer, may be requisite to
open the pores sufficiently and to extract a portion of the
salt. The water must be several times changed during the
steeping. After the ham has been scraped or brushed as

clean as possible, pare away lightly any part which may be
blackened or rusty.   Lay it into a suitable kettle and cover
it plentifully with cold water; bring it *very slowly* to boil,
and clear off the scum, which will be thrown up in great
abundance So soon as the water has been cleared from
this, draw the pot to the edge of the stove, that the ham
may be simmered slowly but steadily, until it is tender.   On
no account allow it to boil fast.   When it can be probed
very easily with a sharp skewer, lift it out, strip off the skin,
and return the ham to the water to cool.

Baked Ham.—A ham of sixteen pounds must be boiled
three hours, then skin and rub in half a pound of brown
sugar, cover with bread-crumbs, and bake well for two
hours.

Glazed Ham.—Take a cold-boiled ham from which the skin
has been removed, and brush it well all over with beaten
egg.   To a cup of powdered cracker allow enough rich
milk or cream to make into a thick paste, salt it, and work
in a teaspoonful of melted butter.   Spread this evenly, a
quarter of an inch thick, over the ham, and set to brown in
a moderate oven.

Ham and Eggs.—Cut the ham in very thin slices, and fry
long enough to cook the fat, but not long enough to crisp
the lean.   A very little boiling water may be put into the
frying-pan to secure the ham moist and tender.   Remove
the ham when it is done, break eggs gently into the pan,
without breaking the yelks, and fry till done, about three
minutes.   The eggs will not require to be turned.   Cut off
the uneaven edges, place the eggs around the ham, and pour
in the gravy.

Ham or Tongue Toast.—Toast a thick slice of bread and
butter it on both sides.   Take a small quantity of remains
of ham or tongue, grate it, and put it in a stewpan with two

hard-boiled eggs chopped fine, and mixed with a little butter, salt, and cayenne; heat it quite hot, then spread thickly upon the buttered toast. Serve while hot.

Broiled Salt Pork.—Cut the pork in thin slices. Put a little water in the pan, and when it has boiled three minutes pour it off; dredge the pork with flour and brown it.

Bacon Broiled or Fried.—Cut evenly into thin slices, or *rashers;* pare from them all rind and rust; curl them round; fasten them with small, slight skewers, then gently fry, broil, or toast them; draw out the skewers before they are sent to table. A few minutes will dress them either way. They may be cooked without being curled. The slow cooking is necessary that the meat may be well done without being dried or hardened.

Fried Sausage.—Sausages should be used while quite fresh. Melt a piece of butter or dripping in a clean frying-pan; when just melted, put in the sausages, shake the pan for a minute, and keep turning them; do not break or prick them; fry them over a very slow fire till they are nicely browned; when done, lay them on a hair-sieve before the fire to drain the fat from them. The secret of cooking sausages well is to let them heat very gradually. If so done the skins will not burst if they are fresh. The common practice of pricking them lets the gravy out, which is undesirable.

Baked Sausages.—The most wholesome way to cook sausages is to bake them. Place them in a baking-pan in a single layer, and bake in a moderate oven; turn them over when half done, that they may be equally browned. Serve with pieces of toast between them, having cut the toast about the same size as the sausage, and moistened it with a little of the sausage fat.

Sausage Meat.—Many prefer to use sausage meat in bulk.

Small portions of the meat should be packed lightly together and fried slowly until nicely browned. When done, drain through a hair-sieve. Do not pack hard. It will make the sausages tough.

Scrapple.—Boil a hog's head one day, and let it stand five or six hours, or all night. Slip out the bones and chop fine; then return the meat to the liquor; skim when cold; warm and season freely with pepper, salt, sage, and sweet herbs. Add two cupfuls of buckwheat-meal and one cupful of corn-meal. Put into molds, and when cold cut into slices and fry for breakfast.

Boiled Pork.—The shoulder or leg are regarded as the most economical pieces for boiling. They should be well salted first, by about ten days' pickling. Boil precisely as ham is boiled, but not for so long a time, about three hours sufficing to thoroughly cook an ordinary sized leg of pork. After it has come to the boiling point, let the process proceed slowly as possible. Peel off the skin when done and spot the surface with dashes of red and black pepper, or with allspice, or garnish with parsley.

Souse.—Pigs' feet and ears may be soused by cleaning thoroughly, soaking in salt and water several days, and then boiling till the bones can be picked out with ease and the skin peeled off. Cover the meat and gelatinous substance with boiling vinegar, highly spiced with peppercorns and mace. This may be eaten cold or the meat may be fried after dipping in egg and cracker.

Pig's head may be prepared the same way, the meat being chopped fine and mixed with pounded crackers. Mix with herbs, spices, salt, and pepper to taste, and a small quantity of vinegar. Press into a mold, or a jar, and cut in slices. To be eaten cold.

VEGETABLES

BLANK PAGE FOR ADDITIONAL RECIPES

VI.—VEGETABLES.

ALL vegetables should be used when fresh as possible. Wash them thoroughly, and allow them to lie in cold water until ready to be used.

Great care must be taken to remove gravel and insects from heads of lettuce, cabbage, and cauliflower. To do this, lay them for half an hour or more in a pan of strong brine, placing the stalk ends uppermost. This will destroy the small snails and other insects which cluster in the leaves, and they will fall out and sink to the bottom.

Strong-flavored vegetables, like turnips, cabbage, and greens, require to be put into a large quantity of water. More delicate vegetables, such as peas, asparagus, etc., require less water. As a rule, in boiling vegetables, let the water boil before putting them in, and let it continue to boil until they are done. Nothing is more indigestible than vegetables not thoroughly cooked. Just when they are done must be ascertained to a certainty in each particular case, without depending upon any general directions.

Never let boiled vegetables stand in the water after coming off the fire; put them instantly into a colander over a pot of boiling water, and let them remain there, if you have to keep them back from the table.

An iron pot will spoil the color of the finest greens; they should be boiled by themselves in a tin, brass, or copper vessel.

91

Potatoes are good with all meats. Carrots, parsnips, turnips, greens, and cabbage belong with boiled meats; beets, peas, and beans are appropriate to either boiled or roast.

RECIPES.

Boiled White Potatoes.—Peel off a strip about a quarter of an inch wide, lengthwise, around each potato. Put them on in cold water, with a teaspoonful of salt in it. Let them boil fifteen minutes, then pour off half the water and replace it with cold water. When the edge of the peel begins to curl up they are done. Remove them from the pot, cover the bottom of a baking-tin with them, place them in the oven, with a towel over them, for fifteen minutes, leaving the oven door open. Then serve with or without the skins.

The use of cold water in boiling potatoes, as in this recipe, is exceptional. Hot water is generally used, but for this purpose cold seems preferable.

Roasted White Potatoes.—Select the largest and finest potatoes for roasting. Wash them thoroughly and put in the oven with their skins on. Roast about one hour, turning them occasionally with a fork. When done, send them to the table hot, and in their skins.

Potatoes Roasted with Meats.—To roast potatoes with beef, poultry, and other meats, peel the potatoes, lay them in a pan, and cook them in the gravy. It is quite proper to roast both white and sweet of potatoes in the same pan.

Mashed Potatoes.—Steam or boil pared potatoes until soft, in salted water; pour off the water and let them drain perfectly dry; sprinkle with salt and mash; have ready hot milk or cream, in which has been melted a piece of butter; pour this on the potatoes, and stir until white and very light. A solid, heavy masher is not desirable. An open wire tool is much better.

Stewed Potatoes.—Take sound raw potatoes, and divide each into four parts, or more, if they be very large. Put them into the stewpan; add salt, pepper, and a piece of fresh butter; pour in milk, with a little cream, just to keep the potatoes from burning. Cover the saucepan, and allow the potatoes to stew until thoroughly soft and tender.

Fried Potatoes.—Boil some good and large potatoes until nearly done; set them aside a few minutes; when sufficiently cool, slice or chop them; sprinkle them with pepper and salt, and fry in butter or fresh lard until they are of a light brown color. Serve hot.

Saratoga Potatoes.—Peel and slice the potatoes on a slaw-cutter, into cold water; wash them thoroughly, and drain; spread between the folds of a clean cloth, rub and pat until dry. Fry a few at a time in boiling lard; salt as you take them out. Saratoga potatoes are very nice when eaten cold. They can be prepared three or four hours before needed, and if kept in a warm place they will be crisp and nice. They may be used for garnishing game and steaks.

Potato Cakes.—Mash thoroughly a lot of potatoes just boiled; add a little salt, butter and cream; fry brown on both sides, after making into little cakes.

Boiled Sweet Potatoes.—Take large, fine potatoes, wash clean; boil with the skins on in plenty of water, but without salt. They will take at least one hour. Drain off the water, and set them for a few minutes in a tin pan before the fire, or in the oven, that they may be well dried. Peel them before sending to the table.

Roasted Sweet Potatoes.—Sweet potatoes are roasted in the same manner as white, but they require a little longer time.

Fried Sweet Potatoes.—Choose large potatoes, half boil them, and then, having taken off the skins, cut the potatoes in slices and fry in butter, or in nice drippings.

Stewed Tomatoes.—Pour boiling water on the tomatoes to be used, and then peel and slice them. Stew them gently, without adding any water, fifteen minutes; then add some pulverized cracker or bread crumbs, sufficient to thicken it a little, and salt and pepper to your taste. Stew fifteen minutes longer, and add a large piece of butter.

The thickening suggested is not essential. Many prefer the pure tomatoes. Try both ways and adopt the more pleasing.

Broiled Tomatoes.—Cut large tomatoes in two, from side to side, not from top to bottom; place them on a gridiron, the cut surface down; when well seared, turn them and put on butter, salt, and pepper; then cook with the skin side down until done.

Fried Tomatoes.—Cut the tomatoes in slices without skinning; pepper and salt them well; then sprinkle a little flour over them and fry in butter until browned. Put them on a hot platter; then pour milk or cream into the butter and juice, and when this is boiling hot, pour it over the tomatoes.

Tomatoes Baked Whole.—Select a number of sound, ripe tomatoes. Cut a round hole in the stem side of each, and stuff it with bread-crumbs, nicely peppered and salted; cover the bottom of the pan with the tomatoes, the opened side upward; put in a very little water, dredge with flour, and bake till brown. Serve hot.

Baked Sliced Tomatoes.—Skin the tomatoes, slice in small pieces; spread a thick layer in the bottom of a pudding dish; cover with a thin layer of bread-crumbs, and sprinkle salt, pepper, and a few small pieces of butter over them; add another layer of tomatoes, then of crumbs, etc., until the dish is filled; sprinkle over the top a layer of fine rolled crackers; bake one hour. Canned tomatoes, put up whole, may be used nicely this way.

Tomatoes a la Creme.—Pare and slice ripe tomatoes; one pound of fresh ones or a quart can; stew until perfectly smooth, season with salt and pepper, and add a piece of butter the size of an egg. Just before taking from the fire, stir in one cup of cream, with a tablespoonful of flour stirred smooth in a part of it; do not let it boil after the flour is put in. Have ready in a dish some pieces of toast; pour the tomatoes over this and serve.

Boiled Green Corn.—Take off the outside leaves and the silk, letting the innermost leaves remain on until after the corn is boiled, which renders the corn much sweeter. Boil for half an hour in plenty of water, drain, and after fully removing the leaves, serve.

Baked Corn.—Grate one dozen ears of sweet corn, one cup of milk, a small piece of butter; salt to taste, and bake in a pudding dish for one hour.

Corn Fritters, see Fritters.

Lima Beans.—Shell, wash, and put into boiling water; when boiled tender, drain and season them. Dress with cream, or with a large lump of butter, and let the whole simmer for a few moments before serving.

Succotash.—Take ten ears of green corn and one pint of Lima beans; cut the corn from the cob, and stew gently with the beans until tender. Use as little water as possible. Season with butter, salt, and pepper—milk, if you choose. If a few of the cobs are stewed in the succotash, it will improve the flavor, as there is great sweetness in the cob.

String Beans.—Remove the strings of the beans with a knife, and cut off both ends. Cut each bean into three pieces, boil tender, add butter when they are done, pepper and salt, and serve hot.

Boiled Beans.—Dried beans must soak over night in soft water; put them in a strong bag, leaving room for them to swell; let them boil in a plenty of water until done; hang up the bag that all the water may drain off; then season with butter, pepper, and salt to the taste.

Baked Beans.—Put the beans to soak early in the evening, in a dish that will allow plenty of water to be used. Change the water at bed-time. Next morning early, parboil two hours; pour off nearly all the water; take raw pork, scored on top; put the beans in a *deep dish*, a stoneware jar is very nice, the pork in the middle, sinking it so as to have it just level with the surface. Add half a teaspoonful of soda, two tablespoonfuls of molasses, and bake at least six hours. As the beans bake dry, add more water, a little at a time, until the last hour, when it is not necessary to moisten them.

Boiled Green Peas.—The peas should be young and freshly shelled; wash and drain them carefully; put them into fast-boiling, salted water; when quite tender drain, and add pepper, butter, and a little milk. Serve hot.

Boiled Asparagus.—Scrape the stems of the asparagus lightly, but make them very clean, throwing them into cold water as you proceed. When all are scraped, tie them in bunches of equal size; cut the hard ends evenly, that all may be of the same length, and put into boiling water. Prepare several slices of delicately browned toast half an inch thick. When the stalks are tender, lift them out and season with pepper and salt. Dip the toast quickly into the liquor in which the asparagus was boiled, and dish the vegetable upon it, the points, or the butts, meeting in the centre of the dish. Pour rich melted butter over it, and send to the table hot.

Boiled Beets.—Wash, but do not cut them, as cutting destroys the sweetness; let them boil from two to three hours, or until they are perfectly tender; then take them up, peel and slice them, and pour vinegar, or melted butter, over them, as may be preferred.

Potato Hillocks.—Whip boiled potatoes light with a little butter and milk, and season with salt and pepper. Beat in a raw egg, to bind the mixture ; shape into small conical heaps, set in a greased pan in the oven, and as they brown, glare with butter. The oven must be very hot. Slip a cake-turner under each hillock and transfer to a hot platter. — *Marion Harland.*

Potato Pie. — Pare and cut four good-sized potatoes into dice, cover them with boiling water, boil ten minutes, drain. Add to them one tablespoonful chopped parsley, one of chopped ham and one of chopped onion. Season with salt and pepper and turn into a baking dish. Add one teaspoonful of baking powder and a half of salt to one pint of flour, mix and add sufficient milk to make a soft dough. Roll out and cover the top of the baking dish, just as you would an ordinary pie. Brush with milk and bake in a quick oven twenty minutes. Serve hot with cream sauce. — *Mrs. S. T. Rorer.*

Stuffed Onions. — Select large onions, the Spanish variety preferred, and cook them in a steamer until tender, but not broken. Let them cool, then cut off a slice from the top and scoop out the inside, leaving not more than two or three layers. Chop the part removed, and chop with it some sweet green pepper (one teaspoon for each onion). Into the onion cups put several boiled chestnuts (shelled), and fill the spaces with the chopped mixture. Add a teaspoon of butter and a little salt, and stand the onions in a pan of water. Bake until very soft, and when nearly done cover the top with buttered cracker crumbs and return to the oven until the crumbs are crisp. When the crumbs are crisp, have ready a tomato sauce and pour it over them on the serving dish. — *Mrs. Lincoln.*

Fried Egg-plant.—Pare and cut in slices quarter of an inch thick; sprinkle with salt; cover and let stand for an hour. Pour off the juice or water which exudes; wipe each slice dry; dip first in beaten egg, then in rolled cracker or bread crumbs. Season with pepper and salt, and fry brown in butter. Serve very hot.

Fried Egg-plant No. 2.—Put into water and boil until soft, then cut in two and scoop out all the inside; season; take a tablespoonful of the remaining pulp at a time, dip in egg and bread-crumbs, and fry in hot lard. Serve hot.

Baked Egg-plant.—Boil them till somewhat tender, in order to remove the bitter flavor. Then slit each one down the side, and take out the seeds. Have ready a stuffing made of grated cracker, butter, minced herbs, salt, pepper, nutmeg, and beaten yelk of eggs. Fill with this the cavity left by the seeds, and bake the plants in a hot oven. Serve with well-seasoned gravy poured around them in the dish.

Boiled Cabbage.—Strip off the loose or withered leaves, and wash well; then split in two, or if the head be very large, into four pieces, and put into boiling water with some salt; let it boil slowly, skimming carefully and frequently. When done, strain through a colander. Serve in a vegetable-dish and lay inside, among the leaves, some bits of butter; season with pepper, and serve while hot.

Boiled Cauliflower.—Trim off all the outside leaves; wrap in a cloth and put into boiling water well salted; boil until tender, and then serve with drawn butter.

Cabbage a la Cauliflower.—Cut the cabbage fine, as for slaw; put it into a stewpan, cover with water, and keep closely covered; when tender, drain off the water; put in a small piece of butter, with a little salt, one-half a cupful of cream, or one cupful of milk. Leave on the stove a few minutes before serving.

Boiled Turnips.—Pare and cut into pieces; put them into boiling water well salted, and boil until tender; drain thoroughly and then mash and add a piece of butter, pepper, and salt to taste. Stir until they are thoroughly mixed, and serve hot.

Boiled Onions.—Skin them carefully and put them to boil; when they have boiled a few minutes, pour off the water, add clean cold water, and then set them to boil again. Pour this away also, and add more cold water, when they may boil till done. This change of waters will make them white and clear, and very mild in flavor. After they are done, pour off all the water, and dress with a little cream, salt, and pepper to taste.

Fried Onions.—Peel and slice fresh, solid onions very evenly, then fry them in a pan of hot butter till slightly browned.

Boiled Leeks.—Trim off the coarser leaves of young leeks, cut them into equal lengths, tie them in small bunches, and boil in plenty of water, previously salted. Serve on toast, and send melted butter to the table with them.

Boiled Squash.—Remove the seeds; boil till very tender; then press out all the water through a colander, and mash, with butter, pepper, and salt.

Fried Squash.—Pare the squash, cut in slices, dip in egg seasoned with pepper and salt, then into cracker dust, and fry to a nice brown.

Boiled Parsnips.—Scrape thoroughly, then wash and boil in a little water well salted. When done, dress with butter and a little pepper, or drawn butter, if desired.

Fried Parsnips.—Having boiled your parsnips, split open the largest ones, season with pepper and salt, dredge a little flour over them, and fry to a light brown.

7

Boiled Spinach.—Boil the spinach in plenty of water, drain, and press the moisture from it; chop it small, put it into a clean saucepan, with a slice of fresh butter, and stir the whole until well mixed and very hot. Smooth it in a dish, and send it quickly to table.

Boiled Greens.—Turnip-tops, mustard-tops, cabbage-leaves, beet-tops, cowslips, dandelions, and various similar articles are much relished in the spring, boiled in salt and water or with salt pork. When done sufficiently they will sink to the bottom.

Stewed Celery.—Clean the heads thoroughly; take off the coarse, green, outer leaves; cut the stalks into small pieces, and stew in a little broth; when tender, add some rich cream, a little flour, and butter enough to thicken the cream. Season with pepper, salt, and a little nutmeg, if that is agreeable.

Boiled Artichokes.—Soak the artichokes and wash them in several waters; cut the stalks even; trim away the lower leaves, and the ends of the other leaves; boil in salted water with the tops downward, and let them remain until the leaves can be easily drawn out. Before serving, remove the surrounding leaves, and send the remainder to the table with melted butter.

Broiled Mushrooms.—In order to test mushrooms, sprinkle salt on the gills; if they turn *yellow*, they are poisonous; if they turn *black*, they are good. When satisfied at this point, pare, and cut off the stems, dip them in melted butter, season with salt and pepper, broil them on both sides over a clear fire, and serve on toast.

Stewed Mushrooms.—Being sure you have the genuine mushrooms, put them in a small saucepan, season with pepper and salt, add a spoonful of butter and a spoonful or two of gravy from roast meat, or, if this be not at hand, the same quantity of good, rich cream; shake them about over the fire, and when they boil they are done.

Boiled Rice.—Wash a cupful of rice in two or three waters; let it lie for a few minutes in the last water, then put it into three quarts of fast-boiling water, with a little salt; let it boil twenty minutes, then turn into a colander, drain, and serve, using such sauce or dressing as may be desired.

Boiled Hominy.—Soak one cupful of fine hominy over night in three cupfuls of water, and salt to taste; in the morning turn it into a quart pail; then put the pail into a kettle of boiling water, cover tightly, and steam one hour; add one teacupful of sweet milk, and boil fifteen minutes additional, then serve hot.

Stewed Macaroni.—Break the macaroni into small pieces, wash it, and put into salted hot water; cook about twenty minutes; drain, and put in a vegetable dish a layer of macaroni, sprinkle with grated cheese, bits of butter, pepper and salt; proceed in this manner until the dish is full, but omit the cheese at the last. Set the dish in the oven for a few minutes, and let it get thoroughly *hot*.

Baked Macaroni.—For baked macaroni, proceed as in stewed, but, when prepared fully as above, pour a few spoonfuls of milk over the top, and bake half an hour.

Macaroni with Tomatoes.—Have water boiling in a large saucepan; throw into it macaroni, broken, but not too short; let it cook twenty to thirty minutes, pour over it some cold water, and strain it quite dry; cut an onion into small dice, throw it into cold water and squeeze it dry in a cloth; put some olive oil, butter, or clarified fat into a saucepan; the oil, of course, is best. Throw into it the onion, and let it cook, shaking occasionally, until the onion is almost melted away. Have some cooked tomatoes ready to add to this

sauce. If it is too thick, add some cold water by teaspoonfuls at a time. Let all simmer for ten minutes longer.
Sprinkle some grated cheese over your macaroni, which
must be piping hot, in a dish. Pour the sauce over this and
serve. A quarter of a pound of macaroni makes a large
dish, and takes about a third of a can to half a can of
tomatoes.

Sliced Cucumbers.—Peel and slice the cucumbers as thin as
possible; lay the slices in salted water for an hour; then
pour off the water; cover them with vinegar, half a teaspoonful of pepper, and salt as may be necessary.

Stewed Oyster-plant.—Cut off the tops of a bunch of
salsify, or oyster-plant, close to the root; scrape and wash
well, and slice lengthwise or round; stew until tender in
salted water; drain and put in a stewpan, cover with milk;
to one pint of salsify add a tablespoonful of butter rolled in
flour; season with salt and pepper; let it stew a few minutes and add a little vinegar, if liked.

Mock Fried Oysters.—Scrape one bunch of salsify, and boil
until tender; mash through a colander, add one beaten egg,
a small piece of butter, salt and pepper to taste; drop by the
spoonful into hot lard and fry brown.

Egg-Plant. — Cut the plant into slices one-third of an
inch thick, without removing the skin. Sprinkle salt
over each slice, pile them, and cover with a weight to
press out the juice. Drain, and dip each slice first in
fine crumbs, then in beaten egg, and again in crumbs,
and sauté them in hot fat.—THE PEERLESS COOK BOOK :
Mrs. D. A. Lincoln. Roberts Brothers, Publishers.

Water-Cresses. — Wash well, pick off decayed leaves,
and leave in ice-water until you are ready to eat them.
They should then be shaken free of wet and piled lightly in a glass dish. Eat with salt.—*Marion Harland.*

SAUCES

BLANK PAGE FOR ADDITIONAL RECIPES

VII.—SALADS AND SAUCES.

SALADS DEFINED—HOW DRESSED, COMBINED, AND SERVED.
SAUCES DEFINED—THEIR USES AND COMPOSITION. HOW TO
PREPARE INGREDIENTS FOR SALADS, WHAT VEGETABLES TO
EMPLOY, FRESHNESS, EXCELLENCE, ETC. THIRTY-SIX RECIPES
FOR SALADS AND SAUCES.

UNDER the head of salads all preparations of uncooked herbs or vegetables is placed. They are usually dressed with salt, vinegar, oil, and spices. Sometimes they are combined with meat or shell fish, as chicken, veal, lobster, etc. They are used chiefly as relishes with other food.

Sauces are generally used to impart a relish to articles of food. Sometimes vegetables are employed as the basis of sauces, but they are compounded chiefly of savory condiments, that they may add zest to eating.

Meat or fish used in salads should not be minced, but rather picked apart, or cut in pieces of moderate size. Cabbage, celery, asparagus, cauliflower, water-cress, and all kinds of lettuce are the vegetables best adapted for use in salads. They must be used when quite fresh and crisp, and all the ingredients used in their dressing must be of the best quality and flavor.

All condiments are in some sense sauces, but the term is usually confined to those which are the result of compounding a variety of articles.

RECIPES.

Coldslaw.—With a sharp knife, or, better, with a knife made for the purpose, cut up into fine shavings a firm head of cabbage; sprinkle with as much salt and pepper as you deem necessary; beat up the yelk of one egg, add a lump of butter the size of a walnut, a gill of cream, the same quantity of vinegar, a tablespoonful of sugar, an even teaspoonful of mustard, and a pinch of bruised celery seed. Heat these condiments together, without boiling, and pour over the sliced cabbage; then toss it with a fork until thoroughly mixed. Allow time for it to cool before serving.

Coldslaw, No. 2.—Take equal parts of chopped cabbage and the green stalks of celery. Season with salt, pepper, and vinegar.

Maryland Coldslaw.—Halve the cabbage and lay it in cold water for one hour; shave down the head into small slips with a sharp knife. Put in a saucepan a cup of vinegar, and let it boil; then add a cup of cream, with the yelks of two eggs, well beaten; let it boil up, and pour over the cabbage. As soon as the cabbage is cut it should be sprinkled with a little salt and pepper.

Cabbage Salad.—Take one head of fine, white cabbage, minced fine; three hard-boiled eggs; two tablespoonfuls of salad oil; two teaspoonfuls white sugar; one teaspoonful salt; one teaspoonful pepper; one teaspoonful made mustard; one teacupful vinegar. Mix and pour upon the chopped cabbage.

Lettuce Salad.—Take a good-sized head of lettuce and pull the leaves apart. Wash them a moment, then shake off the water and dry the leaves. Examine them carefully, wipe off all grit, and reject those that are bruised. Take the yelks of two hard-boiled eggs; add one-half teaspoonful of mixed mustard, and mix to a paste with a silver fork; then add slowly, mixing carefully, about one-half a cup of vinegar, one teaspoonful of sugar, and salt to taste; cut the lettuce small as may be desired with a sharp knife, and pour the dressing over it; garnish with hard-boiled eggs.

Potato Salad.—Steam and slice the potatoes; add a very little raw onion chopped very fine, and a little parsley, and pour over the whole a nice salad dressing. Serve either warm or cold, as may be preferred.

Potato Salad, No. 2.—Cut up three quarts of boiled potatoes. *while hot*, into neat pieces; add a tablespoonful of chopped parsley, a tablespoonful of chopped onion, a teaspoonful of pepper, and one of salt; also add a cupful of oil, and mix; then add a cupful of warm stock, a wineglassful of vinegar (from the mixed-pickle bottle); mix the ingredients together carefully, and do not break the potatoes any more than is absolutely unavoidable. Set the whole in the ice-box and serve cold. The onion and parsley may be omitted, and boiled root celery added, or a little stalk celery chopped fine.

Chicken Salad.—Boil a small chicken until very tender. When entirely cold, remove the skin and fat, cut the meat into small bits, then cut the white part of the stalks of celery into pieces of similar size, until you have twice as much celery as meat. Mix the chicken and celery together; pour on **Slade's Salad Cream,** and stir all thoroughly. Cold veal used in place of chicken will also make a very excellent salad.

Chicken Salad, No. 2.—Take three chickens, boil until very tender; when cold, chop them, but not too fine; add twice the quantity of celery cut fine, and three hard-boiled eggs sliced. Make a dressing with two cups of vinegar, half a cup of butter (or two tablespoonfuls of oil), two eggs beaten, with a large tablespoonful of mustard, saltspoonful of salt, two tablespoonfuls of sugar, tablespoonful of pepper, or a little cayenne pepper; put the vinegar into a tin pan and set in a kettle of boiling water; beat the other ingredients together thoroughly and stir slowly into the vinegar until it thickens. Cool it and pour over the salad just before serving.

Molasses Sauce. — One cupful of molasses, half a cupful of water, one tablespoonful of butter, a little cinnamon or nutmeg (about half a teaspoonful), one-fourth of a teaspoonful of salt, three tablespoonfuls of vinegar. Boil all together for twenty minutes. Juice of lemon can be used instead of vinegar. — NEW COOK BOOK: *Miss Maria Parloa. Estes & Lauriat, Publishers.*

Fruit-Syrup Sauce. — One cup fruit-syrup, one-half cup sugar, one teaspoonful corn-starch, one teaspoonful butter. Use the syrup from apricots, peaches, cherries, quinces, or any fruit you prefer. The amount of sugar will depend upon the acidity of the fruit. Mix the cornstarch with the sugar, add the syrup, and boil five minutes. Add butter last. — THE PEERLESS COOK BOOK: *Mrs. D. A. Lincoln. Roberts Brothers, Publishers.*

Lobster Sauce. — One small lobster, four tablespoonfuls of butter, two of flour, one-fifth of a teaspoonful of cayenne, two tablespoonfuls of lemon-juice, one pint of boiling water. Cut the meat into dice. Pound the "coral" with one tablespoonful of the butter. Rub the flour and the remainder of the butter to a smooth paste. Add the water, pounded "coral" and butter, and the seasoning. Simmer five minutes and then strain on the lobster. Boil up once and serve. — NEW COOK BOOK: *Miss Maria Parloa. Estes & Lauriat, Publishers.*

Cranberry Sauce. — Put three pints of washed cranberries in a granite stewpan. On top of them put three cups of granulated sugar and three gills of water. After they begin to boil, cook them ten minutes, closely covered, and do not stir them. Remove the scum. They will jelly when cool, and the skins will be soft and tender. — THE BOSTON COOK BOOK: *Mrs. D. A. Lincoln. Roberts Brothers, Publishers.*

Tomato Sauce, —Halve the tomatoes and squeeze out the seeds and watery pulp. Stew the solid portions gently with a little gravy or strong broth until they are entirely softened. Strain through a hair sieve and reheat with additional gravy, a little cayenne pepper and salt. Serve hot.

Green Tomato Sauce.—Cut up two gallons of green tomatoes; take three gills of black mustard seed, three table-spoonfuls of dry mustard, two and a half of black pepper, one and a half of allspice, four of salt, two of celery seed, one quart each of chopped onions and sugar, and two and a half quarts of good vinegar, a little red pepper to taste. Beat the spices and boil all together until well done.

Chili Sauce.—Take ten pounds of ripe tomatoes, peeled and sliced; two pounds of peeled onions chopped fine; seven ounces of green peppers finely chopped, without the seeds; six ounces of brown sugar; four ounces salt; a pint and a half of vinegar. Boil all together in a porcelain-lined kettle for several hours, until thick as desired; put up in tight cans or jars, and use with soups and gravies.

Celery Sauce.—Pick and wash two heads of celery; cut them into pieces one inch long, and stew them in a pint of water, with one teaspoonful of salt, until the celery is tender. Rub a large spoonful of butter and a spoonful of flour well together; stir this into a pint of cream; put in the celery, and let it boil up once. Serve hot with boiled poultry.

Mint Sauce.—Wash the sprigs of mint, let them dry on a towel, strip off the leaves, and chop them very fine; put in a sauce-boat with a cupful of vinegar and four lumps of sugar; let it stand an hour, and before serving stir all together. Mint sauce, if bottled, will keep a long time, and be just as good, if not better, than when freshly made.

Asparagus Sauce.—Take a dozen heads of asparagus; two teacupfuls drawn butter; two eggs; the juice of half a lemon; **salt and** white pepper. Boil the tender **heads** in a very little salt water. Drain and chop them. Have ready a pint of drawn butter, with two raw eggs beaten into it; add the asparagus, and season, squeezing in the lemon juice last. The butter must be hot, but do not cook after putting in the asparagus heads. This is a delightful sauce for boiled fowls, stewed fillet of veal, or boiled mutton.

Mushroom Sauce.—Pick, rub, and wash a pint of young mushrooms, and sprinkle with salt to take off the skin. Put them into a saucepan with a little salt, a blade of mace, a little nutmeg, a pint of cream, and a piece of butter rolled in flour; boil them up and stir till done.

Caper Sauce.—Make a drawn butter sauce, and add two or three tablespoonfuls of French capers; remove from the fire and add a little lemon juice.

Cranberry Sauce.—Cover a quart of cranberries with water and let it simmer gently till thoroughly cooked. Strain the skins out through a colander, and add to the juice two cupfuls of sugar; let it simmer again for fifteen minutes, and pour into a mold previously wet in cold water.

Strawberry Sauce.—Rub half a cupful of butter and one cupful of sugar to a cream; add the beaten white of an egg and one cupful of strawberries thoroughly mashed.

Lemon Sauce.—One-half a cupful of butter, one cupful of sugar, yelks of two eggs, one teaspoonful of corn-starch. Beat the eggs and sugar until light; add the grated rind and juice of one lemon. Stir the whole into three gills of boiling water until it thickens sufficiently for the table.

Lemon Sauce, No. 2.—One large tablespoonful of butter, one small tablespoonful of flour, one cupful of sugar, **grated rind** and juice of one lemon.

Vanilla Sauce.—Put half a pint of milk in a small saucepan over the fire; when scalding hot add the yelks of three eggs, and stir until it is as thick as boiled custard; remove the saucepan from the fire, and when cool add a tablespoonful of extract of vanilla and the beaten whites of two eggs.

Venison Sauce.—Mix' two teaspoonfuls of currant jelly, one stick of cinnamon, one blade of mace, grated white bread, ten tablespoonfuls of water; let the whole stew till thoroughly cooked, when done serve with venison steak.

Anchovy Sauce.—Stir two or three teaspoonfuls of prepared essence or paste of anchovy, into a pint of melted butter; let the sauce boil a few minutes, and flavor with lemon juice.

Lobster Sauce.—Break the shell of the lobster into small pieces. Pour over these one pint of water or veal-stock and a pinch of salt; simmer gently until the liquid is reduced one-half. Mix two ounces of butter with an ounce of flour, strain the liquid upon it and stir all, over the fire, until the mixture thickens, but do not let it boil. Add two tablespoonfuls of lobster meat chopped fine, the juice of half a lemon, and serve.

Oyster Sauce.—Strain fifty oysters; put the juice into a saucepan; add one pint of new milk; let it simmer, and then skim off whatever froth may rise. Rub a large spoonful of flour and two of butter together; stir this into the liquor; add a little salt and pepper. Let this simmer five minutes, but do not add the oysters till just as they are to be sent to the table, as oysters much cooked are hard. For turkeys, etc., this is a splendid dressing.

Plain French Dressing.—A plain French dressing is made simply of salt, pepper, oil, and vinegar. Three tablespoonfuls of oil to one of vinegar, saltspoon heaping full of salt, an even saltspoonful of pepper mixed with a little cayenne.

Mayonnaise Sauce.—Work the yelks of two raw eggs to a smooth paste, and add two saltspoonfuls of salt, half a saltspoonful of cayenne, a saltspoonful of dry mustard, and a teaspoonful of oil; mix these thoroughly and add the strained juice of half a lemon. Take what remains of half a pint of olive oil and add it gradually, a teaspoonful at a time, and every fifth teaspoonful add a few drops of lemon juice until you have used two lemons and the half-pint of oil.

Mayonnaise Sauce, No. 2.—Rub the yelks of three hard-boiled eggs with the yelk of one raw egg to a smooth paste; add a heaping teaspoonful of salt, two saltspoonfuls of white pepper, and two saltspoonfuls of made mustard; mix thoroughly and work a gill of oil gradually into the mixture, alternated with a teaspoonful of vinegar, until you have used three tablespoonfuls of vinegar. Should the sauce appear too thick, add a wineglassful of cream.

Butter Sauce.—Mix well together two tablespoonfuls of butter, some chopped parsley, juice of half a lemon, salt, and pepper. For broiled meat or fish.

Brown Butter Sauce.—Put butter into a frying-pan and let it stand on the fire until very brown; then add a little parsley and fry a moment longer.

Drawn Butter Sauce.—Take one-quarter pound of butter; rub with it two teaspoonfuls of flour. When well mixed, put into a saucepan with one-half pint of water; cover it, and set the saucepan into a larger one full of boiling water. Shake it constantly till completely melted and beginning to boil; season with salt and pepper.

Boiled Egg Sauce.—Add to half a pint of drawn butter sauce two or three hard-boiled eggs, chopped.

CROQUETTES & FRITTERS

BLANK PAGE FOR ADDITIONAL RECIPES

VIII.—CROQUETTES AND FRITTERS.

THE term *croquette* (pronounced cro-ket) is from a French verb, meaning " to crunch." It designates all that class of preparations made of minced meat, or other ingredients, highly seasoned and fried in bread-crumbs.

Fritters, like croquettes, are fried, but they are made of batter containing other ingredients, as taste may dictate. Both these preparations are used as accessories of the dinner or tea table rather than as principal dishes.

RECIPES.

Rice Croquettes.—Put a quarter of a pound of rice into a pint of milk. Let it simmer gently until the rice is tender and the milk absorbed. It must then be boiled until thick and dry, or it will be difficult to mold. Add three tablespoonfuls of sugar, one of butter, one egg, and flavor to taste with vanilla or cinnamon ; beat thoroughly for a few minutes, and when cold form into balls or cones, dip these into beaten egg, roll lightly in bread-crumbs, and fry in hot butter.

Hominy Croquettes.—To a cupful of cold boiled hominy (small grained) add a tablespoonful of melted butter and stir hard; moisten by degrees with a cupful of milk, beating to a soft, light paste. Put in a teaspoonful of white sugar and a well-beaten egg. Roll into oval balls with floured hands, dip in beaten egg, then in cracker-crumbs, and fry in hot lard.

111

Potato Croquettes.—Season cold mashed potatoes with pepper, salt, and nutmeg. Beat to a cream, with a tablespoonful of melted butter to every cupful of potato. Add two or three beaten eggs and some minced parsley. Roll into small balls; dip in beaten egg, then in bread-crumbs, and fry in hot lard.

Oyster-Plant Croquettes.—Wash, scrape, and boil the oyster-plant till tender; rub it through a colander, and mix with the pulp a little butter, cream, salt, cayenne, and lemon juice; mix the ingredients thoroughly together to a smooth paste, and set the dish in the ice-box to get cold; then shape it into small cones, dip them in beaten egg, roll in crumbs, and fry crisp and brown.

Chicken Croquettes.—Add to the quantity of minced chicken; about one-quarter the quantity of bread-crumbs, also one egg well beaten to each cupful of meat; pepper, salt, and chopped parsley to taste, add the yelks of two hard-boiled eggs rubbed smooth. Add gravy or drawn butter to moisten it, make into cones or balls, roll in cracker-dust or flour, and fry in hot lard.

Veal Croquettes.—Make these the same as chicken croquettes, by substituting for the chicken cold minced veal and ham in equal parts. The salt may be omitted, as the ham usually supplies it sufficiently. Turkey, duck, or the remains of any cold game or meat may be used in the same way with very satisfactory results.

Oyster Croquettes.—Take the hard ends of the oysters, leaving the other end for a soup or stew; scald them, then chop fine, and add an equal weight of potatoes rubbed through a colander; to one pound of this combination add two ounces of butter, one teaspoonful of salt, half a teaspoonful of pepper, half a teaspoonful of mace, and one-half gill of cream, make in small rolls, dip them in egg and grated bread, fry in deep, hot lard.

Lobster Croquettes.—Chop the lobster very fine; mix with pepper, salt, bread-crumbs, and a little parsley; moisten with cream and a small piece of butter; shape with your hands; dip in egg, roll in bread-crumbs, fry in hot lard.

Plain Fritters.—Take one pint of flour, four eggs, one pint of boiling water, and one teaspoonful of salt. Stir the flour into the boiling water gradually, and let it boil three minutes, stirring constantly. Remove from the fire and stir in the yelks of the eggs, afterward the whites, they having been well beaten. Drop this batter by large spoonfuls into boiling lard and fry to a light brown. Serve hot, powdered with white sugar.

Bread Fritters.—Grate stale bread until you have a pint of crumbs; pour a pint of boiling milk upon these, a tablespoonful of butter having been dissolved in it, and let the whole stand for an hour. Then beat up the mixture and flavor with nutmeg. Stir in gradually a quarter pound of white sugar, two tablespoonfuls of brandy, six well-beaten eggs, and currants enough to flavor the whole. The currants should be washed, dried, and floured. Drop by large spoonfuls into boiling lard and fry to a light brown. Serve with wine and powdered sugar.

Potato Fritters.—Break open four nicely baked potatoes; scoop out the insides with a spoon, and mix with them a wineglassful of cream, a tablespoonful of brandy, two tablespoonfuls of powdered sugar, the juice of one lemon, half a teaspoonful of vanilla extract, and well-beaten yelks of four and the whites of three eggs; beat the batter until it is quite smooth; drop large tablespoonfuls of the mixture into boiling fat and fry to a light brown; dust them with powdered sugar and send to table hot.

Corn Fritters.—Scrape twelve ears of corn, mix with **two**
8

eggs, one and one-half cups of milk, salt and pepper to taste, and flour enough to hold all together. Fry in hot fat.

Hominy Fritters.—Two teacupfuls of cold boiled hominy; stir in one teacupful of sweet milk and a little salt, four table-spoonfuls of sifted flour, and one egg; beat the white separately and add last; drop the batter by spoonfuls in hot lard and fry to a nice brown.

Rice Fritters.—Boil a quarter of a pound of rice in milk till it is tender, then mix it with a pint of milk, two eggs, one cup of sugar, a little salt and cinnamon, and as much flour as will make a thick batter. Fry them in thin cakes and serve with butter and white powdered sugar.

Parsnip Fritters.—Boil four good-sized parsnips in salted water until tender; drain them, beat them to a pulp, and squeeze the water from them as much as possible; bind them together with a beaten egg and a little flour. Shape into cakes and fry in hot lard.

Fruit Fritters.—The following recipe will serve for many kinds of fruit or vegetable fritters: Make a batter of ten ounces of flour, half a pint of milk, and two ounces of butter; sweeten and flavor to taste; stir in the whites of two eggs well beaten; dip the fruit in the batter and fry. Small fruit and vegetables should be mixed with the batter.

Apple Fritters.—Take one egg, two tablespoonfuls of flour, a little sifted sugar and ginger, with milk enough to make a smooth batter; cut a good sized apple into slices and put them into the batter. Put them into a frying-pan, with the batter which is taken up in the spoon. When fried, drain them on a sieve and sift on powdered sugar.

Currant Fritters.—Take two cupfuls dry, fine bread-crumbs, two tablespoonfuls prepared flour, two cups of milk, one-half pound currants, washed and well dried; five eggs whipped very light and the yelks strained, one-half cup powdered sugar, one tablespoonful butter, one-half teaspoonful mixed cinnamon and nutmeg. Boil the milk and pour over the bread. Mix and put in the butter. Let it get cold. Beat in, next, the yelks and sugar, the seasoning, flour, and stiff whites, finally the currants dredged white with flour. The batter should be thick. Drop great spoonfuls into the hot lard and fry. Drain them and send hot to table. Eat with a mixture of wine and powdered sugar.

Oyster Fritters.—Take one and one-half pints of sweet milk, one and one-fourth pounds of flour, four egg (the yelks having been beaten very thick); add milk and flour; stir the whole well together, then beat the whites to a stiff froth and stir them gradually into the batter ; take a spoonful of the mixture, drop an oyster into it, and fry in hot lard; let them be a light brown on both sides.

Clam Fritters.—Take a dozen chopped clams, one pint of milk, three eggs. Add liquor from the clams, with salt and pepper, and flour enough to produce thin batter. Fry in hot lard.

Cream Fritters.—Take one cup of cream, the whites of five eggs, two full cups prepared flour, one saltspoonful of nutmeg, a pinch of salt. Stir the whites into the cream in turn with the flour, put in nutmeg and salt, beat all hard for two minutes. The batter should be rather thick. Fry in plenty of sweet lard, a spoonful of batter for each fritter. Drain and serve upon a hot, clean napkin. Eat with jelly sauce. Do not cut them open, but break or pull them apart.

French Fritters.—Take two cupfuls of flour, two teaspoonfuls of baking powder, two eggs, milk enough for stiff batter, and a little salt. Drop into boiling lard and fry light brown. Serve with cream and sugar or sauce.

Spanish Fritters.—Cut stale bread into small, round slices about an inch thick; soak them in milk, and then dip them into well-beaten egg which has been sweetened to taste. Sprinkle thickly with cinnamon and fry in hot lard.

Venetian Fritters.—Take three ounces of whole rice, wash and drain into a pint of cold milk. Let it come slowly to a boil, stirring often, and let it simmer till quite thick and dry. Add two ounces of powdered sugar, one of fresh butter, a pinch of salt, the grated rind of half a lemon. Let the whole cool in the saucepan, and while still a little warm mix in three ounces of currants, four ounces of chopped apples, a teaspoonful of flour, and three well-beaten eggs. Drop the batter in small lumps into boiling fat, allowing them to fry till the under side is quite firm and brown; then turn and brown the other side. When done, drain through a hair sieve, and powder with white sugar when about tc serve.

BLANK PAGE FOR ADDITIONAL RECIPES

IX.—EGGS.

NUTRITIOUS VALUE OF EGGS—TEST OF FRESHNESS—PACKING EGGS
—PRESERVING EGGS. THIRTY-THREE WAYS OF COOKING EGGS.

HIGH chemical authorities agree that there is more nutriment in an egg than in any substance of equal bulk found in nature or produced by art. They are much used for food the world over, and few articles are capable of more varied employment.

The freshness of an egg may be determined in various ways. In a fresh egg, the butt end, if touched on the tongue, is sensibly warmer than the point end. If held toward the light and looked through ("candled"), a fresh egg will show a clear white and a well-rounded yelk. A stale egg will appear muddled. Probably the surest test is to put the eggs into a pan of cold water. Fresh eggs sink quickly; bad eggs float; suspicious ones act suspiciously, neither sinking nor floating very decidedly. Of all articles of food, doubtful eggs are most certainly to be condemned.

On the packing of eggs, the following conclusions may be regarded as established among egg-dealers: By cold storage, temperature forty to forty-two degrees Fahrenheit, kept uniform, with eggs packed properly or in cases, they will keep in good condition from six to nine months; but they must be used soon after being taken out of the cold storage, as they soon spoil. Eggs become musty from being packed in bad material. They will become musty in cases, as a change of temperature causes the eggs to sweat and the wrapping-paper to become moist and taint the eggs.

117

Well-dried oats, a year old, makes the best packing.   Eggs
become " mixed " by jarring in shipping.   Fresh eggs mix
worse than those kept in cold storage.   Eggs which have
been held in cold storage in the West should be shipped in
refrigerator cars in summer.   Eggs will keep thirty days
longer if stood on the little end than in any other position.
They must be kept at an even temperature and in a pure
atmosphere.   Eggs laid on the side attach to the shell and
are badly injured.   To prevent imposition as to the freshness
of the eggs, the egg gatherers should " candle " them when
they get them from the farmers.   Eggs keep better in the
dark than in the light.

Methods of preservation for domestic purposes are, to
pack them in bran or salt, the small end down ; to grease
them with linseed oil, or dip them in a light varnish.   For
extra long keeping, slack one pound of lime in a gallon of
water ; when this is entirely cold, place it in a jar and fill
with fresh eggs.   Do not agitate the contents when. eggs
are removed from the jar.   Eggs kept so will continue good
for a year.

The French method of preserving eggs is to dissolve
beeswax and olive oil and anoint the eggs all over.   If left
undisturbed in a cool place, they will remain good for two
years.

RECIPES.

Boiled Eggs.—Put into a saucepan of *boiling* water with a
tablespoon, being careful not to break or crack them.   Boil
steadily three minutes, if you want them soft ; ten, if hard.

Another way is to put them on in cold water, and let it
come to a boil.   The inside, white and yelk, will be then of
the consistency of custard.

Still another way is to put them in water, heated to the
boiling point, and let them stand from five to seven minutes
without boiling.   If desired for salad, boil them ten minutes;

then throw them in cold water; roll them gently on a table
or board, and the shell can be easily removed. Wire egg
racks, to set in boiling hot water with the eggs held in place,
are exceedingly convenient.

Boiled Eggs, with Sauce.—Boil hard, remove the shell, set
in a hot dish, and serve with seasoning and sauce to taste.

Poached Eggs.—Have the water well salted, but do not let
it boil hard. Break the eggs separately into a saucer, and
slip them singly into the water; when nicely done, remove
with a skimmer, trim neatly, and lay each egg upon a small
thin square of buttered toast, then sprinkle with salt and
pepper. Some persons prefer them poached rather than
fried with ham; in which case substitute the ham for toast.

Poached Eggs with Ham Sauce.—Mince fine two or three
slices of boiled ham, a small onion, a little parsley, pepper,
and salt; stew together for a quarter of an hour; put the
poached eggs in a dish, squeeze over them the juice of a
lemon, and pour on the sauce hot but not boiling.

Poached Eggs a la Creme.—Nearly fill a clean frying-pan
with water boiling hot; strain a tablespoonful of vinegar
through double muslin, and add to the water with a little
salt. Slip your eggs from the saucer upon the top of the
water (first taking the pan from the fire). Boil three minutes and a half; drain, and lay on buttered toast in a hot
dish. Turn the water from the pan and pour in half a cupful of cream or milk. If you use the latter, thicken with a
very little corn-starch. Let it heat to a boil, stirring to prevent burning, and add a great spoonful of butter, some pepper, and salt. Boil up once and pour over the eggs. Or
better still, heat the milk in a separate saucepan, that the
eggs may not have to stand. A little broth improves the
sauce.

Steamed Eggs.—Butter a tin plate and break in your eggs; set in a steamer; place over a kettle of boiling water, and steam until the whites are cooked; they are more orna mental when broken into patty tins, as they keep their form better; the whites of the eggs, when cooked in this manner, are tender and light, and not tough and leathery, as if cooked by any other process.

Eggs in this style can be eaten by invalids, and are very much richer than by any other method.

Whirled Eggs.—Put a quart of water, slightly salted, into a saucepan over the fire, and keep it at a fast boil. Stir with wooden spoon or ladle in one direction until it whirls rapidly. Break six eggs, one at a time, into a cup and drop each carefully into the centre, or vortex, of the boiling water. If kept at a rapid motion, the egg will become a soft, round ball. Take it out carefully with a perforated spoon, and put it on a slice of buttered toast laid upon a hot dish. Put a bit of butter on the top. Set the dish in the oven to keep warm, and proceed in the same way with another egg, having but one in the saucepan at a time. When all are done, dust lightly with salt and pepper and send up *hot*.

Eggs a la Mode.—Remove the skin from a dozen tomatoes, medium size, cut them up in a saucepan, add a little butter, pepper, and salt; when sufficiently boiled, beat up five or six eggs, and just before you serve, turn them into a saucepan with the tomato, and stir one way for two minutes, allowing them time to be well done.

Baked Eggs.—Mix finely chopped ham and bread-crumbs in about equal proportions, season with salt and pepper, and moisten with milk and a little melted butter; half fill your small patty pans with the mixture, break an egg over the top of each, sprinkle with fine bread-crumbs, and bake; serve hot.

Baked Eggs, No. 2.—Butter a clean, smooth saucepan, break as many eggs as will be needed into a saucer, one by one, and if found good, slip each into the saucepan. No broken yelk must be allowed, nor must they crowd so as to risk breaking the yelk after put in. Put a small piece of butter on each, and sprinkle with pepper and salt. Set into a well-heated oven, and bake till the whites are set. If the oven is rightly heated, it will take but a few minutes, and the cooking will be far more delicate than fried eggs.

Eggs sur le Plat.—Melt butter on a stone-china or tin plate. Break the eggs carefully into this; dust lightly with pepper and salt, and put on top of the stove until the whites are well set. Serve in the dish in which they are baked.

Scrambled Eggs.—Put into a frying-pan enough butter to grease it well; slip in the eggs carefully without breaking the yelks; add butter, and season to taste; when the whites begin to set, stir the eggs from the bottom of the pan, and continue stirring until the cooking is completed. The appearance at the end should be *marbled*, rather than *mixed*.

Scrambled Eggs with Ham.—Put into a pan, butter, a little pepper and salt, and a little milk; when hot, drop in the eggs, and with a knife cut the eggs and scrape them from the bottom as the whites begin to set; add some cold ham chopped fine, and when done, serve in a hot dish.

Toasted Eggs.—Cover the bottom of an earthenware or stone-china dish with rounds of delicately toasted bread, or with rounds of stale bread dipped in beaten egg and fried quickly to a golden-brown in butter or nice dripping. Break an egg carefully upon each, and set the dish immediately in front of a glowing fire. Toast over this as many slices of *fat* salt pork or ham as there are eggs in the dish, holding the meat so that it will fry very quickly and all the dripping fall upon the eggs. When these are well set, they are done. Turn the dish several times while toasting the meat, that the eggs may be equally cooked. Do not send the pork to table, but pepper the eggs lightly and remove with the toast to the dish in which they go to the table.

Egg Toast.—Beat four eggs, yelks and whites, together thoroughly; put two tablespoonfuls of butter into a saucepan and melt slowly; then pour in the eggs and heat, without boiling, over a slow fire, stirring constantly; add a little salt, and when hot spread on slices of nicely browned toast and serve at once.

Egg Baskets.—Boil quite hard as many eggs as will be needed. Put into cold water till cold, then cut neatly into halves with a thin, sharp knife; remove the yelk and rub to a paste with some melted butter, adding pepper and salt. Cover up this paste and set aside till the filling is ready. Take cold roast duck, chicken, or turkey, which may be on hand, chop fine and pound smooth, and while pounding mix in the paste prepared from the yelks. As you pound, moisten with melted butter and some gravy which may have been left over from the fowls; set this paste when done over hot water till well heated. Cut off a small slice from the end of the empty halves of the whites, so they will stand firm, then fill them with this paste; place them close together on a flat, round dish, and pour over the rest of the gravy, if any remains, or make a little fresh. A few spoonfuls of cream or rich milk improves this dressing.

Fricasseed Eggs.—Boil six eggs hard; when cold, slice with a sharp knife. Have ready some slices of stale bread, fried to a nice brown in butter or drippings. Put a cupful of good broth in drawn butter over the fire, season it with pepper, salt, and a trace of onion; let it come to a boil. Dip the slices of egg first into raw egg, then into cracker dust or bread-crumbs, and lay them gently into the gravy upon the side of the range. Do not let it actually boil, lest the eggs should break, but let them lie thus in the gravy at least five minutes. Place the fried bread upon a platter, lay the sliced eggs evenly upon this, pour the gravy over all, and serve hot.

Curried Eggs.—Boil six or eight fresh eggs quite hard, and put them aside until they are cold. Mix well together from two to three ounces of good butter, and from three to four dessertspoonfuls of currie-powder; shake them in a stewpan, or thick saucepan, over a clear but moderate fire for some minutes, then throw in a couple of mild onions finely minced, and fry gently until they are soft; pour in by degrees from half to three-quarters of a pint of broth or gravy, and stew slowly until they are reduced to pulp; mix smoothly a small cup of thick cream with two teaspoonfuls of wheaten or rice flour; stir them to the currie, and simmer the whole until the raw taste of the thickening is gone. Cut the eggs into half-inch slices, heat them through in the sauce without boiling them, and send to the table as hot as possible.

Plain Omelet.—Beat thoroughly yelks of five eggs, and a dessertspoonful of flour, rubbed smooth in two-thirds of a cupful of milk. Salt and pepper to taste, and add a piece of butter the size of a hickory-nut. Beat the whites to a stiff froth, pour the mixture into the whites, and without stirring pour into a hot, buttered omelet pan. Cook on top of the range for five minutes; then set pan and all into the oven to brown the top nicely.

Baked Omelet.—Beat the yelks of six eggs, and add the whites of three eggs beaten very light; salt and pepper to taste, and a tablespoonful of flour mixed in a cup of milk. Pour into a well-buttered pan and put into a hot oven; when thick, pour over it the whites of three eggs beaten light; then brown nicely, without allowing the top to become crusted. Serve immediately.

Omelet a la Mode.—Beat the yelks and whites of six eggs separately until light, then beat together and add one tablespoonful of cream. Have in the omelet pan a piece of butter; when the butter is boiling hot, pour in the omelet and shake until it begins to stiffen, and then let it brown, and season to taste. Fold double and serve hot.

If a larger omelet is desired, a tablespoonful of milk to each egg may be added, and one teaspoonful of corn-starch or flour to the whole.

Cheese Omelet.—Butter the sides of a deep dish and cover with thin slices of rich cheese; lay over the cheese thin slices of well-buttered bread, first covering the cheese with a little red pepper and mustard; then another layer of cheese; beat the yelk of an egg in a cup of cream or milk, and pour over the dish, and put at once into the oven; bake till nicely browned. Serve hot, or it will be tough and hard, but when properly cooked it will be tender and savory.

Meat or Fish Omelet.—Make the same as plain omelet. When it is done, scatter thickly over the surface cold, boiled ham, tongue, poultry, fish, or lobster, chopped fine, and season nicely to taste; slip the broad knife under one side of the omelet and double, inclosing the meat. Then upset the frying-pan upon a hot dish, so transferring the omelet without breaking. Or the minced meat may be stirred in after the ingredients are put together, and before cooking. Be careful not to scorch the egg.

Omelet with Oysters.—Allow one egg for each person, and beat yelks and whites separately, very light; season to taste, and just before cooking add the oysters, which have been previously scalded in their own liquor.

Egg Sandwiches.—Hard boil some fresh eggs, and, when cold, cut them into moderately thin slices, and lay them between slices of bread and butter cut thin, and season well with celery salt. For picnic parties or for traveling, these sandwiches are very nice.

Deviled Eggs.—Boil the eggs hard, remove the shell, and cut in two as preferred. Remove the yelks, and add to them salt, cayenne pepper, melted butter, and mixed mustard to taste ; then stuff the cavities of the hard whites, and put the halves together again. Serve garnished with parsley. For picnics, etc., each egg can be wrapped in tissue paper to preserve its form.

Pickled Eggs.—Boil the eggs until very hard ; when cold, shell them, and cut them in halves lengthways. Lay them carefully in large-mouthed jars, and pour over them scalding vinegar, well seasoned with whole pepper, allspice, a few pieces of ginger, and a few cloves of garlic. When cold, tie up closely, and let them stand a month. They are then fit for use. With cold meat, they are a most delicious and delicate pickle.

Egg Balls.—Rub the yelks of hard-boiled eggs with the raw yelk of an egg, well beaten, and season to taste. Roll this paste into balls the size of marbles, adding flour if necessary to thicken, and boil two minutes. A valuable embellishment and enrichment of soups.

Soft-boiled Eggs.—Put the eggs in a warm saucepan and cover with boiling water. Let them stand where they will keep hot, but not boil, for ten minutes. This method will cook both whites and yolks. — NEW COOK BOOK : *Miss Maria Parloa. Estes & Lauriat, Publishers.*

Sweet Omelet. — Beat four eggs without separating ; add a piece of butter the size of a walnut and four table-spoonfuls of warm water. Put another piece of butter in a frying-pan. When melted and hot turn in the egg and shake until set, then lift carefully the side, drain the liquid portion underneath, shake again until the omelet is cooked. Fill the centre with jam and fold over one side and then the other. Turn it into another heated pan; turn on to a heated dish and serve.

Creamed Eggs for Luncheon. — One-half dozen hard-boiled eggs cut in halves. Make a white sauce as follows: Two teaspoonfuls butter, two level tablespoonfuls flour; melt butter and stir in flour; then add slowly one-half pint milk, seasoning with salt and pepper and a little celery. Pour over eggs and serve in a dish garnished with parsley.

Eggs Scrambled in Tomatoes. — Fry one small slice of onion in three tablespoonfuls butter until crisp, then remove onion; add to the butter one large cup tomato, one teaspoonful sugar, one teaspoonful Worcestershire sauce. Season with salt and pepper and cook five minutes. Add four eggs beaten and cook the same as scrambled eggs. Serve with entire wheat or brown bread toast.

Omelet Souffle. — Separate six eggs, beat the whites to a very stiff froth; beat and add the yolks of three, three tablespoonfuls of powdered sugar, the grated rind of half a lemon, a tablespoonful of lemon juice. Mix quickly and turn into a baking dish or form on a platter. Dust thickly with powdered sugar and bake in a quick oven about five minutes.

BREAD

BLANK PAGE FOR ADDITIONAL RECIPES

X.—BREAD, BISCUIT, HOT CAKES, ETC.

AN immense department is opened up by the title of this chapter; and it is a department of immense importance. Bread is confessedly the "staff of life," and, therefore, it should be good. And whatever takes the place of bread, be it biscuits, hot cakes, muffins, or what not, should also be good, or nothing is gained by the exchange. Many a housekeeper can make excellent pies, cakes, etc., but when bread is needed, she flies to the bakery, confessing her total inability to prepare this indispensable commodity.

But even bread may become distasteful as a steady diet. To vary it with the long line of splendid substitutes which are possible, and which are discussed in this chapter, is a most desirable ability. This department, therefore, is worthy of every housewife's devout study.

I.—BREAD.

ESSENTIALS TO MAKING GOOD BREAD ; HOW TO KNOW GOOD FLOUR ; YEAST ; RAISING BREAD ; BAKING BREAD. TWELVE RECIPES FOR BREAD.

THREE things are essential to the making of good bread, namely, good flour, good yeast, and judicious baking. A fourth might be added, experience, without which none of the domestic arts can be successfully carried on.

RECIPES.

Wheat Bread.—Put seven pounds of flour into a breadpan ; hollow out the centre, and add a quart of lukewarm water, a teaspoonful of salt, and a wineglassful of yeast. Have ready more warm water, and add gradually as much as will make a smooth, soft dough. Knead it well, dust a little flour over it, cover it with a cloth, and set it in a warm place four hours; then knead it again for fifteen minutes and let it rise again. Divide it into loaves, and prick them with a fork, and bake in a quick oven from forty minutes to an hour.

Potato Bread.—Three and one-half quarts of sifted flour, three boiled potatoes, one quart warm water, one teacupful of yeast, one even tablespoonful salt. Mix at night; put the flour in a large bowl; hollow a place in the centre for the mashed potatoes, water, and salt. Stir in flour enough to make a smooth batter; add yeast; stir in the rest of the flour. Put the dough on the floured board; knead fifteen minutes, using barely enough flour to prevent sticking. Flour the bowl, lay the dough in it, cover and leave it to rise. In the morning, divide in four parts; mold into loaves; when light, prick, and bake in a moderate oven.

Salt Rising Bread.—Pour a pint of hot water in a two-quart pail or pitcher on one-half tablespoonful of salt; when it has cooled a little, add one and one-third pints of flour; mix well, and leave the pitcher in a kettle of water, as warm as that used for mixing. Keep it at the same temperature until the batter is nearly twice its original bulk, which will be in from five to eight hours. It may be stirred once or twice during the rising. Add to this a sponge made of one quart of hot water, two and one-half quarts of flour—adding as much more as may be necessary to make a soft dough; mix well, and leave in a warm place to rise. When light, mold into loaves, keeping them as soft as possible; lay in buttered tins. When light again, prick and bake.

Milk Bread.—Let two quarts of milk come to a boil; stand it aside to cool, and when it becomes tepid, add flour to it gradually until it makes a batter just soft enough to beat up with a spoon. To this add one cake of compressed yeast thoroughly dissolved in lukewarm water. The batter should then be well beaten. Cover with a towel and set in a warm place to rise. When light, add two tablespoonfuls of salt, one of lard, one of light brown sugar, and flour enough to make a soft dough. Knead steadily for about half an hour. This quantity should make four or five medium-sized loaves. Put them in greased pans and let them rise again. When light, prick with a fork and bake in a quick oven.

Vienna Bread.—The Vienna bread that became so famous on the Centennial Exhibition grounds in 1876 was made on the following recipe: Sift in a tin pan four pounds of flour; bank up against the sides; pour in one quart of milk and water, and mix into it enough flour to form a thin batter, and then quickly and lightly add one pint of milk, in which is dissolved one ounce of salt and one and three-quarter ounces of yeast; leave the remainder of the flour against the sides of the pan; cover the pan with a cloth, and set in a place free from draught for three quarters of an hour; then mix in the rest of the flour until the dough will leave the bottom and sides of the pan, and let it stand two and a half hours; finally, divide the mass into one-pound pieces, to be cut in turn into twelve parts each; this gives square pieces about three and a half inches thick, each corner of which is taken up and folded over to the centre, and then the cases are turned over on a dough-board to rise for half an hour, when they are put in a hot oven that will bake them in ten minutes.

Rye Bread.—Scald two handfuls of corn-meal with a quart of boiling water, and add a quart of milk and a tablespoonful of salt. When cool, add a teacupful of yeast, and enough rye flour to make it as stiff as wheat-bread dough. After it has risen put it in pans and bake an hour and a half.

Brown Bread.—Take one cup of bread-crumbs, one pint of

sweet milk, one cup of molasses, butter the size of an egg, one teaspoonful of soda, corn-meal enough to make a stiff batter, with salt to taste. Turn the whole into a buttered basin and steam for two hours; then bake in a quick oven half an hour.

Boston Brown Bread.—Take three and three-fourth cupfuls of Indian corn-meal, two and one-half cupfuls rye-meal, two-thirds cupful molasses, one quart milk, either sweet or sour; two even teaspoonfuls soda, dissolved in the milk; steam in a tin pudding boiler five hours; take off the cover and set in the oven to brown.

Corn Bread.—Two heaping cupfuls Indian meal, one cup-ful wheat flour, two heaping teaspoonfuls **Plume Baking Powder**; mix well together while dry; one teaspoonful salt, two tablespoonfuls white sugar, two eggs, one tablespoonful lard, two and a half cupfuls cold milk; beat the eggs, melt the lard, and dissolve the salt and sugar in the milk before add-ing them to the flour; bake in buttered pans in a *quick* oven.

Graham Bread.—Three quarts of Graham flour; one quart of warm water; one gill of yeast; one gill of sirup; one tablespoonful of salt; one even teaspoonful of soda. Mix thoroughly and put in well-buttered pans to rise. Bake about an hour and a half.

This same mixture may be thinned and baked in gem pans for Graham gems.

Rice Bread.—After a pint of rice has been boiled soft, mix it with two quarts of rice flour or wheat flour. When cold, add half a teaspoonful of yeast, a teaspoonful of salt, and enough milk to make a soft dough. When it has risen, bake in small buttered pans.

Unleavened Bread.—Mix wheat flour into a stiff dough with warm water or milk; add a little lard, or suet, and bake in thin cakes. Bake as soon as mixed, and eat hot.

II.—TOAST.

WHAT TOAST IS GOOD FOR.   SIX METHODS OF PREPARING TOAST.

AS a palatable method of disposing of stale bread, as well as to furnish a variety of agreeable dishes, toast is an important factor in the culinary economy of the home. As a dish for invalids it is indispensible.

RECIPES.

Dry Toast is produced by browning stale baker's bread over glowing coals. A toasting fork, or rack, of which there are various patterns, is a great convenience. Do not burn the toast, nor allow it to be so browned as to harden it. It should be eaten hot, as it becomes tough when allowed to cool.

Buttered Toast.—For buttered toast, the slices should be thicker than for dry toast. Butter the slices as toasted, and keep warm until served. Excessive buttering should be avoided.

Egg Toast.—On slices of buttered toast lay poached eggs. Serve with Worcestershire sauce for breakfast.

French Toast.—Beat three eggs light, add one cupful of milk, with pepper and salt to taste. Dip into this slices of bread, then fry them in hot butter to a delicate brown.

Milk Toast.—Toast the bread an even, delicate brown, and pile into a hot dish. Boil milk with a little salt, a teaspoonful of flour, and one of butter, rubbed together; pour it over the toast and serve hot.

Cream Toast.—Take slices of baker's bread from which the crust has been pared and toast it to a golden brown. Have on the range a shallow bowl or pudding-dish, more than half full of boiling water, in which a tablespoonful of butter has been melted. As each slice is toasted, dip in this for a second, sprinkle lightly with salt, and lay in the deep heated dish in which it is to be served. Have ready, by the time all the bread is toasted, a quart of milk scalding hot, but not boiling. Thicken this with two tablespoonfuls of corn-starch or best flour ; let it simmer until cooked ; put in two tablespoonfuls of butter, and when this is melted, the beaten whites of three eggs. Boil up once, and pour over the toast, lifting the lower slices one by one, that the creamy mixture may run in between them. Cover closely, and set in the oven two or three minutes before serving.

III.—FANCY BREADS.

FANCY BREADS AND PLAIN CAKES ; THEIR GENERAL USEFULNESS.
EIGHT RECIPES FOR FANCY BREADS.

SOME special preparations come naturally between bread and cake. For convenient classification, they are grouped here under the title of Fancy Breads, though they might as well be classed as Plain Cakes. They serve a good purpose for variety, for luncheon, etc. See plainer forms of cakes.

RECIPES.

Sally Lunn.—One quart of flour, a piece of butter the size of an egg, three tablespoonfuls of sugar, two eggs, two tea-cupfuls of milk, two teaspoonfuls of cream tartar, one of soda, and a little salt. Scatter the cream of tartar, the sugar, and the salt into the flour ; add the eggs, the butter (melted), and one cup of milk ; dissolve the soda in the remaining cup, and stir all together steadily a few moments. Bake in two round pans.

Sally Lunn, No. 2.—Rub into a quart of flour two teaspoonfuls of baking-powder ; beat together nearly half a cup of butter and two tablespoonfuls of sugar; put into the flour and mix with a pint of milk; then add two eggs, beaten light. Mix and bake as above.

Johnny Cake.—One quart of buttermilk or sour milk, one quart Indian meal, one quart of flour, one cup of molasses, a teaspoonful of soda, two scant teaspoonfuls if the milk is sour, a teaspoonful of salt. Bake in shallow pans in a quick oven.

Hoe Cake.—Scald one quart of Indian-meal in enough water to make a thick batter; add a teaspoonful of salt, one of molasses, and two of butter. Bake on a board before a hot fire or in a pan.

Scotch Short-cake.—Two pounds of fine flour, one pound of fresh, sweet butter, half a pound of finest sifted sugar; throughly knead together without water; roll out to half an inch in thickness, and place it on paper in a shallow pan; bake very slowly until of proper crispness. The cake, to be good, must be very brittle.

Pumpkin Bread.—Stew and strain a sufficient quantity of pumpkin; add enough Indian-meal to stiffen it, with yeast and a little salt; when sufficiently raised, bake as in ordinary bread.

Pone.—This is a dish prepared by the Indians, called also *paune.*. Take two cupfuls of corn-meal, two of wheat flour, one of sugar, and half a cup of melted butter. Add one egg, one teaspoonful of salt, one of soda, and two of cream of tartar. Mix with enough milk to make a moderately stiff batter, and bake in a hot oven.

Barley Bread.—In Scotland, Norway, and other climates where wheat is not grown, barley bread is used extensively. It is both wholesome and palatable. Mix the barley meal with warm water and a little salt, but no yeast. Mix to a stiff dough, roll into flat cakes, and bake before the fire or in an oven. Eat hot, with butter.

IV.—ROLLS.

A FAVORITE departure from the ordinary forms of bread is furnished in rolls.   They are exceedingly popular for breakfast, served warm.   There are sufficient variations in rolls to make them suitable for use day after day, if this be desired.

RECIPES.

Plain Rolls.—Boil six potatoes in two quarts of water, and when done pour and press the whole through the colander ; when cool, but not cold, add flour to make a thick batter ; add half a cup of yeast, or one-half cake of compressed yeast, and set to rise ; when light, add half a cup of lard and butter mixed, a tablespoonful of sugar, teaspoonful of salt, and flour to make a soft dough ; knead well and set again to rise ; when light, knead down again ; repeat three or four times ; an hour before they are to be used cut in small pieces, roll out, spread with melted butter, and fold over, laying them in a pan so that they will not touch each other ; set them in a warm place, and when light bake quickly. Or, make into an oblong roll without spreading and rolling, and just before putting them into the oven, gash deeply across the top with a sharp knife.

English Rolls.—Two pounds of flour, two ounces of butter, three tablespoonfuls of yeast, one pint of warm milk ; mix well together, and set in a warm place to rise ; knead, and make into rolls ; let them rise again and bake twenty minutes.

Breakfast Rolls.—One quart of sifted flour, three teaspoonfuls baking-powder, half teaspoonful salt; mix well together dry, then add three and half gills of cold milk, or enough to make it the consistency of batter, and drop with a spoon into gem baking-pans, which should have been previously heated very *hot* and buttered.

French Rolls.—One pint of milk, scalded; put into it while hot half a cupful of sugar, and one tablespoonful of butter; when the milk is cool, add a little salt and half a cupful of yeast, or one cake of compressed yeast; stir in flour enough to make a stiff sponge, and when light mix as for bread. Let it rise until light, punch it down with the hand, and let it rise again, and repeat this process two or three times; then turn the dough on to the molding board, and pound with rolling-pin until thin enough to cut. Cut out with a tumbler, brush the surface of each one with melted butter, and fold over. Let the rolls rise on the tins; bake, and while warm brush over the surface with melted butter to make the crust tender.

Vienna Rolls.—One quart sifted flour, two heaping tea-spoonfuls **Plume Baking Powder**; mix well while dry; then add a tablespoonful of butter or lard, made a little soft by warming and stirring, and about three-fourths of a pint, or enough cold, sweet milk for a dough of usual stiffness, with about half a teaspoonful of salt dissolved in it. Mix into a dough easily to be handled without sticking; turn on the board and roll out to the thickness of half an inch, cut it out with a large cake-cutter, spread very lightly with butter, fold one-half over the other, and lay them in a greased pan without touching. Wash them over with a little milk, and bake in a hot oven.

Parker House Rolls.—One teacupful of yeast, or one cake of compressed yeast, a little salt, one tablespoonful sugar, piece of lard size of an egg, one pint milk, flour sufficient to mix. Put the milk on the stove to scald with the lard in it. Prepare the flour with salt, sugar, and yeast. Then add the milk, not too hot. Knead thoroughly, and when mixed set to rise; when light, knead again slightly. Then roll out and cut with large biscuit-cutter. Spread a little butter on each roll and lap together. Let them rise again very light, and bake in a quick oven.

Geneva Rolls.—Into two pounds of flour break three ounces of butter, add a little salt, and make into a sponge with yeast, previously mixed with milk and water. Allow the batter to rise; then mix in two eggs, made lukewarm by the adding of hot milk, and work the sponge to a light dough. Let it stand for three-quarters of an hour longer; mold into small rolls; place them in buttered pans. When light, brush them with beaten yelks of eggs, and bake for twenty minutes or half an hour. Serve hot.

V.—BISCUIT, RUSK, AND BUNS.

SPECIAL CARE REQUISITE IN THIS DEPARTMENT; ATTENTION TO INGREDIENTS, OVEN, ETC.; HOW TO BAKE THEM; BAKING-POWDER BISCUITS, SODA BISCUITS, ETC.; CARE OF PANS. FIFTEEN RECIPES FOR BISCUITS, BUNS, ETC.

GREAT care is requisite in making biscuits that quantities be accurately observed and that the ingredients used are of proper quality. Flour should be a few months old. New flour will not make good biscuits. It should always be sifted.

The oven, too, needs careful attention. On its condition the success of biscuit baking will depend. Rolls and biscuit should bake quickly. To make them a nice color, rub them over with warm water just before putting them into the oven; to glaze them, brush lightly with milk and sugar

Baking-powder biscuit and soda biscuit should be made as rapidly as possible, laid into hot pans, and put in a quick oven. Gem pans should always be heated and well greased.

RECIPES.

Potato Biscuit.—Pare ten potatoes, boil them thoroughly, and mash fine; add two cups of lukewarm milk, two table-spoonfuls of white sugar, half a cup of yeast, and flour enough to make a thin batter. Mix well and allow it to rise. Then add four tablespoonfuls of melted butter, a little salt, and enough flour to make a soft dough. Let this rise again; roll into a sheet about an inch thick, and cut into cakes. Set to rise again, and bake in a quick oven.

Light Biscuit.—When kneading bread, set aside a small loaf for biscuits. Into this, work a heaping tablespoonful of lard and butter mixed and a teaspoonful of sugar. The more it is worked the whiter it will be. As it rises, mold it down twice before making into biscuit. Roll out and cut with a biscuit-cutter. The dough should be quite soft.

Soda Biscuits.—One quart of flour, a tablespoonful of but-ter and two of lard, a teaspoonful of salt, and one teaspoon even full of cream of tartar, one teaspoonful of soda; sift the cream tartar with the flour dry; rub the butter and lard very thoroughly through it; dissolve the soda in a pint of milk and mix all together. Roll out, adding as little flour as possible; cut with a biscuit-cutter, and bake twenty minutes in a quick oven.

Tea Biscuit.—Take one quart sifted flour, one tablespoon-ful shortening, half teaspoonful salt, and two teaspoonfuls **Plume** baking-powder; mix well together dry, then add sufficient cold milk or water to form a very soft dough; bake immediately in a quick oven.

Cream Biscuits.—Dissolve one teaspoonful of soda in a quart of sour cream, add to it flour sufficient to make a soft dough and a little salt; or use sour *milk*, and rub a table-spoonful of butter into the flour.

Graham Biscuits.—Take one quart of water or milk, butter the size of an egg, three tablespoonfuls sugar, two of baker's yeast, and a pinch of salt; take enough white flour to use up the water, making it the consistency of batter cakes; add the rest of the ingredients and as much Graham flour as can be stirred in with a spoon; set it away till morning; in the morning grease the pan, flour your hands; take a lump of dough the size of a large egg, roll it lightly between the palms, and let the biscuits rise twenty minutes, then bake in a tolerably hot oven.

Maryland Biscuits.—Take three pints of sifted flour, one tablespoonful of good lard, one pint of cold water, salt to the taste; make into a stiff dough; work it till it cracks or blisters, then break, but do not cut it, into suitable portions, and make into biscuits; stick the top of each with a fork and bake.

Yorkshire Biscuits.—Make a batter with flour sufficient and one quart of boiling hot milk. When the batter has cooled to lukewarmness, add a teacupful of yeast and a half teaspoonful of salt. Set to rise again and let it become very light; then stir in a half teaspoonful of soda, two eggs, and a tablespoonful of melted butter. Add flour enough to make the dough into small, round cakes; let them rise fifteen minutes, and bake in a slow oven.

Short Biscuits.—Mix one quart of flour with a quarter pound of butter melted in boiling water. Add enough cold milk to make a stiff dough. Work into small biscuits and bake in a quick oven.

Flavored Biscuits.—Biscuit dough made as for Light Biscuit may be flavored with any essence, or with lemon or orange peel, as desired.

Tea Rusk.—Three cups of flour, one cup of milk, three-fourths of a cup of sugar, two heaping tablespoonfuls of butter, melted; two eggs, three teaspoonfuls baking-powder. Let them rise, and bake in a moderate oven. Glaze while hot with white of egg, in which has been stirred, not beaten, a little powdered sugar, or sift the powdered sugar in while the egg is still moist on the top. Rusks should never be eaten hot.

Sweet Rusk.—One pint of warm milk—new is best—one-half cup of butter, one cup of sugar, two eggs, one teaspoonful of salt, two tablespoonfuls of yeast; make a sponge with the milk, yeast, and enough flour to make a thin batter, and let it rise over night. In the morning add the sugar, butter, eggs, and salt, well beaten up together, with enough flour to make a soft dough; let it rise again; then work out into round balls, and set to rise a third time. Bake in a moderate oven.

Buns.—One cupful of warm water, one cupful of sweet milk, yeast and sugar, with flour enough to make a stiff batter; let this rise over night; in the morning add a cupful of sugar, a cupful of raisins or currants, mold well; let it rise till light, then make into buns; rise again till very light, and bake. Use any spice desired.

Hot Cross Buns.—Three cupfuls sweet milk; one cupful of yeast; flour to make thick batter. Set this as a sponge over night. In the morning add one cupful of sugar; one-half cupful butter, melted; half a nutmeg; one saltspoonful salt, and flour enough to roll out like biscuit. Knead well, and set to rise five hours. Roll half an inch thick, cut into round cakes, and lay in rows in a buttered baking-pan. When they have stood half an hour, make a cross upon each with a knife, and put instantly into the oven. Bake to a light brown, and brush over with a feather or soft bit of rag, dipped in the white of an egg beaten up stiff with white sugar.

Pop Overs.—Mix four cupfuls of flour, four cupfuls of milk, four eggs, and a little salt. This quantity will make about twenty puffs in gem-pans, which must be baked quick and done to a nice brown.

VI.—MUFFINS AND WAFFLES.

HOW MUFFINS AND WAFFLES DIFFER; THEIR RELATION TO OTHER KINDRED PREPARATIONS; MUFFIN-RINGS AND WAFFLE-IRONS; WHEN TO USE MUFFINS AND WAFFLES; HOW TO SERVE THEM. ELEVEN RECIPES FOR MUFFINS AND WAFFLES.

MUFFINS are baked in rings on a griddle, or in gem-pans, over a quick fire. Waffles are baked in waffle-irons, which inclose the batter and imprint both sides of the cake as it rises in the process of baking. Both muffins and waffles form a medium between bread and biscuits on the one side and griddle-cakes on the other. Muffin-rings were formerly about four inches in diameter, but now, with better taste, they are used much smaller. The approved waffle-irons of to-day are circular, baking four waffles at once, and suspended on a pivot that permits them to be turned with a touch of the fork. Both muffins and waffles are suitable for tea, and with stewed chicken and such delicacies they are really delicious. They should always be served hot and with the best of butter. Waffles and catfish are a famous dish at some eating-houses.

RECIPES.

Muffins.—Two eggs lightly beaten, one quart of flour, one teaspoonful of salt, three teaspoonfuls of **Plume** baking-powder, one tablespoonful of melted butter, one pint of milk, and two teaspoonfuls of vanilla extract, if liked. Beat up quickly to the consistency of a cake batter; bake in buttered gem-pans in a hot oven.

Muffins, No. 2.—One cup of home-made yeast or half of a compressed yeast cake, one pint of sweet milk, two eggs, two tablespoonfuls of melted butter, two tablespoonfuls of sugar. Beat the butter, sugar, and eggs well together ; then stir in the milk, slightly warmed, and thicken with flour to the consistency of griddle-cakes. When light, bake in muffin-rings or on a griddle. If wanted for tea, the batter should be mixed immediately after breakfast. Muffins should never be cut with a knife, but be pulled open with the fingers.

Rice Muffins.—Take one quart of sour milk, three well-beaten eggs, a little salt, a teaspoonful of soda, and enough of rice flour to thicken to a stiff batter. Bake in rings.

Hominy Muffins.—Substitute hominy, well cooked and mashed, for the rice, and proceed as above.

Bread Muffins.—Cut the crust off four thick slices of bread ; put them in a pan and pour on them just enough boiling water to soak them thoroughly. Let them stand an hour, covered ; then drain off the water and stir the bread to a smooth paste. Stir in two tablespoonfuls of flour, a half pint of milk, and three well-beaten eggs. Bake to a delicate brown in well-buttered muffin-rings.

Graham Muffins.—One quart of Graham flour, two teaspoonfuls of baking-powder, a piece of butter the size of a walnut, one egg, one tablespoonful of sugar, one-half teaspoonful of salt, milk enough to make a batter as thick as for griddle-cakes. Bake in gem-pans or muffin-rings in a hot oven.

Corn Muffins.—Mix two cupfuls of corn-meal, two cupfuls of flour, one cupful of sugar, half a cupful of melted butter, two eggs, and one teaspoonful of salt. Dissolve one teaspoonful of soda and two of cream tartar in a little milk, and beat it through. Add milk enough to make a moderately stiff batter, and bake in rings or gem-pans.

Crumpets.—Three cupfuls of warm milk, half a cupful of yeast, two tablespoonfuls of melted butter, one saltspoonful each of salt and soda dissolved in hot water, flour enough to make a good batter. Set these ingredients—leaving out the butter and soda—as a sponge. When very light, beat in the melted butter, with a *very* little flour; stir in the soda hard, fill patty-pans or muffin-rings with the mixture, and let them stand fifteen minutes before baking.

Raised Waffles.—One quart of warm milk, one tablespoonful of butter, three eggs, one gill of yeast, one tablespoonful of salt, and flour to make a stiff batter. Set to rise, and bake in waffle-irons, which must be well heated before used.

Quick Waffles.—One quart flour, two teaspoonfuls **Plume Baking Powder,** one teaspoonful salt; mix dry; then stir in one tablespoonful melted butter, two well-beaten eggs, and enough cold, sweet milk for a batter thin enough to pour; bake at once in waffle-irons.

Rice Waffles.—Mix a teacupful and a half of boiling rice with a pint of milk, rubbing it smooth over the fire. Take from the fire and add a pint of cold milk and a teaspoonful of salt. Stir in four well-beaten eggs with enough flour to make a thin batter, and bake as above. Waffles should always be served hot. Powdered sugar with a flavor of powdered cinnamon makes a pleasing dressing for them.

VII.—GRIDDLE-CAKES.

WHAT GRIDDLE-CAKES ARE ; HINTS ABOUT GRIDDLES ; HOW TO COOK GRIDDLE-CAKES ; HOW TO SERVE THEM ; WHEN TO SERVE THEM ; WITH WHAT TO SERVE THEM. TEN RECIPES FOR GRIDDLE-CAKES.

CAKES made of a batter so thin that it flows easily upon a griddle, and that can, therefore, be quickly baked and be served hot, are griddle-cakes, and great favorites they are.

All new griddles are hard to manage, but as the only way to get old ones is to make them out of new ones, we are shut up to the necessity of using the new, though they do not work so well. Opinions divide between iron griddles and those of soapstone. The latter require no greasing. Hence trouble is saved, and the smoke of the fat used in the constant greasing of a hot iron griddle is entirely avoided. But still, many housekeepers prefer the old style.

A hot griddle is essential to good griddle-cakes. But it must not be hot enough to burn before it bakes. A cold griddle will make cakes tough, unpalatable, and decidedly unwholesome.

Hot cakes may well be served with powdered sugar, **Golden Tree Brand Maple Syrup** or any molasses in the market. Cold days are the gala days for hot cakes. Time immemorial, buckwheat cakes and sausage have gone to the table side by side. There is delightful harmony in this union; but to serve hot cakes and fish together would introduce discord into the best regulated family. There is an eminent fitness between hot cakes and certain other dishes, and it must never be disregarded.

RECIPES.

Buckwheat Cakes.—One quart of buckwheat-meal, one pint of wheat-flour or Indian-meal, half a teacupful of yeast, salt to taste; mix the flour, buckwheat, and salt with as much water moderately warm as will make it into a thin batter; beat it well, then add the yeast; when well mixed, set it in a warm place to rise; as soon as it is very light, grease the griddle and bake the cakes to a delicate brown. Butter them with good butter and serve hot.

Graham Griddle-cakes.—Scald a cupful of Indian-meal in a pint of boiling water, and strain it over night. Thin it with a quart of milk, and make into a sponge with a cupful of

Graham flour, a large tablespoonful of molasses, and half a cupful of yeast. In the morning, add salt to taste, a cupful of white flour, half a teaspoonful of soda, dissolved in hot water, and a tablespoonful of butter or lard. Stir in enough water to make batter of the right consistency, and bake on a hot griddle.

Flannel Cakes.—Three eggs, one quart of sweet milk, about one quart of flour, a small teaspoonful of salt, two table-spoonfuls of prepared baking-powder; beat the yelks, and half of the milk, salt, and flour together; then the remainder of the milk; and last, the whites of the eggs well beaten. Bake in small cakes on a hot griddle.

Flannel Cakes, No. 2.—One quart of milk, three eggs, one cupful of yeast, one dessertspoonful of salt, flour enough for a thinnish batter, and a teaspoonful of butter; set to rise; bake like buckwheat cakes. Cakes half Indian and half wheat are very nice, and good cakes may be made even without the eggs.

Rice Cakes.—Soak a cupful of rice five or six hours in enough warm water to cover it. Then boil slowly till soft. While still warm, but not hot, stir in a tablespoonful of but-ter, a tablespoonful of sugar, a teaspoonful of salt, and a quart of milk. When cold, add three eggs, beaten very light. Sift a half teaspoonful of cream of tartar into a quarter cupful of rice flour, and add them to the batter, first beating into it a quarter teaspoonful of soda dissolved in hot water.

Rice Cakes, No. 2.—Boil a cupful of rice until quite soft, setting it aside until cool. Beat three eggs very light, and put them into the rice, with a pint of flour, into which you have sifted three teaspoonfuls of prepared baking-powder. Add a teaspoonful of butter and one of salt, making it into a batter with a quart of milk. Bake on a griddle.

Hominy Cakes.—Mix with cold boiled hominy an equal quantity of white flour until perfectly smooth; add a teaspoonful of salt and thin off with buttermilk, in part of which a teaspoonful of soda has been dissolved; when of the proper consistency for griddle cakes, add a dessertspoonful of melted butter, and bake as usual.

Sour Milk Cakes.—One pint sour milk, one teaspoonful of soda, a little salt, two eggs, and flour to make a thin batter; bake on a hot griddle.

Indian Griddle Cakes.—One large cupful Indian-meal, four tablespoonfuls of wheat flour, two tablespoonfuls of **Plume** baking-powder, one teaspoonful salt, mix together dry, then add sufficient cold water for a batter; bake at once on a hot griddle.

Slapjacks.—One pint of milk, three eggs, one teaspoonful of soda, and one of salt, flour enough to make a thin batter. Butter your griddle, and fry them the size of a teaplate; when one is done, turn it on the dish, sprinkle with a little white sugar, and continue in this way till they are all fried. Always fry them with butter. A little nutmeg may be grated with the sugar on each cake.

VIII.—YEAST AND YEAST CAKES.

NATURE OF YEAST; ACTION OF YEAST IN DOUGH; CAUSES OF LIGHT BREAD AND HEAVY BREAD; CARE OF YEAST. TWO RECIPES FOR YEAST AND YEAST CAKES.

IN this chapter, yeast has been so often referred to that its special consideration seems important just here. Analytically considered, it consists of an innumerable quantity of infinitesimal fungi, called the *yeast-plant*. The remarkable characteristic of these minute plants is, that under favoring conditions they multiply to an incredible

10

extent in a very short time. Thus the production of yeast, in proper mixtures, is an easy matter.

When yeast is placed in dough, it immediately produces fermentation, in the process of which gases are generated, which permeate the dough, filling it with gas-vessels and so producing the spongy appearance so familiar in raised bread. If this process goes too far, it sours the dough and unfits it for food. If arrested by placing the dough in a hot oven, the gases will be driven off by the heat, and the thin dough walls will be set and baked. If the oven be slow, the gases will be driven off, the dough walls will collapse, and heavy bread will be the result. The proper use of yeast is most important, therefore. It must be watched as carefully as any other tender plant. Excessive heat or cold, or rough mechanical usage will quickly destroy it.

RECIPES.

Patent Yeast.—Boil two ounces of hops in four quarts of water for a half hour. Strain and cool till lukewarm, then add a handful of salt, a half pound of sugar, and a pound of flour, all mixed well and beaten up together. After it has stood forty-eight hours, add three pounds of potatoes, boiled and well-mashed. Let it stand twenty-four hours, stirring it often; then strain and bottle. It is ready for immediate use, or will keep several months. Keep in a cool place.

Yeast Cakes.—Thicken good yeast with Indian-meal till it becomes a stiff batter. A little rye will make it adhere better. Make into cakes an inch thick and two by three inches in area. Dry them in the air, but not in the sun. Keep them in a bag in a cool, dry place. One of these cakes is enough for four quarts of flour. To use them, soak in milk or water several hours and use as other yeast.

PUDDINGS

BLANK PAGE FOR ADDITIONAL RECIPES

XI.—PASTRY AND PUDDINGS.

THAT pastry may be wholesome and appetizing, great care in the selection of ingredients and in their manipulation is absolutely essential. One fact must always be borne in mind—that inferior ingredients cannot be made into superior compounds—though the finest ingredients may be ruined by careless or unskillful handling. Some suggestions of general application are therefore desirable.

Be careful to have all the materials *cool*, and the butter and lard hard; use cold water (ice-water if convenient); use a cool knife, and work on a marble slab if it can be had.

Put the ingredients together quickly, handling as little as possible; slow mixing and much contact with the hands or fingers make tough crust. Always use well-sifted flour.

Except in puff-paste, lard and butter in about equal proportions make the best crust; if made of butter alone, it is almost sure to be tough. That of lard alone, though tender, is usually white and insipid. Beef drippings, or the drippings of fresh pork, make a very light and palatable crust, lighter and more tender indeed than that made with butter alone, much better tasted than that made with lard alone, and quite equal to that made with butter and lard combined. Never use mutton drippings in crust.

Use very little salt and very little water; pour the latter in gradually, only a few drops at a time, unless you want tough crust.

Use plenty of flour on your paste-board, to keep the paste from sticking. Work the crust of one pie at a time, and always roll from you—one way only.

The filling for the pie should be perfectly cool when put in, or it will make the bottom crust heavy.

In making juicy pies, cut a slit in the top to let the steam escape, else the pie will be puffed unduly.

The oven should be hot, but not sufficiently so to scorch or to set the paste before it has had time to rise; if too slack, the paste will not rise at all, but will be white and clammy. The best paste has a tinge of yellow. If permitted to scorch or brown, even the best paste becomes rancid.

RECIPES.

Pie Crust.—Take one-half cupful of lard, one-half cupful of butter, one quart of sifted flour, one cupful of cold water and a little salt. Rub the butter and lard *slightly* into the flour; wet it with the water, mixing it as little as possible. This quantity will make two large or three small pies.

Pie Crust Glaze.—To prevent juice from soaking the under crust, beat up the white of an egg, and before filling the pie, brush over the crust with the beaten egg. Brush over the top crust also, to give it a beautiful yellow brown.

Puff Paste.—Take one pound of sifted flour, on which sprinkle a very little sugar; take the yelks of one or two eggs, and beat into them a little ice-water, and pour gently into the centre of the flour, and work into a firm paste, adding water as is necessary; divide three-quarters of a pound or a pound of firm, solid butter, as you prefer, into three parts; roll out the paste, and spread one part of the butter on half of the paste; fold the other half over, and roll out again, repeating the process until the butter is all rolled in; then set the paste on the ice for fifteen or **twenty**

minutes, after which roll out again three times, each time rolling it the opposite direction; then put on the ice again until cold, when it is ready for use. Such paste will keep several days in a refrigerator, but should not be allowed to freeze.

Paste Shells.—Take sufficient rich puff-paste prepared as in the preceding recipe, roll very thin, cut to shape, and bake in a brisk oven in tin pans. Baked carefully, before filling with fruit, the paste rises better. When cool, the shells may be filled with stewed fruit, jelly, preserves, rich cream whipped to a stiff froth, raspberries, strawberries, or sliced peaches. These are delicious light desserts. Raspberries, strawberries, or sliced peaches, smothered with whipped cream on these shells, are really exquisite.

Apple Pie.—Line a pie plate with paste, and fill it heaping full with tart apples, sliced very thin. Sweeten and spice to taste, mixing well into the apples. Put in plenty of butter, and moisten well with cream. Bake until the apples are thoroughly done. Use no upper crust.

Apple Meringue Pie.—Stew and sweeten ripe, juicy apples. Mash smooth, and season with nutmeg. Fill the crust, and bake until just done. Spread over the apple a thick meringue, made by whipping to a stiff froth the whites of three eggs for each pie, sweetening with a tablespoonful of powdered sugar for each egg. Flavor this with vanilla; beat until it will stand alone, and cover the pie three-quarters of an inch thick. Set back in the oven until the meringue is well set. Eat cold.

Peach Meringue Pie.—Proceed as above in all respects, simply substituting peaches for apples. Whipped cream will make a delightful substitute for the whipped egg in either of these meringue pies.

Peach Pie.—Bake rich shells about two-thirds done; if your peaches are fully ripe, cut them into halves or quarters put in the shell, sweeten and flavor to taste, cover or not as you choose, and finish baking in a *quick* oven; if the peaches are ripe, but not soft, it will improve the flavor to sugar them down some hours before you wish to use them; if not ripe, they should be stewed.

Gooseberry Pie.—Stew the gooseberries with plenty of white sugar, and use plain puff-paste for crust.

Cherry Pie.—Having removed the stones, put in sugar as may be needed, and stew the cherries slowly till they are quite done, if you use shells, or till nearly done if you use paste. A few of the pits added in stewing increase the richness of the flavor; but they should not go into the pies. If baked slowly the cherries need not be stewed at all.

Rhubarb Pie.—Remove the skin from the stalks; cut them in small pieces; pour boiling water over and let stand for ten minutes; drain thoroughly; then fill the pie-dish evenly full; put in plenty of sugar, a little butter, and dredge a trifle of flour evenly over the top; cover with a thin crust, and bake the same as apple pie. Equal quantities of apple and rhubarb used in the same manner make a very good pie.

Pumpkin Pie.—Stew the pumpkin until thoroughly done, and pass it through a colander. To one quart of stewed pumpkin, add three eggs, and one pint of milk. Sweeten, and spice with ground ginger and cinnamon to taste. Add butter, rose water, and a little brandy. The quantity of milk used will vary as the pumpkin may be moist or dry.

Sweet Potato Pie.—Scrape clean two good-sized sweet potatoes; boil; when tender, rub through the colander; beat the yelks of three eggs light; stir with a pint of sweet milk into the potato; add a small teacupful of sugar, a pinch of salt; flavor with a little fresh lemon, or lemon extract; bake to a nice brown; when done, make a meringue top with the whites of eggs and powdered sugar; brown this a moment in the oven.

Dried-Apple Pie. — To a pint of stewed dried-apples, passed through a colander, add a pint of sweet milk, three eggs, and three large tablespoonfuls of sugar, beaten well together as for custard. Spice with a teaspoonful of cinnamon and half a teaspoonful of ground cloves. Bake with upper and under crusts. This quantity will make two pies.

Prune Pie. — Stew the prunes until soft, then cool and remove the stones. Fill your dish with them, sweeten, and spice with a little cinnamon, nutmeg and cloves. Bake with upper and under crust.

Squash Pie. — One cup of stewed squash, one-half cup of sugar, two eggs, and milk enough to fill a pie-plate. First line pie-plate with crust, then beat eggs and sugar together, adding squash and milk. Season with cinnamon, nutmeg and allspice, to suit the taste. Bake till well done.

Tomato Pie. — Take ripe tomatoes, wash, peel, and cut in thin slices; fill a pie-plate, lined with good paste, with them; sprinkle well with sugar, and sift a little cinnamon and grated nutmeg over them; add two teaspoonfuls of vinegar and one of lemon-essence; cover with crust and bake.

Raisin Pie. — Take juice and yellow rind of one lemon; one cup of raisins, one cup of water, one cup of rolled crackers, one cup of sugar. Stone the raisins and boil in water to soften them. Bake with upper and under crusts.

Orange Pie. — One orange grated, five crackers rolled fine, a pint of sweet milk, two eggs well beaten, sugar to sweeten. Bake as a custard.

Custard Pie.—Take one quart of milk, five eggs, four table-spoonfuls of sugar, a small piece of butter. Sift over the top Durkee's mixed spice.

Lemon Pie.—Let two cupfuls of water come to a boil; put in two tablespoonfuls of corn-starch dissolved. When it has boiled enough, take it from the stove, add the juice and rind of two lemons, two cupfuls of sugar, a piece of butter the size of a walnut, and the yelks of two eggs. Beat the whites of these eggs with pulverized sugar, and put on the top of the pies when done. Put into the oven to brown.

Orange Pie.—Beat the yelks of three eggs until light, and add to them the juice and grated rind of one orange, three-quarters of a cupful of sugar, and a tablespoonful of corn-starch mixed in half a cupful of water. Bake without upper crust, using the whites of the eggs for meringue.

Cream Pie.—One pint of milk, scalded; two tablespoonfuls of corn-starch, three tablespoonfuls of sugar, yelks of two eggs. Wet the starch with a little cold milk; beat the eggs and sugar until light, and stir the whole into the scalding milk. Flavor with lemon or vanilla, and set aside to cool. Line a plate with pie-crust and bake; fill it with the cream, and cover with frosting made of the whites of the eggs, beaten dry, with two tablespoonfuls of sugar. Bake to a delicate brown.

Cocoanut Pie.—One quart of milk, half a pound of grated cocoanut, three eggs, six tablespoonfuls of sugar, butter the size of an egg. Bake in open shells.

Cheese-cake Pie.—This may be made from the above recipe, substituting cottage-cheese for the cocoanut. Sprinkle the top with **Slade's Spices.**

Mince Pie.—Seven pounds beef, three and a half pounds beef suet, five pounds of raisins, two pounds of currants, one-half peck apples, four pounds sugar, three-quarters of a pound of citron, one-quarter of a pound of preserved lemon, two large oranges, four nutmegs, half an ounce of cinnamon, half an ounce of cloves, and three pints of brandy. This quantity of mince-meat will make from twenty to twenty-five pies. When making the pies, moisten the meat with sweet cider.

Tarts.—Use the best of puff-paste; roll it out a little thicker than pie-crust, and cut with a large biscuit-cutter twice as many as you intend to have of tarts. Then cut out of half of these a small round in the centre, which will leave a circular rim of crust; lift this up carefully, and lay it on the other pieces. Bake in pans, so providing both the bottom and the top crusts. Fill with any kind of preserves, jam, or jelly.

Pineapple Tart.—Take a fine, large, ripe pineapple; remove the leaves and quarter it without paring, grate it down till you come to the rind; strew plenty of powdered sugar over the grated fruit; cover it, and let it rest for an hour; then put it into a porcelain kettle, and steam in its own sirup till perfectly soft; have ready some empty shells of stiff-paste, or bake in patty-pans. When they are cool, fill them full with the grated pineapple; add more sugar, and lay round the rim a border of puff-paste.

Tea Baskets.—Make a short, sweetened pie-crust; roll thin, and partly bake in sheets; before it is quite done take from the oven, cut in squares of four inches or so, take up two diagonal corners and pinch together, which makes them basket-shaped; now fill with whipped cream, or white of egg, or both, well sweetened and flavored, and return to the oven for a few minutes.

Strawberry Short-cake.—Make a good biscuit crust, and roll out about one-quarter of an inch thick, and cut into two cakes the same size and shape; spread one over lightly with melted butter, and lay the other over it, and bake in a

hot oven. When done, they will fall apart. Butter them
well as usual. Mix the berries with plenty of sugar, and
set in a warm place until needed. Spread the berries and
cakes in alternate layers, berries on the top, and over all
spread whipped cream or charlotte russe. The juice that
has run from the fruit can be sent to the table in a tureen
and served with the cake as it is cut.

Strawberry Short-cake, No. 2.—Take one quart of flour and
sift into it two teaspoonfuls of sea-foam, a little salt, quarter
of a pound of butter rubbed in, with milk enough to moisten
properly. Handle as little as possible, divide into two parts,
roll each flat, and place in two jelly pans. Bake quickly,
then split apart the top and bottom of each crust; spread on
plenty of butter, have the strawberries washed and drained
in a sieve, crush them slightly, and sweeten well. Spread
plenty of berries over each layer of the crust, and have some
of the crushed and sweetened berries in a deep dish. When
the cake is cut and served, cover each piece with the crushed
berries, using this as sauce.

Batter Pudding.—Beat the yelks and whites of four eggs
separately, and mix them with six or eight ounces of flour
and a saltspoonful of salt. Make the batter of the proper
consistency by adding a little more than a pint of milk; mix
carefully; butter a baking-tin, pour the mixture into it, and
bake three-quarters of an hour. Serve with vanilla sauce.

Apple Batter Pudding.—Core and peel eight apples, put in
a dish, fill the places from which the cores have been taken
with brown sugar, cover and bake. Beat the yelks of four
eggs light, add two teacupfuls of flour, three teaspoonfuls
of **Plume Baking Powder** sifted with it, one pint of milk,
and teaspoonful of salt, then the whites well beaten; pour
over the apples and bake. Use sauce with it.

Suet Pudding.—Take a pint of milk, two eggs well beaten,
half a pound of finely chopped suet, and a teaspoonful of

salt. Add flour gradually till you have a pretty thick batter; boil two hours, and eat with molasses.

Suet Pudding, No. 2.—One cupful of suet or butter, one cupful of molasses, one bowlful of raisins and currants, one egg, one cupful of sweet milk, one teaspoonful of saleratus dissolved in milk; one-fourth teaspoonful of cloves, and one-half of nutmeg. Mix stiff with flour and steam three hours. A fine sauce for this pudding may be made thus: One cupful of butter and two cupfuls of sugar, beat into a cream; add three eggs beaten very light; stir in two tablespoonfuls of boiling water. Flavor with wine, brandy, or vanilla.

Hasty Pudding.—Wet a heaping cupful of Indian-meal and a half cupful of flour with a pint of milk; stir it into a quart of boiling water. Boil hard for half an hour, stirring from the bottom almost constantly. Put in a teaspoonful of salt and a tablespoonful of butter, and simmer ten minutes longer. Turn into a deep, uncovered dish, and eat with sugar and cream, or sugar and butter with nutmeg.

Baked Hasty Pudding.—Take from a pint of new milk sufficient to mix into a thin batter two ounces of flour, put the remainder, with a *small* pinch of salt, into a clean saucepan, and when it boils quickly, stir the flour briskly to it; keep it stirred over a gentle fire for ten minutes, pour it out, and when it has become a little cool, mix with it two ounces of fresh butter, three of powdered sugar, the grated rind of a small lemon, four large or five small eggs, and half a glass of brandy or as much orange-flower water. Bake the pudding half an hour in a gentle oven.

Minute Pudding.—Take six eggs, two tablespoonfuls of sugar, one cupful of flour, a lump of butter large as an egg, and half a nutmeg; you may add, if desired, a half pound of raisins; mix well and bake quick.

Corn Pudding.—Twelve ears of sweet corn grated to one

quart of sweet milk ; add a quarter of a pound of good butter, quarter of a pound of sugar. and four eggs; bake from
three to four hours.

Farina Pudding.—Boil one quart of milk, stir in slowly
three tablespoonfuls of farina, let it boil a few minutes ; beat
two eggs and four tablespoonfuls of sugar with one pint of
milk, and mix thoroughly with the farina ; when it has
cooled so as to be little more than lukewarm, put in pans,
and bake in a *moderate* oven. Serve with cream sauce.

Plain Tapioca Pudding.—A cup not quite full of tapioca to
a quart of milk ; let it stand on the side of the range till it
swells; add while hot a tablespoonful of butter and a cupful
of white sugar, and let it cool; then add five eggs (three
will do quite well), well beaten, and flavor to your taste. To
be baked from three-quarters of an hour to an hour. It is
very nice when dressed with wine sauce, but may be eaten
with plainer dressing.

Tapioca and Apple Pudding. — One coffeecupful **Slade's
Quick Tapioca,** one dozen good-flavored, tart apples,
pared and cored, one quart water, a little salt. Cover
tapioca with the water and set it in a tolerably warm place
to soak five or six hours, stirring occasionally. Lay the
apples in a deep dish, put a little sugar and spice in the
centre, pour over the tapioca, and bake one hour.

Peaches may be substituted for apples, which will
make a delightful dish. Serve with hard sauce.

Vermicelli Pudding.—Into pint and a half of boiling milk
drop four ounces fresh vermicelli, and keep it simmering
and stirred gently ten minutes, when it will have become
very thick ; then mix with it three and one-half ounces
sugar, two ounces butter, and a little salt. When the
whole is well blended, pour it out, beat for a few minutes to
cool it, then add by degrees four well-beaten eggs and the

grated rind of a lemon ; pour a little clarified butter over the top ; bake it from one-half to three-fourths of an hour.

Sago Pudding.—Two large spoonfuls of sago boiled in one quart of water, the peel of one lemon, a little nutmeg ; when cold add four eggs and a little salt. Bake about one hour and a half. Serve with sugar and cream.

Arrow-root Pudding.—Boil one quart of milk, and stir into it four heaping tablespoonfuls of arrow-root dissolved in a little milk, mixed with four well-beaten eggs and two table-spoonfuls of white sugar. Boil three minutes. Eat with cream and sugar. This pudding is improved by flavoring with lemon. It should be prepared for table by pouring into wet molds.

Cocoanut Pudding.—One cocoanut finely grated (use both the meat and milk), one quart of milk, one cupful of sugar, five eggs, half a cupful of butter, a little salt, and a tea-spoonful of rose-water. Boil the milk, and pour upon the cocoanut, add the eggs well beaten, and the other ingredients, and bake in a deep dish, with or without an under-crust.

Cocoanut Pudding, No. 2.—Put a pint of milk to boil in a farina kettle. Take four tablespoonfuls of corn-starch and dissolve it in a little cold milk, then stir it into the boiling milk. Add half a cupful of sugar, the well-beaten whites of four eggs, half a grated cocoanut, and a teaspoonful of vanilla extract; turn into a mold to cool. For a suitable sauce put a pint of milk to boil, beat the yelks of four eggs with two tablespoonfuls of sugar till light, then add the boiling milk, with a tablespoonful of vanilla extract. Cook for two minutes in a farina kettle, then turn out to cool.

Rice Pudding.—One quart of milk, three eggs, half a cup-ful of rice, three-fourths of a cupful of sugar, half a cupful of butter, one cupful of raisins, seeded. Soak the rice in a pint of the milk an hour, then set the saucepan containing it where it will slowly heat to a boil. Boil five minutes; remove and let it cool. Beat the eggs, add the sugar and butter, the rice and the milk in which it was cooked, with the pint of unboiled milk, and finally the raisins. Grate nutmeg on the top, and bake three-quarters of an hour, or until the custard is well set and of a light brown. Serve with hard brandy sauce.

Rice Pudding, No. 2.—Three-quarters of a cupful of soaked rice, one cupful of sugar, three pints of milk, one tablespoonful of butter. Season with lemon rind or spice to taste. Bake three-quarters of an hour.

Cottage Pudding.—Three cupfuls flour, or sufficient to make the batter; one teaspoonful butter, one cupful sugar, two eggs, one cupful milk, half a teaspoonful soda, one teaspoonful each of cream of tartar and salt; mix the cream of tartar with the flour, beat the whites of the eggs; put the butter, sugar, and yelks of the eggs together; then work in the milk, soda, and salt, adding gradually the flour and whites of the eggs; there should be flour enough to make a fairly stiff batter; butter a mold or dish, and bake; it may be turned out or served from the dish; to be eaten with any liquid sauce.

Rennet Pudding.—Take one quart of milk, and warm it enough to remove the chill; in summer it does not need warming at all; stir into it three tablespoonfuls of granulated sugar, two of rose-water, and four of rennet wine; stir it gently, not more than a minute; let it stand, and do not move it till it is curdled, then place it gently in the ice chest and grate nutmeg on the top. Be careful not to shake it in moving, for if the curd is disturbed it will turn to whey.

Lemon Pudding.—Take the yellow part of the rind of one, and the juice of two large, juicy lemons. Beat to a cream half a pound of butter, and the same of powdered sugar. Beat six eggs very light, and stir them gradually into the mixture. Add a glass of wine or brandy. Put the whole into a dish with a broad edge; put round two or three layers of puff-paste. Bake half an hour, and when cold sprinkle white sugar over it. Oranges may be used in the same way. To be eaten cold.

Orange Pudding.—Two oranges—the juice of both and grated peel of one; juice of one lemon; one half-pound lady's-fingers—stale and crumbled; two cupfuls of milk; four eggs, one-half cupful sugar; one tablespoonful corn-starch, wet with water; one tablespoonful butter, melted. Soak the crumbs in the cold milk, whip up light, and add the eggs and sugar, already beaten to a cream with the batter. Next add the corn-starch, and when the mold is buttered and water boiling hard, stir in the juice and peel of the fruit. Do this quickly, and plunge the mold directly into the hot water. Boil one hour; turn out and eat with very sweet brandy sauce.

Apple Pudding.—Fill an earthen baking-dish with finely chopped apples; season with sugar and nutmeg, add a little water, set it on the back of the range until the apples are tender; then make a crust of one teacupful of sweet milk, one tablespoonful of butter, a little salt, one teaspoonful baking-powder, flour enough to roll out; lay the crust on top of the apples and bake. To be eaten hot with sweet sauce, flavored with lemon or vanilla. Other kinds of fruit may be used in the same manner.

Bread Pudding.—One pint bread-crumbs; one quart milk; rind of one lemon grated into milk; yelks four eggs, beaten and mixed with one-half cupful sugar. Bake one-half hour. Spread meringue on top.

Fruit Bread Pudding.—Soak three large cupfuls of very fine bread-crumbs, through which has been mixed two teaspoonfuls of cream tartar, in a quart of milk; next, beat in three eggs well whipped, and a cupful of sugar; add half a cupful of finely chopped suet, a little salt, nutmeg, and cinnamon.   Whip the batter very light, and then add fruit as follows, it having been well dredged with flour: Half pound of raisins, seeded and cut in too ; one tablespoonful of finely sliced citron; half a pound of Sultana raisins, washed well and dried.   Add a teaspoonful of soda, dissolved in hot water; heat for three minutes ; put into a buttered mold, and boil hard for two hours.   Eat with brandy sauce.

Delmonico Pudding.—One quart of milk, four eggs, using the white of one only ; three tablespoonfuls of sugar, two tablespoonfuls of corn-starch, one cupful of cocoanut, a little salt.   Put the milk in a farina boiler to scald ; wet the starch in cold milk ; beat the eggs and sugar, and stir all into the scalding milk ; add the cocoanut, and pour the whole into a pudding-dish ; whip dry the three whites, reserved as above, with three tablespoonfuls of sugar ; flavor with lemon or vanilla; spread over the pudding and bake a light brown. Eat hot or cold.

Almond Pudding.—Turn boiling water on to three-fourths of a pound of sweet almonds ; let it remain until the skin comes off easily; rub with a dry cloth; when dry, pound fine with one large spoonful of rose-water; beat six eggs to a stiff froth with three spoonfuls of fine white sugar; mix with one quart of milk, three spoonfuls of pounded crackers, four ounces of melted butter, and the same of citron cut into bits; add almonds; stir all together, and bake in a small pudding-dish with a lining and rim of pastry. This pudding is best when cold. It will bake in half an hour in a quick oven.

Cup Custard. — One quart of milk, five eggs, teaspoonful of butter, sugar to taste. Pour into buttered cups, season with **Slade's Pure Spices,** and bake. This can be baked in a pudding-pan, if preferred.

Rice Custard. — Into a quart of boiling water stir two tablespoonfuls of rice flour, dissolved in a little cold milk ; add two well-beaten eggs to the boiling mixture ; sweeten and flavor to taste.

Chocolate Custard. —Three pints of sweet milk, four table-- spoonfuls of **Bensdorp's Chocolate**, grated, three table-spoonfuls of corn starch, and two eggs. Put the chocolate and a little milk on to boil, stir it until smooth, then add a little cold milk. Beat up the eggs in the remainder of the milk and pour all into the chocolate. Stir until it thickens ; take off the fire, and add sugar and **Metcalf's Water White Vanilla** to taste. Place in a glass dish, and when cold, drop large spoonfuls of the whites of eggs, beaten very light with sugar, over the top, in the centre of each a little currant jelly.

Baked Indian Pudding. — Boil one pint of milk ; while boiling stir in one cupful of Indian meal; let it cool a little, and add three eggs well-beaten, one pint of cold milk, one tablespoonful of flour, one-half cupful of sugar, one cupful of molasses, one teaspoonful of ginger, one of cinnamon, and a little salt. Bake an hour and a half.

Dutch Pudding. — Soak one-half cup Irish moss in cold water fifteen minutes ; pick over, wash it, and tie it in a lace bag or net; put it into the double boiler, with one quart of milk ; mix one tablespoonful **Bensdorp's Royal Dutch Cocoa** and two tablespoonfuls sugar, and make it into a smooth paste with a little of the hot milk, then add enough more milk to make it thin enough to pour ; stir this thoroughly into the milk in the double boiler, and cook until the milk thickens when dropped on a cool plate. Strain into wet moulds, and when hard, serve with sugar and cream. — *Mrs. D. A. Lincoln.*

Brown Betty.—One loaf of stale bread crumbled fine, one-half cupful of milk, and twelve apples. Alternate layers of bread and sliced apples, sugared, buttered, and spiced. Moisten with the milk. Bake in a tin pudding-pan for three hours.

Poor Man's Plum Pudding.—One cupful of molasses, one cupful of suet chopped very fine, beaten smoothly together; one teaspoonful of salt and one of soda mixed through a half-pound of flour, one pint of milk, one pound of raisins, seeded and chopped, and a half-pound of sliced citron. Boil three hours.

English Plum Pudding.—Two pounds of chopped suet, three pounds of seeded raisins, two pounds of currants, one-half pound of citron, two pounds of sugar, five eggs, one pint of milk, one-half pint of brandy, two nutmegs, a little salt, flour sufficient to make it very stiff. Put it into one or two bags, and boil in a large quantity of water seven or eight hours. Serve with sauce.

Spice Pudding.—One cupful of sour milk, one cupful of butter, four cupfuls of flour, two cupfuls of currants, one cupful of sugar, four eggs, four teaspoonfuls of cinnamon, one teaspoonful of cloves, and one teaspoonful of soda. Bake in a quick oven, and serve with brandy sauce.

Paradise Pudding.—Stew until tender three ounces of rice in a pint and a quarter of milk, add four ounces of raisins, three ounces of suet chopped fine, two and a half ounces of sugar, two eggs, a little nutmeg and lemon peel. Boil three hours. Serve with hard sauce.

Jelly Pudding.—Two cupfuls *very* fine stale biscuit or bread-crumbs; one cupful of rich milk—half cream, if you can get it; five eggs, beaten very light; one-half teaspoonful of soda, stirred in boiling water; one cupful of sweet jelly, jam, or marmalade. Scald the milk and pour over the crumbs. Beat until half cold, and stir in the beaten yelks, then whites, finally the soda. Fill large cups half full with the batter; set in a quick oven and bake half an hour. When done, turn out quickly and dexterously; with a sharp knife make an incision in the side of each; pull partly open, and put a liberal spoonful of the conserve within. Close the slit by pinching the edges with your fingers. Eat warm with sweetened cream.

Cabinet Pudding.—Take of the remains of any kind of cake broken up two cupfuls, half a cupful of raisins, half a can of peaches, four eggs, one and a half pints of milk. Butter a plain pudding mold and lay in some of the broken cake, one-third of the raisins, stoned, one-third of the peaches; make two layers of the remainder of the cake, raisins, and peaches. Cover with a very thin slice of bread, then pour over the milk beaten with the eggs and sugar. Set in a saucepan of boiling water to reach two-thirds up the side of the mold, and steam three-quarters of an hour.

Turn out carefully on a dish, and serve with peach sauce, made as follows: Place the peach juice from the can into a small saucepan; add an equal volume of water, a little more sugar, and eight or ten raisins; boil ten minutes, strain, and just before serving add six drops of bitter almond.

Delicious Pudding.—Bake a common sponge cake in a flat-bottomed pudding-dish; when ready for use, cut in six or eight pieces; split and spread with butter, and return them to the dish. Make a custard with four eggs to a quart of milk, flavor and sweeten to taste; pour over the cake and bake one-half hour. The cake will swell and fill the custard. Any stale cake will do about as well as sponge cake.

Bird's-nest Pudding.—Make the foundation of the nest of corn-starch or blanc-mange. Cut strips of lemon peel, boil in a sirup of water and sugar till tender, and arrange around the blanc-mange to represent straw. Extract the contents of four eggs through a small hole, and fill the shells with hot blanc-mange or corn-starch. When cold, break off the shells, and lay the molded eggs in the nest.

Snow Pudding.—Soak an ounce of gelatine in a pint of cold water for one hour; then place it over the fire, stir gently, and remove as soon as it is dissolved; when almost cold, beat to a stiff froth with an egg-beater. Beat the whites of three eggs to a stiff froth, and add it to the gelatine froth, together with the juice of three lemons, and pulverized sugar to the taste. Mix the whole well together, pour into a mold, and set aside to cool. Serve on a dish with soft custard made from the yelks of the eggs.

Cherry Pudding.—Two eggs, one cupful sweet milk, flour enough to make a stiff batter, two teaspoonfuls of baking-powder, and as many cherries as can be stirred in. Eat with sauce made of the cherries.

Blackberry Mush.—Put the berries into a preserving kettle and mash with sugar enough to make sweet; set over the fire, and when it begins to simmer, stir in very gradually one tablespoonful, or more if needed, of corn-starch to a quart of fruit; stir until well cooked, and eat either hot or cold with cream; raspberries also may be used this way.

Roley-poley.—Make a good biscuit dough, and roll about three-quarters of an inch thick, and spread with berries, preserves, or slices of apple; roll up and tie in a cloth; boil or steam an hour and a half.

Berry or Fruit Puddings.—One quart sifted flour, two table-spoonfuls shortening, half teaspoonful salt, and two tea-spoonfuls baking-powder; mix well, then form a soft dough of milk or water, roll out thin, and spread with any kind of berries, fruit, or preserves; roll it up, tie in a cloth, and place in the steamer, or boil in a mold. This makes fine dumplings.

German Puffs.—Two cups of sweet milk, two cups of flour, three eggs, and a little salt. Bake in buttered cups.

Indian Puffs.—Into one quart of boiling milk stir eight tablespoonfuls of corn-meal and four tablespoonfuls of brown sugar; boil five minutes, stirring constantly; when cool, add six well-beaten eggs· bake in buttered cups half an hour. Eat with sauce.

White Puffs.—One pint rich milk; whites of four eggs whipped stiff; one heaping cupful prepared flour; one scant cupful powdered sugar; grated peel of half a lemon; a little salt. Whisk the eggs and sugar to a meringue, and add this alternately with the flour to the milk. Cream, or half cream half milk, is better. Beat until the mixture is very light, and bake in buttered cups or tins. Turn out, sift powdered sugar over them, and eat with lemon sauce.

Oak Balls.—Three cupfuls each of flour and milk, three eggs, whites and yelks beaten separately and very light, three tablespoonfuls of melted butter, a little salt. Pour in well-buttered muffin-rings, and bake to a nice brown.

Apple Dumplings.—Make a biscuit dough, and cover the apples (pared and cored), singly; tie in cloths and drop in boiling water. Let it boil half an hour. If preferred, mix flour and a little salt, and scald with boiling water. When cold enough to handle, roll it out and cover the apples. Or a pie-crust may be made for a cover and the dumplings may be baked in the oven.

Peach Dumplings.—These may be made according to the preceding recipe, substituting peaches for apples.

Lemon Dumplings.—Take suet, four ounces; moist sugar, four ounces; bread-crumbs, one-half pound; one lemon. Grate the rind of the lemon, squeeze out the juice, mix all the ingredients. Put in buttered teacups and bake three-quarters of an hour.

Amsterdam Pudding.—Pour one cup scalded milk in one cup fine cracker crumbs; add one tablespoonful butter; mix two teaspoonfuls **Bensdorp's Royal Dutch Cocoa** with one-half cup sugar, add it to the milk; add one teaspoonful vanilla and the whites of four eggs beaten very stiff. Boil in a buttered melon pudding mould one hour. Serve hot with a

Yellow Sauce.—Yolks of four eggs well beaten, with one-fourth cup of sugar; add one-half cup of water and one-fourth cup of lemon juice; mix well, and stir it over the fire until it thickens.—*Mrs. D. A. Lincoln.*

White Sauce.—Boil a few thin strips of lemon peel in half a pint of good veal gravy just long enough to give it their flavor. Stir in a thickening of arrowroot, or flour and butter; add salt and a quarter of a pint of boiling cream.

Cream Sauce.—Beat the yolks of three eggs, three tablespoonfuls of white sugar, and vanilla flavor. Turn on it a pint of boiling milk, and stir well.

Wine Sauce.—Take one pint bowl of white sugar, not quite a quarter of a pound of butter, one glass of wine, one grated nutmeg, and a tablespoonful of warm water; beat together steadily for half an hour.

Hard Sauce.—One cupful butter, three cupfuls sugar; beat very hard, flavoring with lemon juice; smooth into shape with a knife dipped into cold water.

DESSERTS

BLANK PAGE FOR ADDITIONAL RECIPES

XII.—CREAMS, JELLIES, AND LIGHT DES-SERTS.

LIGHT DESSERTS FOR HOME USE; FROZEN PREPARATIONS; FREEZERS; HOW TO FREEZE CREAMS, ETC.; HOW TO TURN OUT THE MOLDS; WHIPPED CREAMS, JELLIES, ETC. FORTY-FIVE RECIPES FOR CREAMS, JELLIES, BLANC-MANGES, ETC.

THERE is a delightful range of light desserts which need to be introduced more generally into our homes. They have too long been allowed to rest in the confectioner's under the erroneous notion that they were beyond the capacity of the ordinary housekeeper.

Prominent among these desserts are ice-cream and water-ices with all their splendid possibilities of variety.

RECIPES.

Vanilla Ice-cream.—Two quarts of pure cream, fourteen ounces of white sugar, flavored with vanilla bean or extract of vanilla to taste; mix well, and freeze as directed above. Pure cream needs no thickening or boiling. Milk may be boiled or thickened with arrow-root or corn-starch, but it will not produce ice *cream*.

Lemon Ice-cream.—For the same quantity of cream and sugar, as above, stir in the juice of from four to eight lemons, according to size and juiciness, and grate in a little of the rind. Then freeze as above.

Orange Ice-cream.—Proceed as in lemon cream, using oranges, and regulating the quantity of sugar as the fruit is more or less sweet.

Chocolate Ice-cream.—For one gallon of ice-cream, grate fine about one-half cake of **Bensdorp's Chocolate**; make ice-cream as for the recipe above; flavor lightly with **Metcalf's Water White Vanilla** and stir in the chocolate.

Strawberry Ice-cream.—Mash one pint of fresh, ripe strawberries; sprinkle them with half a pound of fine sugar; let it stand about an hour; strain though a fine sieve, or a cloth; if the sugar is not dissolved, stir it well; add a little water; stir this juice into the cream prepared as above and freeze.

Raspberry Ice-cream.—Make the same as strawberry, substituting the raspberries merely.

Peach Ice-cream.—Take fine, ripe freestone peaches; pare, chop fine, mash, and work as for strawberry cream.

Pine-apple Ice-cream.—Pare the fruit, shred fine, and work as in strawberry cream.

Orange Water-ice.—Take one dozen oranges; grate the skin and squeeze out the juice; add six quarts of water and ten ounces of white sugar to each quart of water; mix well and put into the freezer. Be careful to stir steadily while freezing, or the mixture will cake into lumps. The amount of sugar and of orange-juice may be varied to suit taste.

Lemon Water-ice.—To one quart of water, add the juice of four lemons and one pound of sugar. Then proceed as above. Currants, raspberries, strawberries, and all the juicy fruits may be treated in the same way.

Tutti Frutti.—One quart of rich cream, one and one-half ounces of sweet almonds, chopped fine; one-half pound of **sugar**; freeze, and when sufficiently congealed, add one-half pound of preserved fruits, with a few white raisins chopped, and finely sliced citron. Cut the fruit small, and mix well with the cream. Freeze like ice-cream, and keep on ice until required.

Frozen Fruits.—Take two quarts of rich cream and two teacupfuls of sugar, mix well together and put into a freezer with ice and salt packed around it. Have ready one quart of peaches, mashed and sweetened. When the cream is very cold, stir them in and freeze all together. Strawberries can be used in the same way, but will require more sugar. Cherries are specially delightful in this form.

Whipped Cream.—To one quart of cream whipped very thick, add powdered sugar to taste; then add one tumbler of wine. Make just before using.

Italian Cream.—Divide two pints of cream equally in two bowls; with one bowl mix six ounces of powdered sugar, the juice of two large lemons, and two glassfuls of white wine; then add the other pint of cream, and stir the whole very hard; boil two ounces of isinglass with four small tea-cupfuls of water till reduced one-half; then stir the isinglass, lukewarm, in the other ingredients; put them in a glass dish to harden.

Syllabub.—Whip a small cupful of powdered sugar into a quart of rich cream, and another cupful of sugar into the whites of four eggs. Mix these together, and add a glass of white wine and flavoring to taste.

Spanish Cream. — Soak one-half box of **Swampscott Sparkling Gelatine** in one-half cup water fifteen minutes; add three pints milk, one cup sugar, one teaspoonful of **Metcalf's Water White Vanilla**, and yolks of six eggs; cook ten minutes; stir constantly. Add whites beaten to stiff froth; beat five minutes. Mould and cool.

Strawberry Sherbet. — Dissolve one tablespoonful gelatine in half pint of water; add juice of one lemon; pour over one quart of mashed strawberries mixed with one pint of sugar; freeze in the same manner as ice-cream.

Tapioca Cream.—Soak half a cupful of tapioca in water over night. Let a quart of milk get steaming hot, and add to it the tapioca. Let it boil three minutes, then mix five tablespoonfuls of white sugar with the yelks of four eggs; stir them into the milk and tapioca, and let it come to a boil again. Beat the whites up stiff; stir them rapidly and thoroughly through the boiling tapioca; add two tablespoonfuls of wine and a pinch of salt. Let it stand till cold and garnish with macaroons.

Orange Cream.—Put half a box of gelatine to soak for half an hour in cold water enough to cover it. Take three half-pints of cream, whip half of it, and heat the other half; dissolve the gelatine in the heated cream; then strain it, and return to the boiler again. Take the yelks of five eggs and a cupful of sugar; beat them together till light, and add to the boiling cream; cook about two minutes, stirring constantly; take from the fire, and while it cooks, stir in the whipped cream and the juice of four oranges, and pour into a mold to stiffen. Stir the cream constantly before putting into the mold, to prevent it from thickening in lumps.

Pink Cream.—Three gills of strawberry or currant juice; mix with one-half pound of powdered sugar, one-half pint of thick cream; whisk until well mixed; serve in a glass dish.

Bavarian Cream. — Whip one pint of cream to a stiff froth, laying it on a sieve; boil a pint of rich milk, add one teaspoonful **Metcalf's Water White Vanilla** and two tablespoonfuls sugar; then take it off the fire and add half a box **Swampscott Sparkling Gelatine**, soaked for an hour in half a cupful water. Stir in whites of six eggs well-beaten. When it has become quite cold and begins to thicken, stir it without ceasing a few minutes, until it is very smooth ; then stir in the whipped cream lightly until it is well mixed. Put it into a mold or molds, and set it on ice or in a cool place.

Turret Cream.—Soak one box of gelatine in a cupful of milk four hours. Scald three cupfuls of milk; add one cupful of the sugar; when this is dissolved, add the soaked gelatine. Stir over the fire until almost boiling hot; strain and divide into two equal portions. Return one to the fire and heat quickly. When it nears the boiling-point, stir in the beaten yelks of three eggs. Let all cook together two minutes, and turn out into a bowl to cool. When it has cooled, churn one pint of cream very stiff, and beat the whites of the eggs until they will stand alone. Divide the latter into two heaps. As the yellow gelatine begins to " form," whip one-half of the whites into it, a little at a time. To the white gelatine add the rest of the whites in the same manner, alternately with the whipped cream. Season the yellow with vanilla, the white with lemon juice beaten in at the last. Wet the inside of a tall, fluted mold with water, and arrange in the bottom, close to the outside of the mold, a row of crystallized cherries. Then put in a layer of the white mixture; on this crystallized apricots or peaches cut into strips ; a layer of the yellow, another border of cherries, and so on until your mold is full. When firm, which will be in a few hours if set on ice, wrap a cloth wrung out in hot water about the mold, and invert upon a flat dish. Eat with sweet cream, or, if you like, with brandied fruit. Not only is this a very palatable dish, but it is also very beautiful, well repaying the trouble of its preparation.

Velvet Cream.—Half an ounce of isinglass dissolved in one and a half cupfuls of white wine ; then add the juice and grated peel of a lemon, three-quarters of a pound of loaf sugar; simmer all together until mixed well; strain and add one and a half pints rich cream, and stir until cool; pour into molds and let stand till stiff enough to turn out.

Calf's Foot Jelly. — Take one pair of calf's feet and put them into a gallon of water; let it boil half away and skim constantly; strain it when cold; take the fat from the top and bottom, then warm it; add sugar, the juice of three lemons, a pint of Madeira wine, and the whites of seven eggs; boil it half an hour, strain through a flannel bag, and cool in molds.

Wine Jelly. — One box of **Swampscott Sparkling Gelatine** dissolved in one pint of cold water, one pint of wine, one quart of boiling water, two cupfuls of granulated sugar, and three lemons. Cool in molds.

Wine Jelly, No. 2. — Soak one package of **Swampscott Sparkling Gelatine** in a large cupful of cold water. Add to this all the juice and half the rind of a lemon, two cupfuls of white sugar, and a half teaspoonful of bitter almond or two peach leaves, and cover for half an hour; then pour on boiling water, stir and strain. After adding two cupfuls of pale sherry or white wine, strain again through a flannel bag. Cool in molds.

Jelly Oranges. — Soak a package of **Swampscott Sparkling Gelatine** about fifteen minutes in a cup of cold water. Cut from the top of each of a dozen fine oranges a round piece, leaving a hole just large enough to admit the bowl of a small spoon. Clean out the pulp, so as not to tear the edges of the hole. Scrape the inner skin from the sides with your forefinger, and when the oranges are emptied lay them in cold water. Strain the juice of all and grated peel of three of the oranges through coarse, thin muslin over three cupfuls of sugar, squeezing rather hard to get the coloring matter.

Stir this until it is a thick sirup, and add a quarter teaspoonful of cinnamon. Pour two cupfuls of boiling water upon the soaked gelatine, and stir over the fire until well dissolved ; add the juice and sugar, stir all together, and strain through a flannel bag into a pitcher, not shaking or squeezing it, lest it should become cloudy. Wipe off the outside of the oranges, set them close together in a dish, the open ends uppermost, and fill *very* full with the warm jelly, as it will shrink in cooling. Set it away in a cold place where there is no dust. Next day cut each in half with a sharp knife, taking care to sever the skin all around before cutting into the jelly. If neatly divided, the rich amber jelly will be a fair counterfeit of the orange pulp. Pile in a glass dish, with green leaves around, as you would the real fruit. This is a delicious dish, and it is highly ornamental on the table.

Apple Jelly. — Soak half a package **Swampscott Sparkling Gelatine** in one cupful cold water. Pare, core and slice a dozen well flavored pippins, throwing each piece into cold water as it is cut to preserve the color. Pack them in a glass or stoneware jar with just cold water enough to cover them ; cover the jar loosely, that the steam may escape ; set in a pot of warm water and bring to a boil. Cook until the apples are broken into pieces. Have ready in a bowl the soaked gelatine, two cupfuls powdered sugar, the juice of two lemons, and the grated peel of one. Strain the apple pulp scalding hot over them ; stir until the gelatine is dissolved ; strain again through a flannel bag, without shaking or squeezing it ; wet a mold with cold water, fill it, and set in a cold place until firm. This preparation is greatly improved if formed in a mold with a cylinder in the centre, the cavity being filled and heaped with whipped cream.

Coffee Jelly. — Take half a box of sparkling gelatine, three-quarters of a pound of sugar, pint of strong coffee ;

pour the coffee over the gelatine, and when the gelatine is dissolved stir the sugar in, adding at the same time one-half pint of boiling water; when thoroughly mixed, strain into molds and serve with whipped cream.

Orange Jelly. — Soak one-half box of **Swampscott Sparkling Gelatine** in one-half cup cold water fifteen minutes; add one cup boiling water, juice of one lemon, one cup sugar and one pint orange juice; stir, strain and place in mold, and set on ice to harden.

Lemon Jelly. — Soak one box of **Swampscott Sparkling Gelatine** in one pint of cold water fifteen minutes; add three pints boiling water and stir until dissolved; add the juice of three lemons and grated rind of one; strain and sweeten to taste.

Orange Trifle. — Stir half a package of soaked gelatine into a cupful of boiling water. Mix the juice of two oranges and rind of one with a cupful of powdered sugar, and pour the hot liquid over them. Should the gelatine not dissolve readily, set all over the fire and stir until clear. Strain, and stir in the beaten yelks of three eggs. Heat quickly within a vessel of boiling water, stirring constantly lest the yelks curdle. If they do curdle, strain again through coarse flannel. Set aside until perfectly cold and slightly stiff, then whip in a pint of frothed cream. Wet a mold, fill, and set it on ice.

Orange Dessert. — Pare five or six oranges; cut into thin slices; pour over them a coffeecupful of sugar. Boil one pint of milk; add, while boiling, the yelks of three eggs, one tablespoonful of corn-starch (made smooth with a little cold milk); stir all the time; as soon as thickened, pour over the fruit. Beat the whites of the eggs to a froth; add two tablespoonfuls of powdered sugar; pour over the custard, and brown slightly in the oven. Serve cold.

Apple Snow.—Grate half a dozen apples to a pulp; press them through a sieve; add half a cupful of powdered sugar and a teaspoonful of extract of lemon; take the whites of six eggs, whip them for several minutes, and sprinkle two tablespoonfuls of powdered sugar over them; beat the apple pulp to a froth, and add the beaten egg; whip the mixture until it looks like stiff snow; then pile it high in rough portions on a glass dish; garnish with small spoonfuls of currant jelly.

Floating Island.—Beat the yelks of six eggs until very light; sweeten and flavor to taste; stir into a quart of boiling milk; cook till it thickens; when cool, pour into a low glass dish; whip the whites of the eggs to a stiff froth; sweeten, and place over a dish of boiling water to cook. Take a tablespoon and drop on the whites of the cream, far enough apart so that the "little white islands" will not touch each other. By dropping little specks of bright jelly on each island a pleasing effect will be produced.

Blanc-mange.—Take one quart of milk, one ounce gelatine, and sugar to sweeten to taste; put it on the fire, and keep stirring until it is all melted, then pour it into a bowl and stir until cold; season with vanilla; pour it into a mold, and set in a cool place to stiffen.

Tapioca Blanc-mange.—Take one pint of new milk, half a pound of the best farina-tapioca soaked in water four hours, three-fourths of a cupful of sugar, two teaspoonfuls of almond or vanilla extract, a little salt. Heat the milk, and stir the soaked tapioca. When it has dissolved, add the sugar. Boil slowly fifteen minutes, stirring all the time; take from the fire, and beat until nearly cold. Flavor and pour into a mold dipped in cold water. Sago blanc-mange may be made in the same manner.

Corn-starch Blanc-mange.—One quart of milk, four table-spoonfuls of corn-starch, wet with a little water, three eggs, whites and yolks beaten separately, one cupful of sugar, a little salt, flavor with lemon extract. Heat the milk to boiling; stir in the corn-starch and salt, and boil together five minutes; then add the yolks, beaten light, with the sugar; boil two minutes longer, stirring all the while; beat in the whipped whites while it is boiling hot; pour into a mold wet with cold water, and set in a cold place; eat with sugar and cream.

Chocolate Blanc-mange. — Heat a quart of milk; stir in a cupful of sugar and half a package of gelatine, soaked; strain through flannel; add three large spoonfuls of **Bensdorp's Chocolate,** grated; boil ten minutes, stirring all the time; when nearly cold, beat until it begins to stiffen; flavor with **Metcalf's Water White Vanilla;** whip up once, and put into a wet mold.

Berry Sponge. — Mash one quart of berries; add half cup of sugar; rub through hair sieve; boil half cup of sugar in cup of water; add one-half box **Swampscott Sparkling Gelatine,** soaked, to boiling syrup; take syrup from fire, add juice from berries, juice of one lemon, beaten whites of four eggs; beat until it begins to thicken; cool in molds; serve with cream.

Peach Meringue.—Put on to boil scant quart new milk, omitting half a teacupful, with which moisten two table-spoonfuls corn-starch. When the milk boils, add corn-starch, stir constantly, and when it begins to thicken, remove from fire; add tablespoonful of perfectly sweet butter; let cool; then beat in yolks of three eggs until the custard seems light and creamy; add half teacupful fine sugar; cover the bottom of a well-buttered baking-dish with ripe, juicy peaches, that have been pared, stoned, and halved; sprinkle two tablespoonfuls of sugar over the fruit, pour the custard over gently, and bake in a quick oven twenty minutes; draw it out, and cover with the well-beaten whites of the three eggs; sprinkle a little fine sugar over the top, and set in the oven until brown. Eat warm with sauce, or cold with cream.

Charlotte Russe.—Dissolve half a box of gelatine in cold water. Beat the yelks of four eggs with two cupfuls of white sugar. Whip one quart of sweet cream very stiff, add flavoring, then the yelks and sugar, and blend all the ingredients. Add the whites, turn into a bowl lined with sponge cake or lady-fingers, and set away to cool.

Charlotte Russe, No. 2.—Two tablespoonfuls gelatine soaked in a little cold milk two hours; two coffeecupfuls rich cream; one teacupful milk. Whip the cream stiff in a large bowl or dish; set on ice. Boil the milk and pour gradually over the gelatine until dissolved, then strain; when nearly cold add the whipped cream, a spoonful at a time. Sweeten with pulverized sugar and flavor with vanilla. Line a dish with lady-fingers or sponge cake; pour in the cream and set in a cool place to harden.

Chocolate Charlotte Russe.—Soak one-half box **Swampscott Sparkling Gelatine** in one-half pint of cold water fifteen minutes; grate two squares of **Bensdorp's Chocolate** in one-half pint of cream; add the gelatine and mix thoroughly; set in boiling water and stir until chocolate is dissolved, and then set away to cool; into this stir the yolks of four eggs and whites of four eggs lightly beaten together; add one cup of sugar and one-half pint of whipped cream, and beat the whole together until stiff; line a mould with strips of sponge cake and fill in the centre with the cream; set away to cool. In order that the shape of the mould may more easily be retained, the edges of the cake may be covered with jelly

Figs a la Genevieve.—Dissolve two ounces of best sugar in half a pint of cold water in an enameled stewpan, with half the very thin rind of a large lemon; when this is done, put into it half a pound of Turkey figs, and put the stewpan over a moderate fire, so that the figs may stew very slowly; when quite soft, add one glassful of common port or any other wine, and the strained juice of half a lemon; serve them cold for dessert. About two hours or two hours and a half is the average time for stewing the figs, and the flavor may be varied by using orange peel and juice instead of lemon, and by boiling two or three bitter almonds in the sirup.

Biscuit Glace.—Make a quart of rich boiled custard, flavor it with vanilla, and let it cool. Then mix with it a quart of grated pineapple or mashed peaches. Stir them well together, and add enough sugar to allow for the loss in freezing. Freeze in the usual way, stirring in a pint of cream, whipped, when it is beginning to set in the freezer. Partly fill little paper cases with the mixture, and smooth the tops nicely. Place them carefully in the cleaned and dried freezer, and let them remain embedded in ice for several hours.

CAKE.

BLANK PAGE FOR ADDITIONAL RECIPES

XIII.—CAKES AND CAKE-BAKING.

IN cake-making it is absolutely essential that the best materials be employed. Stale eggs, strong butter, musty flour, or common sugar are not so much as to be thought of in this connection. The idea that such refuse " will do for cooking " is most unworthy. When a luxury, such as cake, is attempted, the maker should certainly be willing to luxuriate in acceptable ingredients.

Flour for cake should be white and dry. It should always be carefully sifted. Sugar should be white, dry, and free from lumps. Eggs and butter should be sweet and fresh; the milk rich and pure. Fruit and extracts must be of the best. The weighing and measuring of ingredients must be accurately done. Guessing at quantities has spoiled many a cake.

For mixing cake, an earthen or wooden dish and a wooden spoon are requisite. Butter and sugar should be beaten together to a cream before using. Butter may be softened for this purpose, if too hard to manage readily, but it must not be melted. Whites and yelks of eggs must be beaten separately, until there is no stringiness visible, and the froth can be taken up on a spoon. Beat eggs in a broad, shallow dish, and in a cool place. It is well to lay the eggs in cold water for an hour before beating them, as they will beat the lighter for such treatment. Sweet milk is best for

179

solid cake; sour milk, for light cake. The two should never be mixed.

Baking-powder should be mixed dry through the flour. Soda and cream of tartar should be dissolved in milk. Flavoring extracts, fruit, and spices must be added the last thing, and fruit should always be well sprinkled with flour before it is put in the dough. Currants and such fruit should be washed, picked over, and dried before using. Almonds should be blanched by pouring boiling water over them till they pop from their skins. Cake should be beaten as little as possible after the flour has been added. When it requires long baking, the bottom and sides of the pan should be lined with paper well buttered. This will insure the easy turning out of the cake when done.

Much of the success in cake-baking depends on the heating of the oven. If the oven is very hot when the cake goes in, it will bake on top before it becomes light. If the oven is too cool, it will rise and fall again before done. If the top of the cake browns too fast, cover it with thick paper. Try it by inserting a broom-splinter or knitting-needle in the thickest part of the cake, and if nothing adheres when it is drawn out, it is done. Turn out of the tins at once, taking care not to expose the cake to draft.

Cake should be kept in earthen pans or crocks, or tin boxes, but never in wooden boxes or drawers. It will keep better for being wrapped in a cloth, and more than is needed should not be cut.

Cake that is to be frosted should be baked in pans with perpendicular sides. The icing should be put on as soon as the cake is removed from the oven. This will insure its drying smooth and hard.

RECIPES.

Loaf Dutch Cake.—Take one cupful of light bread dough, one egg, sugar and salt to taste, half a teaspoonful of soda, half a pound of raisins, and, if desired, a little butter and nutmeg ; work all together very smooth ; let the dough rise about half an hour, and bake as bread.

Bread Cake.—Two coffeecupfuls of bread dough, two tea-cupfuls of sugar, two eggs, one teacupful of butter, two tea-spoonfuls essence of lemon, one nutmeg, a teaspoonful each of cloves, cinnamon, and allspice, a wineglass of brandy, and a coffeecupful of raisins. Let it rise before baking.

Cinnamon Bun.—Put one pint of milk on to boil and mix a cupful of butter in a little lukewarm water; add a tea-spoonful of salt, and half an yeast cake dissolved in luke-warm water; add two quarts of sifted flour; mix all together, and let it stand over night till morning. Now beat two eggs and half a cupful of sugar until light, and mix it with the dough ; use just flour enough on the board to keep the dough from sticking; roll the dough out into a sheet one-fourth of an inch in thickness; spread a little butter, and sprinkle a little sugar on it, then some pulverized cinnamon, a few currants or chopped raisins. Now roll the sheet up into one long roll and cut in pieces about one inch thick ; a sharp knife must be used for this purpose ; put the pieces in a baking-pan, the cut side or end downward, and let them stand in a warm place for an hour, when they will be ready for the oven, which must be moderately heated.

Soft Molasses Cake.—Into one pint of molasses, put one tablespoonful of ginger, one teaspoonful of cinnamon, one tablespoonful of butter; add one teaspoonful of soda and two teaspoonfuls cream of tartar in one-half cupful of milk, one egg, and two and a half cupfuls of flour. Bake half an hour.

Gingerbread.—One cupful of molasses, one cupful of but-ter, two cupfuls of sugar, one cupful of sour milk, four eggs, three cupfuls of flour, one tablespoonful of ginger, and one teaspoonful of soda. Mix well and bake quickly.

Ginger Snaps.—Mix one pint of flour, one cupful of sugar, a piece of butter the size of two eggs; three heaping table-spoonfuls of ginger, and a little salt. Pour into this two cupfuls of heated molasses. Add flour enough to make it roll out thin. Bake three or four minutes.

Cookies.—Six cupfuls of flour, two of sugar, one of butter, one of milk, teaspoonful of soda, flavored with cinnamon or nutmeg, as you like. Roll thin, cut with biscuit-cutter, and bake quick.

Small Sugar Cakes.—One heaping teacupful of sugar; three-quarters teacupful of butter; one-quarter teacupful sweet milk; two eggs, well beaten; two teaspoonfuls cream tartar; one teaspoonful soda, dissolved in hot water; use flour sufficient to enable you to roll out the dough; one saltspoonful salt, nutmeg and cinnamon to taste. Cut into round cakes and bake quickly.

Knickerbocker Cakes.—Beat half a pound of fresh butter to a cream; add half a pound of powdered sugar, three-quarters of a pound of sifted flour, a tablespoonful of orange-flower water, and one of brandy, and four ounces of washed cur-rants; add five well-beaten eggs, and beat the mixture until very light. Line some shallow cake-tins with buttered paper, pour in the mixture until they are half full, and bake in a quick oven.

Scotch Wafers.—Take one pound of sugar, half a pound of butter, one pound of flour, two eggs, two teaspoonfuls of cinnamon. Roll thin and bake quickly.

Shrewsbury Cakes.—Mix a pound of flour and a half pound of butter; stir in a pound of brown sugar and two tablespoonfuls of cinnamon. Mix all thoroughly into a paste with three eggs, roll very thin, using as little flour as possible, and bake in a quick oven.

Soft Cookies.—One egg, two cupfuls of sugar, two cupfuls of cream, one even teaspoonful of soda, salt and flavor to taste. Flour to stiffen so they will drop from the spoon ; leave a space between them, as they spread in baking.

Apees.—One cupful of butter, one large cupful of sugar, three eggs, half a teaspoonful of soda, one teaspoonful of cream tartar, and flour enough to roll out thin. Bake quickly.

Cinnamon Cakes.—Take six ounces of butter, a pound of fine, dry flour, three-quarters of a pound of sifted sugar, and a dessertspoonful of pounded cinnamon. Make these ingredients into a firm paste with three eggs, or four, if needed. Roll it, not very thin, and cut out the cakes with a tin shape. Bake them in a very gentle oven from fifteen to twenty minutes, or longer, should they not be done quite through.

Lemon Cakes.—Lemon cakes can be made on the above recipe by substituting for the cinnamon the rasped or grated rinds of two lemons, and the strained juice of one, when its acidity is not objected to.

Seed Cakes.—Two pounds of flour, one pound of sugar, fourteen ounces of butter, one tablespoonful of caraway seed, half a pint of milk, two tablespoonfuls of saleratus. Rub the butter, sugar, and flour together, then add all the other ingredients; knead all well together into a smooth dough; roll it out quite thin, cut with a round cutter, place the cakes on tins, and bake in a *moderate* oven.

Walnut Cakes.—One pound of sugar, six eggs, three teaspoonfuls of yeast-powder, half a pound of butter, flour to make a dough, and one cupful of walnut kernels ; bake in a moderate oven.

Jumbles.—Three-fourths of a cupful of butter, one and a half cupfuls of sugar, three eggs, three tablespoonfuls of

milk, flour enough to make it roll, and a teaspoonful of baking-powder; roll; sprinkle with granulated sugar and gently
roll it in; cut out, with a hole in centre, and bake.

Currant Jumbles.—One pound each of flour and powdered
loaf sugar, half a pound each of butter and currants, eight
eggs, brandy to taste; cut out as in plain jumbles and bake
on tins.

Cocoanut Cookies.—One cupful of butter, two cupfuls of
sugar, two cupfuls of prepared or grated cocoanut, two
eggs, flour enough to make a stiff batter, and one teaspoonful of soda; drop on buttered paper in pans.

Doughnuts.—Two teacupfuls of sugar, three eggs, one and
a half teacupfuls of buttermilk or sour milk, two teaspoonfuls of saleratus, one teaspoonful of salt, six tablespoonfuls
of melted lard, flour enough to roll out nicely; boil or fry
in lard enough to cover them. If not well covered in the
cooking they will be tough.

Raised Doughnuts.—One pint of sweet milk, one half pint
of lard, one pint of sugar, three eggs. Mix soft at night,
using the milk, one-half the sugar and lard, and one-half
pint of yeast. In the morning, add the rest with the eggs,
one nutmeg, two tablespoonfuls of whisky, and a little
soda. Knead well, and allow to rise. When light, roll out
thin, and after cutting, let rise again before frying. One-
half beef suet and one-half lard is better to fry them in than
all lard.

Crullers.—Two cupfuls of sugar, one-half cupful of butter,
one-half cupful of milk, two eggs, one teaspoonful of soda,
two of cream tartar. Roll out, and cut according to fancy,
and boil in fat.

French Straws.—Mix well eight eggs, ten ounces of sugar,
and half a teaspoonful of cinnamon and nutmeg with flour
enough to form a dough; beat the eggs very thick and add

the sugar, spices, and flour ; knead well, and roll to about half an inch thick ; cut in strips, give each a twist, and boil them in plenty of lard to a rich yellow ; sift sugar on when cool.

Love Knots.—Five cupfuls of flour, two of sugar, one of butter, a piece of lard the size of an egg, two eggs, three tablespoonfuls of sweet milk, half a teaspoonful of soda ; rub the butter, sugar, and flour together fine, add the other ingredients, roll thin, cut in strips one inch wide and five inches long, lap across in true-love knots, and bake in a quick oven.

One, Two, Three, Four Cake.—One cupful of butter, two cupfuls of sugar, three cupfuls of flour, four eggs ; rub well together, and add some milk or cream, with one teaspoonful of soda and two teaspoonfuls of cream of tartar ; flavor with grated lemon rind and juice ; bake carefully in a quick oven.

Tea Cake.—Three and a half cupfuls of flour, two of sugar, one of butter, four eggs, a teaspoonful of soda in a tablespoonful of milk or wine, and a half grated nutmeg. Bake carefully in quick oven.

Tumbler Cake.—Five tumblerfuls of flour, three of sugar, two of butter, four eggs, one of milk, one pint and a half of raisins, stoned, one nutmeg, one teaspoonful of allspice, a teaspoonful of soda dissolved in the milk. Bake in deep pan with a hot oven.

Cider Cake.—Two cupfuls of sugar, one cupful of butter, five eggs, one and one-half cupfuls of cider, with one teaspoonful of soda dissolved in it ; spices or nutmeg to taste ; four and one-half cupfuls of flour, two cupfuls of fruit. Bake quickly.

Puff Cake.—Two cupfuls of sugar, one of butter, one of sweet milk, three of flour, three eggs, one and one-half teaspoonfuls of yeast powder, extract of lemon. Bake quickly

Pinafore Cake.—One cupful of butter, three half cupfuls of sugar, three half cupfuls of flour, one-half cupful of corn-starch, one-half cupful of milk, four eggs, one teaspoonful of cream of tartar, one-half teaspoonful of soda, and a pinch of salt. Flavor to taste.

Cork Cake.—Two cupfuls of sugar, two-thirds of a cupful of butter, three eggs, one cupful of warm milk, three cupfuls of flour, a teaspoonful of baking-powder, and a half pound of currants. Use the whites of two of the eggs for icing, and put the yelks into the cake.

Poor Man's Cake.—One cupful of cream, one of sugar, two of flour, one egg, one teaspoonful of soda, and two of cream tartar.

Cup Cake.—One cupful of butter, two cupfuls of sugar, half a cupful of molasses, one teaspoonful of soda, two of cream tartar in half a cup of milk, two eggs, and two and a half cups of flour.

Moravian Cake.—Two cupfuls of sugar, one cupful of but-ter, five eggs, two cupfuls of flour, half a cupful of sour milk, one teaspoonful of cream tartar, and half a teaspoonful of soda. Flavor with a little grated nutmeg and a teaspoonful of vanilla.

Silver Cake.—Whites of twelve eggs, five cupfuls of flour, three cupfuls of sugar, one cupful of butter, one and one-half cupfuls of sweet milk, one teaspoonful of soda, two tea-spoonfuls of cream tartar, one teaspoonful of almond extract.

Gold Cake.—Substitute the yelks for whites of eggs, and flavor with vanilla, then make it same as preceding recipe.

Lincoln Cake.—Two cupfuls of sugar, half a cupful of but-ter, two eggs, one cupful of cream or sour milk, three cup-fuls of flour, one teaspoonful of cream tartar, half a tea-spoonful of soda, and one teaspoonful of essence of lemon.

Washington Cake.—One pound of flour, one pound of sugar, half a pound of butter, five eggs, one pound of raisins, one cupful of brandy and water, one teaspoonful of soda, two of cream tartar.

Pound Cake.—One pound of butter, one pound of sugar, one pound of flour, and eight eggs. Bake one hour.

White Pound Cake.—Beat to a cream one pound of sugar and one-half pound of butter; two teaspoonfuls of baking-powder in one pound of flour; whites of sixteen eggs beaten very stiff and added last. Cover with frosting before it cools.

Sponge Cake.—Five eggs, half a pound of sugar, quarter pound of flour, juice and rind of half a lemon. Beat yelks of eggs, sugar, and lemon together till light; add half the beaten whites, then half the flour, the balance of the whites and balance of flour. Avoid beating after the ingredients are all together.

Almond Sponge Cake.—Take half a pound of loaf sugar; rub the rind of a lemon on a few of the lumps, and crush the whole to a powder; separate the whites from the yelks of five eggs, beat the yelks, and add the sugar gradually; then beat the whites to a stiff froth; add it to the dish, and sift in flour enough to make a batter; add a tablespoonful of essence of almonds; butter and paper a tin, pour in the mixture until the tin is two-thirds full, and bake one hour in a moderate oven. The bottom of the tin may be studded with small pieces of almonds.

Cream Sponge Cake.—Beat together a cupful of sugar and the yelks of three eggs. Add a half teaspoonful of soda, a teaspoonful of cream tartar, a cupful of flour, and the whites of the eggs. Bake in three layers, and put between them the following filling: One egg, a half cupful of cream, a cupful of sugar, and a piece of butter the size of a walnut. Boil till like a cream, and when cold flavor to taste

Snow Cake.—Take one pound of arrowroot, quarter of a pound of powdered white sugar, half a pound of butter, the whites of six eggs, flavoring to taste. Beat the butter to a cream; stir in the sugar and arrowroot gradually, at the same time beating the mixture; whisk the whites of the eggs to a stiff froth; add them to the other ingredients, and beat well for twenty minutes; flavor with essence of almond, vanilla, or lemon, as may be preferred; pour into a buttered mold or tin, and bake in a *moderate* oven.

Spice Cake.—One cupful each of butter and cold water, three cupfuls of flour, two cupfuls of sugar, three eggs, one teaspoonful of soda, two teaspoonfuls of ground cinnamon, one-fourth pound each of currants and raisins.

Spice Cake, No. 2.—One cupful of butter, two cupfuls of sugar, four eggs, a teaspoonful of cream tartar, half a teaspoonful of soda, half a cupful of sour milk, one cupful of molasses, three cupfuls of flour, a teaspoonful of ground cloves, two teaspoonfuls of cinnamon, two teaspoonfuls of ginger, one nutmeg, and a small pinch of Cayenne pepper.

Coffee Cake.—One cupful of brown sugar, one cupful of butter, one cupful of strained coffee, one cupful of molasses, three eggs well beaten, one pound of raisins, two cupfuls of flour, two teaspoonfuls of baking-powder.

Wine Cake.—Beat to a cream half a cupful of butter with two full cups of powdered sugar; add the yelks of four eggs, and half a glass of sherry wine; beat till very light; add half a cupful of cream with a pinch of soda in it; beat two minutes, and stir in very quickly the whites of the eggs, three and a half cupfuls of prepared flour, and a little grated nutmeg.

Fig Cake.—One cupful butter, two and a half cupfuls sugar, one cupful of milk, six cupfuls of flour, three teaspoonfuls baking-powder, whites of sixteen eggs, and, at the last, one and a quarter pounds of figs, cut and floured. Bake well but do not burn.

Walnut Cake.—One coffeecupful of sugar, two of raisins (stoned and chopped), one cupful and a half of flour, half a cupful of butter, half a cupful of sweet milk, three eggs, two teaspoonfuls of baking-powder, half a nutmeg grated, one teaspoonful of lemon or vanilla, one cup heaping full of nuts, which must be cracked and picked, before anything else is done to the cake. Bake slowly, with a buttered paper in the bottom of the tin.

Hickorynut Cake.—One pound of flour, three-quarters of a pound of sugar, half a pound of butter, half a pint of milk, five eggs, two quarts of hickorynuts, one teaspoonful of soda, and two of cream tartar.

Cocoanut Cake.—One pound of grated cocoanut, one pound of sugar, one-half pound of butter, six eggs, three-quarters of a pound of flour. Flavor to taste.

New Year's Cake.—One and a quarter pound of raisins, seeded, one and a quarter pounds of currants, half a pound of sliced citron, half a pound of butter, half a pound of brown sugar, half a pound of flour, five eggs, half a tumblerful of brandy, half a bottle of rose-water, one teaspoonful of cinnamon, two of cloves, two of mace, and a grated nutmeg.

Currant Cake.—One cupful of butter, two cupfuls of powdered sugar, four eggs, half a cupful of sweet milk, three cupfuls of prepared flour, half a nutmeg grated, and half a pound of currants washed, dried, and dredged with flour.

Citron Cake.—Six eggs, beaten light and the yelks strained; two cupfuls of sugar, three-quarters of a cupful of butter, two and one-half cupfuls of prepared flour, or enough to make good pound cake batter. With some brands you may need three cupfuls; one-half pound of citron cut in thin shreds; juice of an orange, and one teaspoonful of grated peel. Cream the butter and sugar; add the yelks, the whites, and flour by turns, then the orange, and lastly, the citron, dredged with flour. Beat all up hard, and bake in two loaves.

Plum Cake.—Two and a half pounds of raisins, two and a half pounds of currants, one pound of citron, one pound of butter, one pound of sugar, ten eggs, one pound of flour, one-half pint of brandy, and a little molasses.

Fruit Cake.—Take of butter two cupfuls; sugar, four cupfuls; molasses, one cupful; sour milk, two cupfuls; flour, eight cupfuls; eggs, eight; soda, one tablespoonful; cloves, two tablespoonfuls; cinnamon, two tablespoonfuls; raisins, two pounds; currants, two pounds; almonds, one pound; citron, half a pound; two nutmegs; two lemons cut fine; bake four hours.

Wedding Cake.—One pound of powdered sugar, one pound of butter, one pound of flour, twelve eggs, one pound of currants well washed and dredged, one pound of raisins, seeded and chopped, one-half pound of citron cut in slips, one tablespoonful of cinnamon, two teaspoonfuls of nutmeg, one teaspoonful of cloves, one wineglass of brandy. Cream the butter and sugar, add the beaten yelks of the eggs, and stir all *well* together before putting in half of the flour. The spice should come next, then the whipped whites stirred in alternately with the rest of the flour, lastly the brandy. The above quantity is for two large cakes. Bake at least two hours in deep tins lined with well-buttered paper. The icing should be laid on stiff and thickly. Bake this well, and, if kept in a cool, dry place, it will not spoil in two months. Test the cakes well, and be sure they are quite done before taking them from the oven.

Black Cake.—One pound of browned flour, one pound of brown sugar, one pound of citron, two pounds of currants, three pounds of stoned raisins, three-quarters of a pound of butter, one teacupful of molasses, two teaspoonfuls of mace, two teaspoonfuls of cinnamon, one teaspoonful of cloves, one teaspoonful of soda, twelve eggs.

Farmers' Fruit Cake. — Three cupfuls of dried apples, two cupfuls of molasses, one cupful of butter, one cupful of brown sugar, one pound of raisins, one-quarter pound of citron, two eggs, one lemon (both juice and rind), two teaspoonfuls of soda, one pound and small cup of flour. Soak the apples over night, chop fine, and boil till done in the molasses and one cupful of the water they were soaked in. Flavor with nutmeg, cinnamon, and a very little clove. Bake three hours.

Melrose Cake. — Beat yolks of two eggs well, mix with one-half cupful of fresh milk, one and one-third cupfuls of **Automatic Flour**, one cupful of sugar; stir well and add one-quarter cupful melted butter; stir until smooth; fold in the well-beaten whites of the two eggs; flavor with one teaspoonful of **Metcalf's Water White Vanilla**.

Gold Cake. — Take one-quarter of a cupful of good butter, creamed; add the yolks of four eggs and beat well; then add gradually one cupful of sugar, one-half of a cupful of fresh milk, one and one-half cupfuls of **Automatic Flour**; stir well; flavor with one teaspoonful of **Metcalf's Water White Vanilla**.

Chocolate Cake. — Take two cupfuls of sugar, one cupful of butter, five eggs, one-half a teaspoonful of soda, one teaspoonful of cream tartar, one-half a cupful of sour milk; grated nutmeg and vanilla to suit the taste. Bake in layers and put between the layers the following filling: One cupful of **Bensdorp's Chocolate**, grated, and a small cupful of sugar. Put in a dry bowl, and stand the bowl in a pan of boiling water. Stir until the heat of the bowl dissolves the chocolate and sugar into a thick paste. Add a tablespoonful of clear table sirup and two eggs well beaten. Let this cook in the boiling water about ten minutes, then add two teaspoonfuls of vanilla.

Jelly Cake.—Beat three eggs well, the whites and yelks separately; take a cupful of fine white sugar, and beat that in well with the yelks, and a cupful of sifted flour, stirred in gently; then stir in the whites, a little at a time, and a teaspoonful of baking-powder and one tablespoonful of milk; pour it in three jelly-cake plates, and bake from five to ten minutes in a well-heated oven, and when cold spread with currant jelly, and place each layer on top of the other and sift powdered sugar on the top.

Jelly Roll.—Add one cupful of powdered sugar and one cupful of flour to three well-beaten eggs; stir well, and add one teaspoonful of cream of tartar, half a teaspoonful of saleratus dissolved in three teaspoonfuls of water; bake in two pie-pans; spread as evenly as possible; as soon as done, turn the cake, bottom side up, on to a dry towel; spread it evenly with jelly, roll up quickly, and wrap closely in the towel.

Peach Cake.—Bake sponge cake in layers; cut peaches in very thin slices, and spread upon the cake; sweeten, flavor, and whip some sweet cream, and spread over each layer and over the top.

Pineapple Cake.—One cupful of butter, two cupfuls of sugar, one cupful milk, three cupfuls of flour, whites of six eggs and yelks of four, three teaspoonfuls of baking-powder well mixed through flour; bake in jelly-cake pans; grate a pineapple; sprinkle with sugar, spread between the layers; pineapple jam may be substituted; frost the outside; beat two tablespoonfuls of the pineapple into the frosting.

Cocoanut Cake.—Two eggs, one cupful white sugar, one-half a cupful sweet milk, one-quarter cupful of butter, one and one-half cupfuls of flour, one and one-half teaspoonfuls baking-powder. Bake in a moderate oven in pans one inch deep. To prepare the desiccated cocoanut, beat the whites of two eggs to a stiff froth, add one cupful of pulverized sugar and the cocoanut, after soaking it in boiling milk. Spread the mixture between the layers of cake and over the top.

White Mountain Cake.—Make the cake with one pound of flour, one pound of sugar, half a pound of butter, six eggs, one cupful of milk, one small teaspoonful of saleratus dissolved in the milk. Bake four thin cakes in flat pie plates ; frost each of these cakes, laying one on another. When all are done, even the edges with a knife and frost the sides. Use the following frosting preparation : Beat to a standing froth the whites of four eggs made thick with sifted, refined sugar, and add the sugar and juice of one lemon.

Delicate Cake.—Two cupfuls of pulverized sugar, half a cupful of butter, three cupfuls of flour, nearly three-fourths of a cupful of milk, whites of eight eggs, half a teaspoonful of cream tartar, one-fourth teaspoonful soda. This may be baked in jelly cake tins and put together with icing.

Cream Cake.—Take two cupfuls of sugar, two-thirds of a cupful of butter, one cupful milk, one teaspoonful of soda, one and a half teaspoonfuls of cream of tartar, two and a half cupfuls of flour, three eggs. Make the custard for the cake with one cupful of milk, and one teaspoonful of corn-starch dissolved in it, and brought to a boiling heat, with the yelk of one egg dropped in to color it. Flavor with lemon or vanilla ; let it cool. Bake your cake in round pie-tins ; use just enough batter in the tin so that when they are baked two of them put together will make one proper sized cake. Make the custard first, and let it cool ; put the

13

cakes together when they are warm, with plenty oi custard between them.

Orange Cake.—Two cupfuls of sugar, one of butter, five eggs, half a cupful of sour milk, one teaspoonful of cream tartar, half a teaspoonful of soda, and two cupfuls of flour. Bake in four layers, and put between the layers the following filling : Beat two eggs, add to them a small cupful of sugar, heaping tablespoonful of butter. Simmer gently until it thickens. Remove from the fire, add the juice, grated pulp, and part of the rind of one large orange.

Ice-Cream Cake.—Two cupfuls of sugar, half a cupful of butter, three eggs, a cupful of milk, three cupfuls of flour, two teaspoonfuls of baking-powder. Bake in layers. Boil two small cupfuls of sugar and two-thirds of a cupful of water for ten minutes. Beat the white of an egg, and pour it over the mixture when it cooks a little. Beat till cold and stiff, and put between the layers.

Union Cake.—Two-thirds of a cupful of butter, two cupfuls of sugar, one cupful of milk, three cupfuls of flour, four eggs, two-thirds of a teaspoonful of cream tartar, and one-third of a teaspoonful of soda. Divide into three equal parts, and into one part put a cupful of seeded raisins, two-thirds of a cupful of currants, and one-quarter pound of citron. Bake in three pans of the same size. Put icing, flavored with extract of lemon, between the layers and on the top and sides.

Marble Cake.—Two cupfuls of white sugar, one cupful of butter, the whites of seven eggs, two teaspoonfuls of cream tartar, one of soda, three and a half cupfuls of flour, and half a cupful of milk. In another bowl three cupfuls of brown sugar, one of butter, one of molasses, the yelks of seven eggs, two tablespoonfuls of cinnamon, two of allspice, one teaspoonful of cloves, half a nutmeg, half a cupful of milk, three cupfuls of flour, one teaspoonful of soda, and two of cream tartar.   Arrange by dropping in first a tablespoonful of dark batter, then of the light, to imitate marble.

Watermelon Cake.—White part : One-half cupful of butter, one cupful of powdered sugar, whites of three eggs, one-third of a cupful of sweet milk, half a tablespoonful of baking-powder, and three half cupfuls of flour.—Red part : One-half cupful of butter, one cupful of red sugar, yelks of five eggs, one-third of a cupful of sweet milk, one tablespoonful of baking-powder, two cupfuls of flour, and half a pound of seeded raisins.   Put the red part in the centre of the pan, with the white on the outside.   Raisins may be introduced in the red part to represent seeds.   Red sugar can be had of the confectioners.

Neapolitan Cake.—Mix a *yellow* portion thus : Two cupfuls of powdered sugar, one cupful of butter stirred to light cream with sugar; five eggs beaten well, with yelks and whites separately; half a cupful of sweet milk, three cupfuls of prepared flour, a little nutmeg.

Mix a *pink and white* portion thus : One pound of powdered sugar, one pound of prepared flour, half a pound of butter creamed with sugar, the whites of ten eggs whisked stiff.   Divide this batter into two equal portions.   Leave one white, and color the other with a very little prepared cochineal or with red sugar.

Mix a *brown* portion thus : Three eggs beaten light, one cupful of powdered sugar, quarter cupful of butter creamed with sugar, two tablespoonfuls of cream, one *heaping* cupful of prepared flour, two tablespoonfuls of **Bensdorp's Vanilla Chocolate** grated and rubbed smooth in the cream, before it is beaten into the cake.

Bake each of these parts in jelly-cake tins.   The above quantities should make three cakes of each color.

Mix a filling for the cake thus : Two cupfuls sweet milk, two tablespoonfuls corn-starch wet with milk, two eggs, two small cupfuls of fine sugar. Heat the milk, stir in the sugar and corn-starch, boil five minutes, and put in the eggs. Stir steadily until it becomes quite thick. Divide this custard into two parts. Stir into one two tablespoonfuls of grated chocolate and a teaspoonful of vanilla; into the other, bitter almond.

Prepare another filling thus: Whites of three eggs, whisked stiff, one heaping cup of powdered sugar, juice and half the grated peel of one lemon. Whip all together well. Lay the brown cake as the foundation of the pile; spread with the yellow custard; add the pink, coated with chocolate; then add the white and yellow with the frosting between them. Vary the order as fancy dictates. Cover the top with powdered sugar or with icing.

Angel's Food.—Use the whites of eleven eggs, a scant pint of granulated sugar, a large half pint of flour, one teaspoonful of cream tartar (even full), and a teaspoonful of vanilla. Sift the flour four times, then measure; add cream of tartar, and then sift again. Sift the sugar four times, then measure it. Beat the eggs to a stiff froth on a large dish, and on same dish add the sugar quickly and lightly; add the flour in the same way, and last of all the vanilla. Put at once into a moderate oven, and bake forty minutes or more. Do not grease the pans. Turn upside down to cool, putting small blocks of wood under the edges that air may reach the cake.

Macaroons.—Blanch half a pound of almonds with boiling water, and pound them to a smooth paste. Add a tablespoonful of essence of lemon, half a pound of powdered sugar, and the whites of two eggs. Work the paste well together with the back of a spoon. Wet your hands, and roll them in balls the size of a nutmeg, and lay them an inch apart on a sheet of paper. Wet your finger, and press gently over the surface to make them shiny. Bake three-quarters of an hour in a very moderate oven.

Chocolate Macaroons. — Put three ounces of plain **Bensdorp's Chocolate** in a pan, and melt on a slow fire; then work it to a thick paste with one pound of powdered sugar and the whites of three eggs; roll the mixture down to the thickness of about one-quarter of an inch; cut it in small, round pieces with a paste-cutter, either plain or scalloped; butter a pan slightly, and dust it with flour and sugar in equal quantities; place in it the pieces of paste or mixture, and bake in a hot but not quick oven.

Cream Puffs.—Stir one-half pound of butter into a pint of warm water, set it on the fire in a saucepan, and slowly bring it to a boil, stirring often. When it boils, put in three-quarters of a pound of flour, and let it boil one minute, stirring constantly. Take from the fire, and turn into a deep dish to cool. Beat eight eggs light, and whip into this cool paste, first the yelks, then the whites. Drop in great spoonfuls on buttered paper so as not to touch or run into each other, and bake ten minutes. Split them, and fill with the following cream: One quart of milk, four tablespoonfuls of corn-starch, two eggs, two cupfuls of sugar. Stir while boiling, and when thick, add a teaspoonful of butter. When cold, flavor.

Kisses.—Beat the whites of four eggs very stiff, add one-half pound of pulverized sugar, and flavor to taste. Beat until very light, then lay in heaps the size of an egg on paper. Place the paper on a piece of wood half an inch thick, and put in a hot oven. Make the surface shiny by passing over it a wet knife. Bake until they look yellowish, when they are done.

Chocolate Kisses. — Beat stiff whites of two eggs; beat in gradually one-half pound powdered sugar. Scrape fine one and a half ounces **Bensdorp's Chocolate;** dredge with flour, mix the flour well; add gradually to the eggs and sugar; stirring very hard. Cover bottom of a pan with white paper, and place on it spots of powdered sugar the size of half-dollars. Heap the mixture on these spots, smooth with a broad knife, sift with powdered sugar, and bake quickly.

Cocoanut Steeples.—One pound of powdered sugar; one-half pound of grated cocoanut; whites of five eggs. Whip the eggs as for icing, adding the sugar as you go on until it will stand alone, then beat in the cocoanut. Mold the mixture with your hands into small cones, and set these far enough apart not to touch one another upon buttered paper in a baking-pan. Bake in a very moderate oven.

Meringues.—Mix the whites of four eggs, beaten to a stiff froth, with one pound of pulverized sugar, and flavored to the taste. Beat stiff, bake the same as macaroons, when light brown, slip them from the papers, and put the smooth sides together, with jelly between.

Lady-fingers.—One-half pound pulverized sugar and six yelks of eggs, well stirred; add one-fourth pound flour, whites of six eggs, well beaten. Bake in lady-finger tins, or squeeze through a bag of paper in strips two or three inches long.

Lady-fingers, No. 2.—Rub half a pound of butter into a pound of flour; to this add half a pound of sugar, the juice and grated rind of one large lemon, and, lastly, three eggs, the whites and yelks beaten separately, and the whites stirred in after all the other ingredients are well mixed together. This dough, if properly made, will be stiff enough to make rolls about the size of a lady's finger; it will spread when in the oven, so that it will be of the right size and shape. If you wish them to be especially inviting, dip them in chocolate icing after they are baked, and put two together. See that the icing is so hard that it will not run, and set the cakes on a platter in a cool room until the icing is firm.

Eclairs a la Creme.—Three-fourths pound flour, one pint water, ten eggs, one-half cupful butter. Put the water on the fire in a stewpan with the butter; as soon as it boils stir in the sifted flour; stir well until it leaves the bottom and sides of the pan, when taken from the fire; then add the eggs, one at a time. Put the batter in a bag of paper, and press out in the shape of fingers on a greased tin. When cold, fill with cream, prepared as follows: One and one-half pints of milk, two cupfuls sugar, yelks of five eggs, one tablespoonful butter, three large tablespoonfuls corn-starch, two teaspoonfuls extract vanilla. Frosted with chocolate, they are much improved in appearance and flavor.

Icing for Cakes.—In making icing, use at least a quarter of a pound of pulverized sugar to the white of each egg; if not stiff enough, add more sugar. Break the whites into a broad, cool dish, and throw in a small handful of sugar. Begin whipping it in with long, even strokes of the beater, adding the sugar gradually. Beat until the icing is smooth and firm, then add the flavoring. Spread it on the cake with a broad-bladed knife, dipped in cold water. If ornamentation of the icing is desired, it may be done by affixing prepared leaves, flowers, etc., which can be had at the confectioners' stores or at their supply stores. To make letters, tracery, etc., for cakes, roll into a funnel shape a piece of thick, white paper; fill this with icing in the soft state, allowing it to drip out slowly from the small end of the paper cone. Apply this carefully, and allow it to harden.

Orange Icing.—Whites of two eggs, one-half pound of pulverized sugar, and the juice of a large orange, treated as above.

Lemon Icing.—Whites of two eggs, one-half pound of pulverized sugar, juice and part of the rind of one lemon.

Chocolate Icing.—Whites of two eggs, one-half pound of

pulverized sugar, and three tablespoonfuls of grated **Bensdorp's Chocolate.**

Almond Icing.—The whites of three eggs, one cupful of pounded blanched almonds, three-quarters of a pound of pulverized sugar, and a little almond extract.

Banana Icing.—Whites of two eggs, one-half pound of pulverized sugar, and one banana finely crushed through it. This cake should be eaten the same day it is made, as the banana discolors over night.

Cocoanut Frosting.—Whites of two eggs, one-half pound of pulverized sugar. Spread on the cake, then sprinkle thickly with grated cocoanut. This will make a whiter frosting than results from stirring in the cocoanut.

Cooked Frosting.—One cupful of granulated sugar, wet with a little water. Let it boil without stirring until it begins to thicken. Beat the whites of two eggs very light. Strain the boiled sugar into them slowly, beating all the time. Flavor to taste.

FRESH FRUITS & NUTS:

BLANK PAGE FOR ADDITIONAL RECIPES

XIV.—FRESH FRUITS AND NUTS.

FRESH fruits are a most delightful accessory to the
table supply of both rich and poor. They are so great
in variety, so rich in flavor, so beautiful in appearance,
so healthful, and of so long continuance in most parts of the
country, that it behooves every housekeeper to familiarize
herself with the best methods of using fresh fruits to
advantage.

A few years ago each locality depended upon its own
local crop of fruits. Now the railroads bring early fruits
from the far South and late fruits from the far North, so
that at the centres of population the several fruit seasons are
delightfully prolonged. Nor are we restricted to our own
country's production. Such are the facilities for rapid and
safe communication from distant points, that the world lays
her tribute of fruits, sweet and sound, at the door of the
enlightened nations.

Fruits do not take an important place as nutrients. They
belong rather among the luxuries, and yet, as an agreeable
stimulant to digestion, they occupy a front rank. In many
conditions of health, some of the fruits are the only articles
the invalid can enjoy, and their genial influences contribute
greatly to the general improvement of a patient's appetite.

Fruits intended for immediate use should be gathered
early in the morning, while the coolness of the night dews

is upon them. They should be just ripe, neither overdone nor underdone, in nature's great process of preparing them for human food. Fruit for storage is best gathered at the middle of a dry day. It should be *nearly* ripe. If unripe, or overripe it will not keep well. A moist atmosphere, but not one positively damp, is best for the storing of fruit. An ordinary cellar does better than a dry storeroom. Fruit keeps better in the dark than in the light.

All varieties of nuts belong to the albuminous fruits and are very nutritious, though the richer nuts are not easy of digestion owing to their oily properties.

The supply of peanuts once came wholly from Africa, but our Southern States have so successfully cultivated this popular nut that we are now independent. The bulk of the supply is from Virginia, North Carolina, and Tennessee. During a single season the crop of Virginia rose to one million one hundred thousand bushels, of Tennessee, five hundred and fifty thousand bushels, and of North Carolina, one hundred and twenty thousand bushels.

The Texas pecan is especially in demand. While a few years ago several barrels of pecans abundantly supplied the demand, carloads and invoices of one or two hundred barrels are not now uncommon.

In the Eastern States hickory nuts are sufficiently plentiful to ship to New York half a dozen carloads a week when demanded.

The chestnut is becoming scarcer every year, but their great popularity will probably prevent their total disappearance, as they are already being successfully cultivated, and it is expected that in a few years the cultivated nut will equal in quality the high-priced Italian chestnuts.

RECIPES.

Watermelons.—Wipe watermelons clean when they are taken from the ice. They should lie on ice for at least four hours before they are eaten. Cut off a slice at each end of the watermelon, then cut through the centre; stand on end on platter, and slice down, allowing each slice a part of the centre, or heart.

Nutmegs, etc.—Wash nutmegs and muskmelons; wipe dry; cut in two; shake out the seeds lightly, and put a lump of ice in each half. Eat with pepper and salt. A silver spoon is a neat and pleasant article with which to eat small, ripe melons.

Pineapples.—Slice on a slaw-cutter, or very thin with a knife; mix with finely powdered sugar. Set on ice till ready to serve.

Oranges are nice served whole, the skins quartered and turned down. Form in a pyramid with bananas and white grapes.

Orange and Cocoanut.—A layer of oranges sliced, then sugar, then a layer of cocoanut, grated; then another of oranges, and so on until the dish is full. This is by many known as *Ambrosia*.

Sliced Peaches.—Peel and slice ripe peaches. Lay them in a dish with plenty of sugar for an hour or two, till tea time. Eat with cream.

Stewed Peaches.—Make a sirup of sugar and water; halve the peaches, leaving the stone in one half, and drop into sirup. Allow the whole to simmer slowly until fruit is tender; then remove fruit, and let sirup boil till thick; then pour over fruit and serve at once.

Frosted Peaches.—Put half a cupful of water and the beaten whites of three eggs together; dip in each peach, using fine, large freestones, after you have rubbed off the fur with a clean cloth; and then roll in powdered sugar. Set them on the stem end, upon a sheet of white paper, in a sunny window. When half dry, roll again in the sugar.

Expose to the sun and breeze until perfectly dry. Until ready to arrange them in the glàss dish for table, keep in a cool, dry place. Decorate with green leaves.

Fried Peaches.—Cut the peaches in two, and remove the stones. Dust a little flour on the side from which the stone is taken, and fry, only on that side, in a little butter. When done, add sugar and a little butter.

Baked Apples.—Pare and core good, sound, tart apples. Fill them with sugar, butter, and a flavor of spice. Put a little water in the pan, and bake until the apples are thoroughly tender.

Apple Sauce.—Pare, core, and slice nice, juicy apples that are not very sweet; put them in a stewpan with a little grated lemon peel, and water enough to keep them from burning. Stew till soft and tender; mash to a paste, and sweeten well with brown sugar, adding a little butter and nutmeg.

Apples with Lemon.—Make a sirup of sugar and water. Slice a lemon into it, and let boil until clear. Pare and core sound, tart apples, cut into quarters, and lay them carefully into the sirup; let them cook gently until a straw can be run through them, taking care not to break them. Lay the pieces of apple in a glass dish, boil down the sirup, and when slightly cool, pour over the apples.

Apple Float.—Pare, slice, and stew six large apples in as much water as will cover them; when well done, press them through a sieve and sweeten highly with crushed sugar; while cooling, beat the whites of four eggs to a stiff froth, and stir into the apples; flavor with lemon or vanilla; serve with plenty of sweet cream.

Transparent Apple.—Boil tart, ripe, and juicy apples in a little water; then strain through a fine cloth, and add a pound of white sugar to a pint of juice. Boil till it jellies, and then put into molds. It is very nice served with blanc-mange in saucers.

Baked Pears.—Place in a stone jar, first a layer of pears, with their skins on, then a layer of sugar, then pears, and so on until the jar is full. Then put in as much water as it will hold. Bake three hours.

Quinces.—Bake ripe quinces thoroughly; when cold, strip off the skins, place the quinces in a glass dish, and sprinkle them with white sugar; serve with rich cream.

Bananas and Cream.—Peel, slice, and heap up in a glass dessert-dish, and serve raw, with fine sugar and cream.

Fried Bananas.—Cut the bananas into slices, and fry in a little butter. This makes a very rich dish.

Stewed Rhubarb.—Carefully remove the outer stringy skin; then cut in pieces an inch long, and simmer gently till tender in water and sugar, and the rind and juice of a lemon. When done add a bit of butter and nutmeg.

Crystallized Fruit.—Pick out the finest of any kind of fruit; leave in the stones; beat the whites of three eggs to a stiff froth; lay the fruit in the beaten egg, with the stems upward; drain them, and beat the part that drips off again; select them out, one by one, and dip them into finely powdered sugar; cover a pan with a sheet of fine paper, place the fruit on it, and set it in a cool place; when the icing on the fruit becomes firm, pile them on a dish, and set them in a cold place.

Candied Fruits.—Make a very rich sirup with one pound of granulated sugar to a gill of water. Heat over boiling water till the sugar is dissolved. Pare and halve fine, ripe, but solid peaches. Put a single layer of them in the sirup, in a shallow vessel; cook slowly until clear; drain from the sirup, and put to dry in a moderately heated oven. When fairly dry they may be eaten at once; or, after drying twenty-four hours, they may be packed for future use. Plums, cherries, and pears may be candied in the same manner.

Nuts.—Almonds are inseparably joined with raisins in table service; so for evening uses, hickory nuts and apples form a pleasant combination. All the harder-shelled nuts should be well cracked before they are served. With the softer-shelled, nut crackers should be furnished. Nut picks should always be at hand.

Sweet almonds, which are used for dessert, are of several varieties. Those known as the Syrian, or Jordan almonds, are regarded as the best. Those with hard shells are generally richer in flavor than those with the soft. Certainly the harder shell offers the more effective protection. The skin of almonds is not easily digested. For use in cooking they should be *blanched*, but for table use this is not desirable. Walnuts keep well and improve with age. Of the hickory-nut family, the *shell-bark* is considered best. These, too, are the better for age.

PRESERVES

BLANK PAGE FOR ADDITIONAL RECIPES

XV.—JELLIES, JAMS, AND PRESERVES.

TO insure success in preserving fruits, the first thing to
be looked after is the fruit itself. This should be fully
ripe, fresh, sound, and scrupulously clean and dry. It
should be gathered in the morning of a sunny day, as it will
then possess its finest flavor. Care should be taken to remove all bruised or decayed parts. Allowing them to remain will darken the sirup, and consequently impair the
beauty of the preserves. Fruit requiring to be pared should
be laid in water to preserve the color after the paring. The
best sugar is the cheapest; indeed, there is no economy in
stinting the sugar, either as to quality or proper quantity,
for inferior sugar is wasted in scum, and the preserves will
not keep unless a sufficient proportion of sugar is boiled
with the fruit. At the same time, too large a proportion of
sugar will destroy the natural flavor of the fruit, and in all
probability make fruit candy, instead of the result sought.

The usual proportion in making preserves, is a pound of
sugar to a pound of fruit. There are a few fruits which
require more sugar. In making the sirup, use a small cupful of water to a pound of fruit. The sirup should always
be boiled and strained before putting the fruit in.

Fruit should be cooked in brass kettles, or those of bell-
metal. Modern kettles lined with porcelain, are much used

for this purpose. The kettle should be broad and shallow, so that there will be no necessity for heaping the fruit. Never use tin, iron, or pewter spoons, or skimmers, for preserves, as they will convert the color of red fruit into a dingy purple, and impart, besides, a very unpleasant flavor.

Great care should be taken not to place the kettle flat upon the fire, as this will be likely to burn at the bottom.

Glass jars are much the best for preserves, as the condition of the fruit can be observed more readily. Whatever jars are used, however, the contents should be examined every three weeks for the first two months, and if there are any signs of either mold or fermentation it should be boiled over again. Preserves should be stored in a cool, dry place, but not in one into which fresh air never enters. Damp has a tendency to make the fruit mold, and heat to make it ferment.

A jelly-bag should be in every kitchen. It should be made of flannel, pointed at the bottom, so that the jelly will run out chiefly at one point. It is a good plan to sew a strong loop to the top of the bag, so that it may be hung upon a nail near the fire, that the juice of the fruit may run through gradually into a vessel below. The bag should not be squeezed with the hands, if you wish a very clear jelly. After the clear juice has been obtained, the remainder may be pressed, to make a very excellent, but inferior article of jelly or marmalade.

Rinse the tumblers or bowls to be used in cold water just before filling with jelly or marmalade. When the jelly is cold, fit a circle of tissue-paper, dip it in brandy, and place it directly on the surface of the fruit. This simple precaution will save the housekeeper much annoyance by protecting the conserve from mold. Should the fungus form inside the upper cover of the glass, the inner will effectually shield the contents. Paste thick paper over the top of the glass to exclude the air.

RECIPES.

Currant Jelly.—Never gather currants or other soft or small seed fruit immediately after a rain for preserving purposes, as they are greatly impoverished by the moisture absorbed. In this climate, the first week in July is usually considered the time to make currant jelly. Weigh the currants without removing the stems; do not wash them, but remove leaves and whatever may adhere to them; to each pound of fruit allow half the weight of granulated or pure loaf sugar; put a few currants into a porcelain-lined kettle, and press them with a potato-masher, or anything convenient, in order to secure sufficient liquid to prevent burning; then add the remainder of the fruit and boil freely for twenty minutes, stirring occasionally to prevent burning; take out and strain through a jelly-bag, putting the liquid into earthen or wooden vessels. When strained, return the liquid to the kettle, without the trouble of measuring, and let it boil thoroughly for a moment or so; then add the sugar; the moment the sugar is entirely dissolved, the jelly is done, and must be dished, or placed in glasses; it will jelly upon the side of the cup as it is taken up, leaving no doubt as to the result.

Currant Jelly, No. 2.—Take three quarts of fine, ripe, red currants, and four of white; put them into a jar, tie paper over the top, and put them into a cool oven for three or four hours, or else into a pan of boiling water, or set them on the side of the range; when they are thoroughly heated, strain through a jelly-bag. To every pint of juice, add one pound of granulated sugar, and boil from five to fifteen minutes; turn while hot into wet tumblers.

Currant Jelly without Cooking.—Press the juice from the currants and strain it; to every pint put a pound of fine white sugar; mix them together until the sugar is dissolved; then

14

put it in jars; seal them and expose them to a hot sun for two or three days.

Black Currant Jelly.—Boil the currants till the juice flows, then strain through a jelly-bag, and set it over the fire for twenty minutes, after which add half a pound of sugar to a pound of juice, and boil for about ten minutes.

White Currant Jelly.—Strip the fruit off the stems, and pound it in a clean wooden bowl. Drip the juice gently through a jelly-bag. Prepare a very pure, clear sirup of the best white sugar; allow a pint of juice to a pound of sugar; boil it ten minutes only. Put it in glass preserve-tumblers, cover with paper to fit exactly, and keep it dry and cool.

Apple Jelly.—Take twenty large, juicy apples; pare and chop; put into a jar with the rind of four large lemons, pared thin and cut in bits; cover the jar closely, and set in a pot of boiling water; keep water boiling all around it until the apples are dissolved; strain through a jelly-bag, and mix with the liquid the juice of four lemons; to one pint of mixed juice use one pound of sugar; put in kettle, and when the sugar is melted set it on the fire, and boil and skim about twenty minutes, or until it is a thick, fine jelly.

Apple Jelly, No. 2.—Peel and core sour apples; boil them in a very little water, and strain them through a jelly-bag. Measure, and allow a pound of granulated sugar to a pint of juice. Mix the sugar and juice well together, and let it boil from five to ten minutes. Put it warm into glasses; cut some white paper to fit the top, dip it in brandy, and lay on when the jelly is cool; paste or tie thick paper over the glasses, and when cold put away in a dark, dry place.

Crab-apple Jelly.—Wash and quarter Siberian crab-apples. Cover with cold water and let cook until thoroughly tender. Strain through a jelly-bag, and to every pint of juice add one pound of sugar. Let cook until it will jelly A slight flavoring of essence of cinnamon is an improvement.

Quince Jelly.—Take very ripe quinces ; peel and core, and boil in a little water till very soft; drain off the juice through a coarse towel, add an equal measure of sugar, and boil twenty minutes.

Grape Jelly.—Mash the grapes thoroughly and strain out the juice. Add an equal measure of sugar, and boil twenty minutes.

Barberry Jelly.—Pick the berries from the stalks, mash them, and boil fifteen minutes. Squeeze through a jelly-bag; allow a pound of white sugar to a pound of juice; melt the sugar in the juice, and boil half an hour.

Raspberry Jelly.—Crush the raspberries and strain through a wet cloth. Add an equal measure of sugar, and boil from ten to twenty minutes.

Apple Marmalade.—Pare, core, and slice two or three dozen tart, juicy apples ; three-quarters of a pound of sugar to every pint of juice. Stew until tender in just enough cold water to cover them. Drain off the juice through a colander, and put into a preserving-kettle, stirring into it three-quarters of a pound of sugar for every pint of the liquid. Boil until it begins to jelly; strain the juice of two lemons into it; put in the apples, and stew pretty fast, stirring almost constantly, until it becomes thick and smooth. If the apples are not entirely soft, rub them through the colander before adding them to the boiling sirup.

Quince Marmalade.—Take very ripe quinces ; wash, pare and core them ; to each pound of fruit allow one pound of loaf sugar. Boil the parings and cores together, with water enough to cover them, till quite soft; strain the liquid into the preserving-kettle with the fruit and sugar. Boil the whole over a slow fire, stirring frequently until the mass becomes thick.

Pear and Quince Marmalade.—Pare and core two dozen juicy pears and ten fine, ripe quinces. Add three-quarters of a pound of sugar to every pound of fruit and the juice of three lemons. Throw them into cold water, and stew the parings and cores in a little water to make the sirup. When they have boiled to pieces, strain off the liquid; when cold, put in the sliced fruit and bring to a fast boil. When the mass is thick and smooth, cook steadily for an hour or more, working with a wooden spoon to a rich jelly.

Pineapple Marmalade.—Take ripe, juicy pineapples; pare, cut out the specks very carefully, and grate on a coarse grater all but the core. Weigh, and allow a pound of sugar to a pound of fruit. Cook from twenty minutes to half an hour.

Orange Marmalade.—Take eighteen sweet, ripe oranges, six pounds best white sugar. Grate the peel from four of these and reserve it for the marmalade. The rinds of the others will not be needed. Pare the fruit carefully, removing the inner white skin as well as the yellow. Slice the orange; remove the seeds; put the fruit and grated peel in a porcelain kettle, and boil steadily until the pulp is reduced to a smooth mass. Take from the fire, and put through a colander. Stir in six pounds of the best white sugar; return to the fire, and boil fast, stirring constantly half an hour or until thick.

Grape Marmalade.—Put green grapes into a preserving-pan with sufficient water to cover them. Put them on the fire, and boil until reduced to a mash; put the pulp through a sieve which will strain out the seeds; to each pound of pulp add two pounds of the best loaf sugar, and boil to the consistence of a jelly.

Peach Marmalade.—Select peaches which are quite ripe; pare and cut them in small pieces; to every pound of fruit add one pound of sugar; put the fruit and sugar into a preserving-kettle, and mash well together; place it over the fire, and when it begins to boil, stir until it becomes quite thick.

Cherry Jam.—First stone and then weigh some freshly gathered preserving cherries; boil them over a brisk fire for an hour, keeping them almost constantly stirred from the bottom of the pan, to which they will otherwise be liable to stick and burn. Add for each pound of the fruit half a pound of good sugar roughly powdered, and boil quickly for twenty minutes, taking off the scum as it rises.

Blackberry Jam.—To four bowls of blackberries add four bowls of sugar; boil until it jellies.

Raspberry Jam.—Mash the raspberries, and allow a pound of sugar to a pound of fruit. Boil twenty minutes. A few currants added to raspberry jam is considered by many a great improvement.

Barberry Jam.—The barberries should be quite ripe, though they should not be allowed to hang until they begin to decay. Strip them from the stalks, throw aside such as are spotted, and for each pound of fruit allow eighteen ounces of well-refined sugar; boil this, with one pint of water to every four pounds, until it becomes white and falls in thick masses from the spoon; then throw in the fruit, and keep it stirred over a brisk fire for six minutes only; take off the scum, and pour it into jars or glasses.

Strawberry Jam.—Use fine, scarlet berries; weigh and boil them for thirty-five minutes, keeping them constantly stirred; add eight ounces of good sugar to the pound of fruit; mix them well off the fire, then boil again quickly for twenty-five minutes. One pound of white currant juice added at the outset to four of the strawberries will greatly improve this preserve.

White Currant Jam.—Boil together quickly for seven minutes equal quantities of fine white currants, picked very carefully, and of the best white sugar pounded and passed through a sieve. Stir the preserve gently the whole time, and skim it thoroughly.   Just before it is taken from the fire, throw in the strained juice of one good lemon to four pounds of the fruit.

Damson Jam.—The fruit for this jam should be freshly gathered and quite ripe.   Split, stone, weigh, and boil it quickly for forty minutes ; then stir in half its weight of good sugar roughly powdered, and when it is dissolved, give the preserve fifteen minutes additional boiling, keeping it stirred and thoroughly skimmed.

Green Gage Jam.—Rub ripe green gages through a sieve ; put all the pulp into a pan with an equal weight of loaf sugar pounded and sifted.   Boil the whole until sufficiently thick, and put into glasses.

Preserved Peaches.—Weigh the peaches, and allow three-quarters of a pound of sugar to every pound of fruit.   Throw about half the sugar over the fruit, and let it stand over night.   In the morning drain the sirup off the fruit, add the rest of the sugar, and let that come to a boil.   Put the peaches in, and let them boil until you can stick a straw through them.   In cooking the peaches, put a few at a time only in the sirup to cook.

Preserved Peaches, No. 2.—Weigh the fruit after it is pared and the stones extracted and allow a pound of sugar to every pound of peaches.   Put the sugar in a preserving-kettle, and make the sirup ; let it just boil ; lay the peaches in, and let them boil steadily until they are tender and clear.   Take them out with a perforated skimmer and lay upon flat dishes, crowding as little as possible.   Boil the sirup almost to a jelly, until it is clear and thick, skimming off all the scum.   Fill the jars two-thirds full of the peaches, pour on the boiling sirup, and, when cold, cover with brandied tissue-paper, then with thick paper tied tightly over them. Or put them in air-tight jars.

Preserved Quinces.—Use a pound of sugar to each pound of quince after paring, coring, and quartering; take half of the sugar and make a thin sirup; stew in this a few of the quinces at a time till all are finished. Make a rich sirup of the remaining sugar, and pour over them.

Pineapple Preserves.—Use pineapples as ripe as can be had. Pare and cut them into thin slices, weigh them, and allow one pound of the best granulated sugar to each pound of fruit. Take a deep china bowl or dish, and in it put a layer of fruit and sugar alternately, a coating of sugar on the top; let it stand all night. In the morning, take out the fruit and put the sirup into a preserving-kettle. Boil and skim it until it is perfectly clear; then, while it is boiling hot, pour it over the fruit, and let it stand uncovered until it becomes entirely cold. If it stands covered, the steam will fall into the sirup and thin it.

Preserved Pears.—Preserved pears are put up precisely as are peaches, but are only pared, not cored or divided. Leave the stems on.

Watermelon Rind Preserves.—Select rind which is firm, green, and thick; cut in any fanciful shape, such as leaves, stars, diamonds, etc. Then weigh, and to each pound of rind allow one and a half pounds of loaf sugar. To green them, take a brass or copper kettle, and to a layer of grape-vine leaves, which should be well washed, add a layer of the rind, and so on until the last, which should be a thick layer of the leaves, and well covered with a coarse linen cloth. To each pound of the rind, add a piece of alum the size of a pea; then fill up with warm water sufficient to cover the whole, and let it stand upon the stove, where it will steam, but not boil, until the greening is completed, which will be in two or three hours. When green, lay them in clear, cold water, and make your sirup. To each pound of sugar add one and a half pints of water; clarify, put in your rind; slice lemons, two to each pound of rind, and when about half done add the lemons. Boil until the rind is perfectly transparent. A few pieces of ginger-root may be added, which will impart a high flavor, and will blend very delightfully with the lemons.

Preserved Citron.—Proceed the same as above, substituting citron for the watermelon rind.

Preserved Strawberries.—Procure fresh, large strawberries when in their prime, but not so ripe as to be very soft; hull and weigh them; take an equal weight of sugar, make a sirup, and when boiling hot, put in the berries. A small quantity only should be done at once. If crowded, they will become mashed. Let them boil about twenty minutes, or a half an hour; turn into tumblers or small jars, and seal with egg papers while hot.

Preserved Cherries.—Wash, stem, and stone the cherries; save every drop of the juice, and use it in place of water in making the sirup. Make a sirup, allowing a pound of sugar to every pound of fruit; add the fruit, and let it simmer gently for half an hour, skimming as is necessary.

Damson Preserves.—To four pounds of damsons use three pounds of sugar; prick each damson with a needle; dissolve the sugar with one-half pint of water, and put it on the fire; when it simmers, put in as many damsons as will lie on the top; when they open, take them out and lay them on a dish, and put others in, and so on until all have been in; then put them all in the kettle together and let them stew until done; put them in jars and seal them.

Green Gage Preserves.—When the fruit is ripe, wipe them clean, and to one pound of fruit put one-quarter pound of sugar, which will make a fine sirup; boil the fruit in this sirup until it is perfectly done; then use a fresh sirup of one pound of fruit to one pound of sugar; moistening the sugar with water. When the sirup boils put in the fruit, and leave for fifteen minutes; then put the fruit in jars; boil the sirup until thick; when cooled to milkwarm, pour it over the fruit; tie the jars tightly and keep in a warm place.

Strawberries in Wine.—Put a quantity of the finest large strawberries in a bottle, strew in a few spoonfuls of powdered sugar, and fill the bottle up with Madeira or Sherry wine.

Grapes in Brandy.—Take some close bunches of grapes, white or black, not overripe, and lay them in a jar. Put a good quantity of pounded white candy upon them, and fill up the jar with brandy. Tie them close down, and keep in a dry place. Prick each grape with a needle three times.

Brandy Peaches.—Take large, juicy freestone peaches, not so ripe as to burst or mash on being handled. Rub the down from them with a clean thick flannel. Prick every peach down to the stone with a large silver fork, and score them all along the seam or cleft. To each pound of peaches allow a pound of granulated sugar and half a pint of water mixed with half a white of egg, slightly beaten. Put the sugar into a porcelain kettle and pour the water upon it. When it is quite melted, give it a stirring, set it over the fire, and boil and skim it till no more scum rises. Then put in the peaches, and let them cook (uncovered) in the sirup till a straw will penetrate them. Then take the kettle off the fire, and take out the fruit with a wooden spoon, draining it over the kettle. Let the sirup remain in the kettle a little longer. Mix a pint of the very best white brandy for each pound of peaches, with the sirup, and boil them together ten minutes or more. Transfer the peaches to large glass jars, making each about two-thirds full, and pour the brandy and sirup over them, filling the jars full. When cool, cover closely.

Spiced Peaches.—Seven pounds of fruit, one pint vinegar, three pounds sugar, two ounces cinnamon, one-half ounce cloves. Scald together the sugar, vinegar, and spices; pour over the fruit. Let it stand twenty-four hours; drain off, scald again, and pour over fruit, letting it stand another twenty-four hours. Boil all together until the fruit is tender. Skim it out, and boil the liquor until thickened. Pour over the fruit and set away in a jar.

Apple Butter.—Boil down a kettieful of cider to two-thirds the original quantity. Pare, core, and slice juicy apples, and put as many into the cider as it will cover. Boil slowly, stirring often with a flat stick, and when the apples are tender to breaking, take them out with a perforated skimmer, draining well against the sides of the kettle. Put in a second supply of apples and stew them soft, as many as the cider will hold. Take from the fire, pour all together into a tub or large crock; cover and let it stand twelve hours. Then return to the kettle and boil down, stirring all the while until it is the consistency of thick custard and brown in color. Spice well with **D. & L. Slade Co.'s Pure Spices.**

Peach Butter.—To one bushel of peaches allow from eight to ten pounds of granulated sugar; pare and halve the peaches, put into the kettle, and stir constantly, to prevent sticking to the kettle, until perfectly smooth and rather thick; a part of the peach-stones thrown in and cooked with the peaches give it a nice flavor, and they can be afterward skimmed out; add the sugar a short time before taking from the fire; put in jars and cover tight; peaches for butter should be neither too mealy nor too juicy.

CANNED FRUITS & VEGETABLES

BLANK PAGE FOR ADDITIONAL RECIPES

XVI.—CANNED FRUITS AND VEGETABLES.

WIDESPREAD USE OF CANNED GOODS; PHILOSOPHY OF CANNING
FRUITS; HOW TO FILL THE JARS; WHAT JARS ARE BEST; SELEC-
TION OF THE FRUIT; WHERE TO STORE THE CANS; NEED OF
WATCHING THE CANS. TWELVE RECIPES OF CANNING FRUIT
AND VEGETABLES.

CANNED fruits and vegetables of all kinds may now be
found abundantly in the stores. Their prices are so
low that they present a strong inducement to the
housekeeper to omit the labor incident to home canning, and
simply to purchase what is needed.

What is aimed at in all these processes is the entire ex-
clusion of air from the fruit. Its expulsion from them is
effected by using heat enough to cook them, after which the
hermetical sealing does the remaining service. Solder, wax,
and rubber bands do this sealing work.

If it is desired to preserve the fruit whole, it may be put
into the jars before heating. Fill the jars with water, and
set them into a wash-boiler of cold water, the water reaching three-fourths of the way to the tops of the jars. Do not
set them directly on the bottom, but on a little hay, lest the
heat cause them to crack. Bring the water slowly to a boil,
and let it boil about five minutes. The cans may then be
taken out, stirred lightly, or shaken, to expel any remaining
air bubbles; then fill to the brim with boiling water and
close the jars. No air bubbles should remain in the can.
If the fruit can be cooked before canning, the process is
much simpler, as the boiling material itself expels the air.
The cans in this case need simply to be filled and then
sealed.

RECIPES.

Canned Strawberries.—Fill glass jars with fresh strawberries sprinkled with sugar, allowing a little over one-quarter of a pound of sugar to each pound of berries; set the jars in a boiler, with a little hay laid in the bottom to prevent the jars from breaking; fill with cold water to within an inch or two of the tops of the jars; let them *boil* fifteen minutes, then move back to the boiler, wrap the hand in a towel, and take out the jars; fill the jars to the top before sealing, using one or more of the filled jars for that purpose if necessary.

Canned Gooseberries.—Fill very clean, dry, wide-necked bottles with gooseberries gathered the same day and before they have attained their full growth. Cork them tightly, wrap a little hay round each of them, and set them up to their necks in a kettle of cold water, which should be brought very gradually to boil. Let the fruit be gently simmered until it appears shrunken and perfectly scalded; then take out the bottles, and with the contents of one or two fill up the remainder. Use great care not to break the fruit in doing this. When all are ready, pour *scalding* water into the bottles and cover the gooseberries entirely with it, or they will become moldy at the top. Cork the bottles well immediately, and cover the necks with melted resin; keep them in a cool place; and when they are used pour off the greater part of the water and add sugar as for the fresh fruit.

Canned Peaches.—Peel and quarter choice peaches. To peel, place them in a wire basket, dip into boiling water a moment and then into cold water, and strip off the skins. Have a porcelain-kettle with boiling water and another with sirup made with granulated sugar; drop the peaches into boiling water (some previously boil the pits in the water for their flavor) and let them cook until tender; then lift them **out** carefully into a can, pouring over them all the sirup the can will hold, and seal immediately.   Cook only peaches enough to fill one can at a time.

Canned Peaches, No. 2.—Pare and stone peaches enough for two jars at a time. If many are pared, they will become dark colored by standing.   Rinse in cold water ; then cook in a rich sirup of sugar and water about fifteen or twenty minutes, or until they are clear. Put into jars all that are not broken; fill up with the hot sirup, about as thick as ordinary mo‑lasses, and seal. The same sirup will do to cook several jars. After the sirup becomes dark, it, with the broken peaches, can be used for marmalade or peach butter. The same method can be used for pears, plums, and all light fruits.

Canned Pineapple.—Use three-fourths of a pound of sugar to one pound of fruit.   Pick the pineapple to pieces with a silver fork.   Scald and can while hot.

Canned Grapes.—Squeeze the pulp from the skin ; boil the pulp until the seeds begin to loosen, having the skins boiling hard and separately in a little water.   When the pulp seems tender, put it through the sieve ; then add the skins, if ten‑der, with the water they boil in, if not too much. Use a large coffeecupful of sugar for a quart can ; boil until thick, and can in the usual way.

Canned Plums.—Prick each plum with a needle to prevent bursting ; prepare a sirup, allowing a gill of pure water and a quarter of a pound of sugar to every three quarts of fruit. When the sugar is dissolved and the water blood-warm, put in the plums.   Heat slowly to a boil.   Let them boil five minutes—not fast or they will break badly—fill up the jars with plums, pour in the scalding sirup until it runs down the sides, and seal.   Green gages are very fine put up in this way, also damsons for pies.

Canned Pears.—Select finely flavored fruit ; either halve and core them or core whole ; make a sirup of sugar and water, using as little water as will dissolve the sugar. Add a quarter of a pound of sugar to a pound of fruit. Place the fruit in the kettle carefully, and let it come to a boil or until the fruit is well scalded. Turn into the jars hot, and seal at once.

Canned Tomatoes.—Pour boiling water over the tomatoes to loosen the skins. Remove these; drain off all the juice that will come away without pressing hard; put them into a kettle and heat slowly to a boil. The tomatoes will look much nicer if all the hard parts be removed before putting them on the fire. Rub the pulp soft with your hands. Boil half an hour; dip out the surplus liquid, pour the tomatoes, boiling hot, into the cans, and seal. Keep in a cool, dark place.

Canned Beans.—Remove the strings at the sides, and cut into pieces about an inch long; put them into boiling water and scald, then can them.

Canned Asparagus.—Cut away all the hard part of the stem and boil the top portion until nearly done, just as if about to serve at once. Flat cans are best, into which the stems can be laid regularly, the water in which they were boiled being poured over them boiling hot, and the can sealed. If jars or high cans are used, pack the ·asparagus into them until they are full. Fill the cans with water; set them on hay in a boiler of cold water reaching to within an inch of their tops; then bring to a boil and nearly finish cooking the stems. Wrap the hand in a towel; take out the cans and seal or solder them as in other vegetables.

Canned Corn.—Boil sweet corn till nearly done; cut close from the cobs and fill the jars; pour on water in which the corn was boiled; place in a boiler and just bring to a boil, as above · then take out and seal.

PICKLES

BLANK PAGE FOR ADDITIONAL RECIPES

XVII.—PICKLES AND CATSUPS.

PICKLES MORE POPULAR THAN WHOLESOME; GREENING PICKLES; WHAT KETTLES AND JARS SHOULD NOT BE USED IN PICKLING; CHOOSING THE FRUIT, SPICES, ETC.; HOW TO KEEP PICKLES; CATSUPS, HOW MADE, ETC. THIRTY-THREE RECIPES FOR PICKLES AND CATSUPS.

PICKLES are very popular as a relish, but it must be confessed that they are not the most wholesome diet. This is due chiefly to the fact that they are made of hard, crude, and often of unripe fruit. Then, too, the excess of acid and the high seasoning disagree with many constitutions.

It is deemed important that pickles for the market be well greened. To accomplish this end, copperas and other chemicals are employed or copper kettles are used. All this is poisonous, and should be shunned. No metal kettles or spoons should be tolerated in pickling. Glazed jars are not desirable either, as salt and vinegar decompose the glazing and set free the lead which it contains. An ordinary stone jar is the vessel to use, or a porcelain-lined kettle.

Be careful to select perfectly sound fruit or vegetables for pickling, and use none but the very best cider vinegar. Good white wine vinegar does well for some sorts of pickles, but be ever watchful against chemical preparations called vinegar, that destroy instead of preserving the articles put away in them. In the selection of spices there is so much diversity of taste that no general directions will be of practical value. But get the purest articles you can find.

Pickles must be kept from the air. It is a good plan to

put them up in large jars, and for use to empty the large jar at once into smaller ones, using these one at a time. Keep them wholly covered with the vinegar. Water will soon cause the jar of pickles to spoil.

The same hints given above apply to the making of catsup, which is really but a pickle cooked to a more advanced point. It needs to be tightly corked and sealed, that it may keep well.

RECIPES.

Cucumber Pickles.—Make a weak brine, hot or cold; if hot, let the cucumbers stand in it twenty-four hours; if cold, forty-eight hours; rinse and dry the cucumbers with a cloth, take vinegar enough to cover them, allow one ounce of alum to every gallon of vinegar, put it in a brass kettle (or porcelain-lined, if the *greening* is not desired) with the cucumbers, and heat slowly, turning the cucumbers from the bottom frequently; as soon as they are heated through, skim them out into a crock, let the vinegar boil up, turn it over the pickles, and let them stand at least twenty-four hours; drain off the vinegar. Take fresh vinegar, and to every gallon allow two tablespoofuls of white mustard-seed, one of cloves, one of celery-seed, one of stick cinnamon, one large, green pepper, a very little horse-radish, and, if you like, one-half pint of sugar. Divide the spices equally into several small bags of coarse muslin, scald with the vinegar, and pour over the pickles. If you like your pickles hard, let the vinegar cool before pouring over them.

Cucumber Pickles, No. 2.—To a gallon of water add a quart of salt, put in the cucumbers, and let them stand over night. In the morning, wash them out of the brine, and put them carefully into a stone jar. Boil a gallon of vinegar, put in, while cold, quarter of a pound of cloves, and a tablespoonful of alum; when it boils hard, skim it well and turn over the cucumbers. In a week they will be fit for use.

15

Pickled Carrot. — Boil carrots until tender, cut into fancy shapes, and put them into strong vinegar. Spice or flavor to suit taste. This is a pretty garnish and an excellent pickle.

Pickled Barberries. — Soak nice large bunches of barberries in salt and water for a few hours. Remove from the water and pour scalding vinegar over them. Spice the vinegar if you prefer. These are ornamental for salad-garnishing. They may be kept in the brine and freshened when used. — THE PEERLESS COOK BOOK : *Mrs. D. A. Lincoln. Redding & Co., Publishers.*

Pickled Pears. — Take half a peck of pears halved and cored, lay the pieces together, and pack them all closely together in a preserving-kettle. Add two ounces of cinnamon-bark and half an ounce of cloves, two pounds of sugar, and one pint of vinegar; cover them up and set on a slow fire to boil. Boil down until thoroughly cooked. Put in a stone jar and cover with white paper wet with brandy.

Pickled Muskmelon. — Take a ripe melon (cantaloupe), peel, and cut in blocks. Then take two tablespoonfuls of pulverized alum dissolved in hot water, pour over and add cold water until they are covered. (Press them down with a plate.) Let them stand over night, then drain off, and rinse well with cold water. Take a quart of vinegar and two pounds of sugar, boil and turn over. Do this for nine mornings, adding the vinegar and sugar if necessary. The ninth morning tie up in a thin muslin bag an ounce of cloves and two ounces of cinnamon-bark, boil in vinegar, then add your melon and boil for a short time. In putting the pickle away in a jar, place the muslin bag containing the spices among them on the top.

Pickled Onions.—Select small white onions, put them over the fire in cold water with a handful of salt. When the water becomes scalding hot, take them out and peel off the skins, lay them in a cloth to dry; then put them in a jar. Boil half an ounce of allspice and half an ounce of cloves in a quart of vinegar. Take out the spice and pour the vinegar over the onions while it is hot. Tie up the jar when the vinegar is cold, and keep it in a dry place.

Pickled Onions, No. 2.—Take small, white onions and peel them; lay them in salt water for two days; change the water once; then drain and put them in bottles. Take vinegar enough to cover them, spice with whole mixed spices, scald it, and pour over the onions.

Pickled Garlic and Eschalots.—Garlic and eschalots may be pickled in the same way as onions.

Pickled Nasturtiums.—Nasturtiums should be gathered quite young, and a portion of the buds, when very small, should be mixed with them. Prepare a pickle by dissolving an ounce and a half of salt in a quart of pale vinegar, and throw in the berries as they become fit, from day to day. They are used instead of capers for sauce, and by some persons are preferred to them. When purchased for pickling, put them at once into a jar and cover them well with the vinegar.

Pickled Watermelon.—Take the outer part of the rind of the melon, pare and cut in small pieces. To one quart of vinegar add two pounds of sugar, one ounce of cassia buds. In this boil the rind until clear and tender.

Pickled Walnuts.—Walnuts for this pickle must be gathered while a pin can pierce them easily. When once the shell can be felt, they have ceased to be in a proper state for it. Make sufficient brine to cover them well, with six ounces of salt to the gallon of water; take off the scum, which will rise to the surface as the salt dissolves, throw in the walnuts, and stir them night and morning; change the brine every three days, and if they are wanted for immediate eating, leave them in it for twelve days; otherwise, drain them from it in nine, spread them on dishes, and let them remain exposed to the air until they become black; this will be in twelve hours, or less. Make a pickle for them with something more than half a gallon of vinegar to the hundred, a teaspoonful of salt, two ounces of black pepper, three of bruised ginger, a drachm of mace, and from a quarter to half an ounce of cloves (of which some may be stuck into three or four small onions), and four ounces of mustard-seed. Boil the whole of these together for about five minutes; have the walnuts ready in a stone jar, or jars, and pour the vinegar on them as soon as it is taken from the fire. When the pickle is quite cold, cover the jar securely and store it in a dry place. Keep the walnuts always well covered with vinegar, and boil that which is added to them.

Pickled Red Cabbage.—Slice the red cabbage into a colander, and sprinkle each layer with salt; let it drain two days, then put it into a jar and pour boiling vinegar enough to cover, and put in a few slices of red beet-root. Use the purple red cabbage. Cauliflower cut in bunches, and thrown in after being salted, will take on the color of a beautiful red.

Pickled Mushrooms.—Rub the mushroom heads with flannel and salt, throw them in a stewpan with a little salt over them; sprinkle with pepper and a small quantity of mace; as the liquor comes out, shake them well, and keep them over a gentle fire until all the liquor is dried into them again; then put as much vinegar into the pan as will cover them; give it a scald, and pour the whole into bottles.

Pickled Beets.—Wash the beet perfectly, not cutting any of the fibrous roots, lest the juice escape; put in sufficient

water to boil it, and when the skin will come off easily it is
sufficiently cooked, and may be taken out and laid upon a
cloth to cool. Having rubbed off the peel, cut the beet
into thick slices, pour over it cold vinegar prepared as follows: Boil a quart of vinegar with an ounce of whole black
pepper and an equal weight of dry ginger, and let it stand
until quite cold. Keep closely corked.

Pickled Peppers.—Do not pick them till just as they begin
to turn red; then soak them for ten or twelve days in strong
salt and water; take them from the brine and soak them
in clear water for a day. Wipe them dry, and put them
away in cold vinegar; or if you wish them milder, remove
the seeds and scald the vinegar, but do not boil.

Pickled Bell Peppers.—Cut a slit in the side of each pepper
and take out all the seeds. Let them soak in brine (strong
enough to float an egg) two days. Then, washing them in
cold water, put them into a stone jar. Pour over them vinegar boiled with cinnamon, mace, and nutmeg. Whenever
they are wanted to be served, stuff each one with a boiled
tongue cut into dice and mixed with a *mayonnaise* dressing.
Or little mangoes may be made, stuffing each one with
pickled nasturtiums, grapes, minced onions, red cabbage, or
cucumbers, seasoned with mustard-seed, root ginger, and
mace.

Pepper-hash.—Take four dozen peppers, two very large
cabbages, one ounce of *light* mustard-seed. Chop the
peppers fine, cut the cabbage on a cabbage-knife, mix together, salt well, and let it stand over night, putting the
dish or tub so the juice will run down; pour off in the
morning. Add one ounce of cloves, one ounce of allspice;
mix all through, and put the vinegar on cold.

Flint Pickles.—Make a brine of a gallon of water and a
cupful of salt. This must be poured boiling hot on the cucumbers six days in succession. Rinse them in cold water;

put them in a kettle with a teaspoonful of allspice and a teaspoonful of cloves, a handful of cinnamon sticks, a little sliced horse-radish, and cider vinegar to cover them. Let them come to a boil, then take out and put in jars.

East India Pickle.—One hundred cucumbers (large and small), one peck of green tomatoes, one-half peck of onions, four cauliflowers, four red peppers (without the seeds), four heads of celery, one pint of bottled horse-radish. Slice all, and stand in salt twenty-four hours, then drain; pour on weak vinegar; stand on stove until it comes to a boil; then drain again. Take one ounce of ground cinnamon, one ounce of ground tumeric, one-half pound of mustard, one-quarter pound of brown sugar; wet these with cold vinegar; add to this sufficient vinegar to moisten all the pickles. Cook all together ten minutes. Seal in bottles while hot.

French Pickle.—Take one peck of green tomatoes, sliced; six large onions. Throw on them a teacupful of salt over night. Drain thoroughly, then boil in two quarts of water and one quart of vinegar fifteen or twenty minutes; drain in colander; then take four quarts of vinegar, two pounds of brown sugar, one-half pound of white mustard-seed, two tablespoonfuls of cloves, two tablespoonfuls of cinnamon, two tablespoonfuls of ginger, two tablespoonfuls of ground mustard, one teaspoonful of cayenne pepper; put all together and cook fifteen minutes.

Piccalilly.—One peck of green tomatoes sliced, one-half peck of onions sliced, one cauliflower, one peck of small cucumbers. Leave in salt and water twenty-four hours; then put in a kettle with a handful of scraped horse-radish, one ounce of tumeric, one ounce of whole cloves, one-quarter pound of whole pepper, one ounce of cassia buds or cinnamon, one pound of white mustard-seed, one pound of English mustard. Put in kettle in layers, and cover with cold vinegar. Boil fifteen minutes, constantly stirring.

Chow-chow.—One quart of large cucumbers, one quart of small ones; two quarts of onions, four heads of cauliflower, six green peppers, one quart of green tomatoes, one gallon of vinegar, one pound of mustard, two cupfuls of sugar, two cupfuls of flour, one ounce of tumeric. Put all in salt and water one night; cook all the vegetables in brine until tender except the large cucumbers. Pour vinegar and spices over all.

Sweet Pickles.—Such fruit as peaches, plums, cherries, grapes, etc., are very palatable when sweet pickled. The process is the same as for other light pickles, except that the vinegar is sweetened to taste.

Sweet Tomato Pickles.—Eight pounds of peeled tomatoes, four of powdered sugar. Of cinnamon, cloves, and allspice, each one ounce. Boil one hour, and add a quart of boiling vinegar.

Tomato Catsup.—Take one bushel of tomatoes; boil soft, and pass through a sieve. Add half a gallon of cider vinegar, one pint of salt, two ounces of cloves, a quarter pound of allspice, a half ounce of cayenne pepper. Boil until reduced to half the quantity. When cool, bottle and cork tightly.

Tomato Catsup, No. 2.—Take one peck of ripe tomatoes, cut up, boil tender, and strain through a wire sieve; add one large tablespoonful of ground cloves, one large tablespoonful of allspice, one large tablespoonful of cinnamon, one teaspoonful of cayenne pepper, one-quarter pound of salt, one-quarter pound of mustard, one pint of vinegar. Boil gently three hours. Bottle and seal while warm.

Green Tomato Catsup.—One peck of green tomatoes, one dozen large onions, one-half pint of salt; slice the tomatoes and onions. To a layer of these add a layer of salt; let stand twenty-four hours, then drain. Add one-quarter pound of mustard-seed, three dessertspoonfuls of sweet oil, one ounce of allspice, one ounce of cloves, one ounce of ground mustard, one ounce of ground ginger, two tablespoonfuls of black pepper, two teaspoonfuls of celery-seed, one-quarter pound of brown sugar. Put all into a preserving-pan, cover with vinegar, and boil two hours.

Chili Sauce.—Thirty tomatoes, three large onions, three peppers, one tablespoonful each of allspice, cloves, and cinnamon, two nutmegs, two tablespoonfuls of salt, one quart of vinegar, one cupful of sugar. Chop the onions and peppers very fine. Cook the tomatoes somewhat first. Mix thoroughly.

Tomato Soy.—One-half bushel of green tomatoes, three onions, three green peppers, one-quarter pound of mustard-seed, three cupfuls of sugar, three cabbages. Chop the tomatoes and onions together fine; add to one gallon of the tomatoes one cupful of salt; let stand twenty-four hours, drain, and add the peppers (chopped fine), mustard-seed, sugar, and other spices to taste. Moisten all with vinegar and cook until tender. Before bottling, add the cabbages (chopped), and one cupful of chopped horse-radish.

Grape Catsup.—Take five pints of grapes; simmer until soft, then put through a colander; add to them two pints of brown sugar, one pint of vinegar, two tablespoonfuls of allspice, two tablespoonfuls of cinnamon, two tablespoonfuls of cloves, one and one-half teaspoonfuls of mace, one teaspoonful of salt, one and one-half teaspoonfuls of red pepper. Boil till thick; then bottle and seal tightly.

Walnut Catsup.—The vinegar in which walnuts have been pickled, when they have remained in it a year, will generally answer all the purposes for which this catsup is required, particularly if it be drained from them and boiled for a few minutes, with a little additional spice and a few eschalots, but where the vinegar is objected to, it may be made by boiling either the expressed juice of young walnuts for an hour, with six ounces of fine anchovies, four ounces of eschalots, half an ounce of black pepper, a quarter ounce of cloves, and a drachm of mace to every quart.

Walnut Catsup, No. 2.—Pound in a mortar a hundred young walnuts, strewing among them as they are done half a pound of salt; then pour to them a quart of strong vinegar and let them stand until they have become quite black, keeping them stirred three or four times a day; next add a quart of strong, old beer, and boil the whole together for ten minutes; strain it, and let it remain until the next day; then pour it off clear from the sediment, add to it one large head of garlic bruised, half an ounce of nutmegs bruised, the same quantity of cloves and black pepper, and two drachms of mace; boil these together for half an hour, and the following day bottle and cork the catsup well.

A bottle of port wine may be added before bottling, if desired, and a large bunch of sweet herbs.

Oyster Catsup.—Take fine, large fresh oysters, opened carefully, and wash them in their own liquor. To take any particle of shell that may remain, strain the liquor after. Pound the oysters in a mortar, add the liquor, and to every pint put a pint of sherry; boil it up and skim; then add two anchovies, pounded, an ounce of common salt, two drachms of pounded mace, and one of cayenne. Let it boil up, then skim, and rub it through a sieve. Bottle when cold and seal it. What remains in the sieve will do for oyster sauce.

DRINKS.

BLANK PAGE FOR ADDITIONAL RECIPES

XVIII. — BEVERAGES.

WHAT is worth doing at all in culinary lines is worth doing well, and beverages, being in the line of luxuries, should be good, if not positively luxuriant. Employ good materials, and do not stint them in quantity, if you want good results.

Tea is the leaf of the tea-tree cured in various ways, and the difference between good tea and poor tea is due mainly to methods of picking and curing the leaf.

The housekeeper has no means of knowing the quality of the tea she buys until it is ready for drinking, and the dealer has usually no means of knowing the manner in which the tea he sells is picked and cured.

Of the hundred million pounds of tea sent to this country each year, fully three-quarters is of low grade. It is probable that it requires twenty times as many days' labor to produce a given quantity of choice tea as it does to produce the same amount of the lower grades.

In order to be sure of securing choice tea, the housekeeper should buy for her supplies goods sold by dealers who are in a position to know all about the tea sold, from the time it is picked.

The old-established **Oriental Tea Company** still distributes, in the writer's opinion, the most satisfactory brands, notwithstanding the extensive advertising indulged in by some of the newer tea-houses.

The nutritive value of tea is not appreciable, but as an excitant of respiratory action and promoter of digestion it is very valuable. Tea should be kept closely covered in air-tight canisters, in order that the flavor may be retained.

Coffee will grow in any climate where the temperature does not fall below fifty-five degrees. The best brands are obtained, however, when regard is had for climate and soil; when skill is used in gathering and curing; and when the preparation for and roasting of the coffee has been under the direction of trained and experienced experts. But a few years ago the securing of good coffee was a matter of chance. To-day there are several good brands on the market; but the writer has found **Spurr's Revere Coffee** to be by far the most satisfactory.

Coffee should be kept in tight canisters or boxes. The coffee-pot must be scalded clean and occasionally with soda, so that the inside may be absolutely pure.

Chocolate should never be made except it is intended to be used immediately. By allowing it to become cold or by boiling it again, the flavor is injured, the oily particles of the cocoa are separated and rise to the surface also, and they will never blend pleasantly again.

RECIPES.

Tea. — Tea is best made in an earthenware tea-pot, and should never be made in a vessel made of tin. Use boiling water, but do not boil the tea. Allow one teaspoonful for each person. Use the **Oriental Tea Company's** teas — Garden Formosa, first picking, uncolored Japan tea, or for afternoon teas use Scented. Orange Pekoe and Garden Flowery Pekoe.

Iced Tea.—Iced tea should be made several hours before it is needed and set on ice. When ready to use it, sweeten and drink without milk or cream. Use cracked ice to put into the glass. The tea must be extra strong, and do not stint the ice.

Tea a la Russe. — Slice fresh, juicy lemons; pare carefully, lay a piece in the bottom of each cup; sprinkle with white sugar and pour tea, very hot and strong, over them.

Iced Tea a la Russe. — To each goblet of cold tea (without cream) add the juice of half a lemon. Fill up with pounded ice and sweeten well. A glass of champagne added to this makes what is called Russian punch.

Coffee. — To make choicest coffee, take **Spurr's Revere Coffee** ground to about the fineness of granulated sugar, and use one ounce or one tablespoonful to a pint of water. Mix one egg with the ground coffee and put into the coffee pot. Pour the water, which should be boiling hot, on it; allow it to boil for one minute. Then pour in a very little cold water which will settle the grounds and clarify the liquid. Serve at once if you would have it at its best.

The above applies when using an ordinary coffee pot. When using a percolating coffee pot, like the **Gem** coffee pot, the coffee should be ground very fine, the boiling hot water should be poured over it, and then poured from the spout into a hot pitcher, or other vessel, to be again poured over the coffee. This should be repeated two or three times in order to get the full strength of the coffee.

Stronger or weaker coffee can be prepared by using more or less water but the proportions given here will prove most satisfactory.

Whatever process you use always thoroughly cleanse the coffee pot after each service.

Meringued Coffee. — For six cupfuls of coffee take about one cupful of sweet cream, whipped light, with a little sugar. Put into each cup the desired amount of sugar and about a tablespoonful of boiling milk. Pour the coffee over these, and lay upon the surface of the hot liquid a large spoonful of the frothed cream. Give a gentle stir to each cup before sending it from the tray.

Frothed Cafe au Lait. — Pour into the table urn one quart of strong, clear coffee, strained through muslin, and one quart boiling milk, alternating them and stirring gently. Cover and wrap a thick cloth about the urn for five minutes before it goes to table. Have ready in a cream-pitcher the whites of three eggs, beaten stiff, and one tablespoonful of powdered sugar, whipped with them. Put large spoonful of this froth upon each cupful of coffee as you pour it out, heaping it slightly in the centre.

Chocolate. — Scrape fine one square of a cake of **Bensdorp's Chocolate**; add equal weight of sugar; put these into a pint of boiling milk and water, each one-half, and stir well for two or three minutes until the sugar and chocolate are well dissolved. This preparation may be improved by adding a well-beaten egg or two and stirring briskly through the mixture with an egg-beater. A teaspoonful of **Metcalf's Water White Vanilla** extract, added just before sending to table, is a valuable addition.

Frothed Chocolate. — One cupful boiling water; three pints fresh milk; three tablespoonfuls **Bensdorp's Chocolate,** grated; five eggs, whites only, beaten light, and two tablespoonfuls powdered sugar for froth. Sweeten chocolate to taste; heat milk to scalding; wet up chocolate with boiling water, and when milk is hot, stir this into it; simmer gently ten minutes, stirring frequently; boil up briskly once; take from fire; sweeten to taste, taking care not to make it too sweet, and stir in whites of two eggs, whipped stiff, without sugar; pour into the chocolate-pot or pitcher, which should be well heated. Have ready in a cream-pitcher the remaining whites, whipped up with the powdered sugar; cover the surface of each cup with the sweetened *meringue* before distributing to the guests.

Breakfast Cocoa. — Into a breakfast cup put one-half a teaspoonful of **Bensdorp's Royal Dutch Cocoa,** add a tablespoonful of boiling water, and mix thoroughly. Then add equal parts of boiling water and boiled milk, and sugar to the taste. Boiling two or three minutes will improve it.

Luncheon Cocoa. — Put one-half teaspoonful **Bensdorp's Royal Dutch Cocoa** into a cup, and a teaspoonful of sugar. Mix both well, pour one-half cup of boiling water, while stirring it add one-half cup of hot milk, and the Cocoa is ready. The Cocoa is much improved by boiling one minute. — *Mrs. D. A. Lincoln.*

Grape Punch. — Take one pint of grape juice and the juice of six lemons, one pound of granulated sugar and two quarts of water. Mix and serve from a punch bowl. An orange or pineapple may be sliced in if desired.

Lemonade.—Squeeze the juice of lemons, and add sugar and ice-water to taste.

Concentrated Lemonade.—Make a rich sirup of two and a half pounds of sugar and one pint of cold water and boil gradually. Pour it hot on one and a half ounces of citric acid. Bottle tight while hot. One tablespoonful will make a tumblerful of lemonade.

Portable Lemonade.—Mix a quarter pound of white sugar with the grated rind of a large, juicy lemon. Pour upon this the strained juice of the lemon and pack in a jar. One tablespoonful will suffice for a glass of water.

Egg Nog.—To the yelks of six eggs, add six tablespoonfuls of powdered sugar, one quart of new milk, a half pint of French brandy, and one pint of Madeira wine. Beat the whites up separately, and stir them through the mixture just before pouring into glasses for use.

Roman Punch.—Beat stiff the whites of three eggs, with a half pound of powdered sugar. Add three teacupfuls of strong, sweet lemonade, one wineglassful each of rum and champagne, and the juice of two oranges. Ice abundantly, or freeze.

Milk Punch.—Boil one quart of milk, warm from the cow. Beat up the yelks of four eggs and four tablespoonfuls of powdered sugar together; add two glasses of the best sherry wine; pour into a pitcher, and mix with it the boiling milk, stirring all the time. Pour from one vessel to another six times; add cinnamon and nutmeg to taste, and serve as soon as it can be swallowed without scalding the throat.

Currant and Raspberry Shrub.—Pound four quarts of ripe currants and three quarts of red raspberries in a stone jar or wide-mouthed crock with a wooden beetle. Squeeze out every drop of the juice; put this into a porcelain, enamel, or very clean bell-metal kettle, and boil hard ten minutes. Put in four pounds of loaf sugar at the end of the ten minutes, and boil up once to throw the scum to the top; skim and let it get perfectly cold; then skim off all remaining impurities; add one quart of the best brandy and shake hard for five minutes. Bottle, seal the corks, and lay the bottles on their sides in dry sawdust.

Currant Wine.—One quart of currant juice, three pounds of brown sugar, and one gallon of water; dissolve the sugar in the water, then add the juice; when it ferments, add a little fresh water each day till it is done fermenting, which will be in from a month and a half to two months; turn it off, scald the keg, put it in again, and cork tightly,

Raspberry Wine.—Bruise the raspberries with the back of a spoon; strain them through a flannel bag; add one pound of loaf sugar to one quart of juice; stir well and cover closely, letting it stand for three days, stirring well each day. Pour off the clear juice and add one quart of juice to two quarts of sherry wine; bottle it and use in two weeks.

Raspberry Brandy.—Using brandy instead of wine, as above, will produce a very valuable medicinal drink, Raspberry Brandy.

Raspberry Vinegar.—Take three pints of red berries; pour over them one pint of cider vinegar and let stand twenty-four hours. Strain, and to one pint of juice add one pound of sugar; boil one-half hour, and when cold, bottle for use.

Cherry Brandy.—Use either morello cherries or small black cherries; pick them from the stalks; fill the bottles nearly up to the necks, then fill up with brandy (some use whisky, gin, or spirit distilled from the lees of wine). In three weeks or a month strain off the spirit; to each quart add one pound of loaf sugar clarified, and flavor with tincture of cinnamon or cloves.

Sherbet.—In a quart of water boil six or eight sticks of rhubarb ten minutes; strain the boiling liquor on the thin shaved rind of a lemon. Two ounces of clarified sugar, with a wineglassful of brandy, stir to the above, and let it stand five or six hours before using.

Ginger Beer.—Two ounces of ginger to a pint of molasses; add a gallon of warm water; stir it well, and add half a pint of lively yeast. If you wish it sweeter or hotter, add ginger or molasses before putting in the yeast, to suit your taste.

Spruce Beer.—To three gallons of boiling water, add two pounds of molasses and two ounces of essence of spruce. Let the mixture cool, and when lukewarm, add a scant gill of yeast and set aside to ferment. While the fermentation goes on, skim frequently. When it becomes inactive, put in stone bottles and tie the corks down. White sugar may be used instead of molasses, and will give a better color.

Quick Beer.—To fourteen quarts of water add one quart of molasses, one quart of hop yeast, and four tablespoonfuls of ginger. Mix well; strain through a fine sieve; bottle immediately. Ready for use in twenty-four hours.

Imperial.—Mix in a jug one-half ounce of cream tartar and one quart of boiling water; flavor with lemon peel or essence of lemon, and sweeten to taste. This is a refreshing and pleasantly stimulating summer drink.

Mead.—Mix six gallons of water with six quarts of strained honey; add the yellow rind of two large lemons, pared thin, and the whites of three eggs beaten to a stiff froth. Mix well and boil three-quarters of an hour, skimming thoroughly. Pour into a tub, add three tablespoonfuls of good yeast, and leave it ferment. When it is well worked, pour into a barrel with some lemon peel, and let it stand six months. Then bottle and tie down the corks. It is ready for immediate use, or will keep for months in a cool place.

CANDIES

BLANK PAGE FOR ADDITIONAL RECIPES

XIX.—CANDIES.

THE great danger in candy-making is that of burning the
sugar. To properly cook the candy requires a heat of
about two hundred and fifty degrees.   Less than that
heat will leave the candy soft and sticky. A very little more
than two hundred and sixty degrees will burn it. Here,
then, is the need of care in candy-making.

In the cooking, allow the heat to reach the bottom of the
pan only. Have a quick fire that the work may be done in
the shortest possible time.   When cooked for about fifteen
minutes, test a spoonful of the mass upon a cold plate. If it
form a viscid, tenacious mass, which forms a long, adherent
thread when drawn out, then it is nearly done, and it needs
special care lest it burn before the work be completed. Test
frequently now, dropping a little in cold water. When the
hardened portion is crisp as a pipestem, the cooking has
gone far enough. Then comes the flavoring and coloring.

When the mass has cooled on a stone or buttered plate,
so that it can be handled, it is ready for *pulling*, rolling into
sticks, shaping into forms, etc. The pulling process is
simply a mechanical means of whitening the candy. It is
literally a *pulling*, the candy being thrown on a hook and
pulled out from it, then being thrown on it again and again
pulled, and so on, as may be desired, the longer pulling giving the whiter candy.

For home-made candies use pure materials and good
fruit. Enough of earths and starch and decayed fruits are
bought in the cheap candies of the stores.

RECIPES.

Molasses Candy.—Three cupfuls of brown sugar, one-half cupful of molasses, one cupful of water, one-half teaspoonful of cream tartar, butter the size of a walnut. Bring to a boil, and when crisp by testing in cold water, flavor; pour out on a buttered plate, and pull to whiteness if desired.

Butter Scotch.—Two cupfuls of sugar, two tablespoonfuls of water, a piece of butter the size of an egg. Boil without stirring, until it hardens on a spoon. Pour out on buttered plates to cool.

Ice-cream Candy.—Take two cupfuls of granulated sugar, half a cupful of water, and add one-quarter of a teaspoonful of cream tartar dissolved in a teaspoonful of boiling water. Put it in a porcelain kettle, and boil ten minutes without stirring it. Drop a few drops into a saucer of cold water or on snow. If it become brittle, it is done; if not, boil till it is. Add a piece of butter half as large as an egg while it is on the fire, and stir it in. Pour into a buttered tin, and set on ice or snow to cool enough to pull it white. Flavor with vanilla just before it is cool enough to pull. Work into strands and cut into sticks.

Cream Candy.—One pound of white sugar, three table-spoonfuls of vinegar, one teaspoonful of lemon extract, one teaspoonful of cream tartar. Add a little water to moisten the sugar, and boil until brittle. Put in the extract, then turn quickly out on buttered plates. When cool, pull until white, and cut in squares.

Cocoanut Candy.—Grate very fine a sound cocoanut, spread it on a dish, and let it dry naturally for three days, as it will not bear the heat of an oven, and is too oily for use when freshly broken. Four ounces will be sufficient for a pound of sugar for most tastes, but more can be used at pleasure. To one pound of sugar, take one-half pint of water, a very little white of egg, and then pour over the sugar; let it stand for a short time, then place over a very clear fire, and let it boil for a few minutes; then set it one side until the scum is subsided, clear it off, and boil the sugar until very thick; then strew in the nut, stir and mix it well, and do not quit for an instant until it is finished. The pan should not be placed on the fire, but over it, as the nut is liable to burn with too fierce a heat.

Almond Candy.—Proceed in the same way as for cocoanut candy. Let the almonds be blanched and perfectly dry, and do not throw them into the sugar until they approach the candying point.

Candied Nuts and Fruits.—Three cupfuls of sugar, one cupful of water; boil until it hardens when dropped in water, then flavor with lemon. It must not boil after the lemon is put in. Put a nut on the end of a fine knitting needle, take out, and turn on the needle until it is cool. If the candy gets cold, set on the stove for a few minutes. Malaga grapes, and oranges quartered, may be candied in the same way.

Chocolate Caramels.—Two cupfuls of sugar, one cupful of warm water, one-half cupful of **Bensdorp's Chocolate,** grated, three-fourths of a cupful of butter. Let it boil without stirring until it snaps in water.

Chocolate Caramels, No. 2.—One cupful rich, sweet cream; one cupful brown sugar; one cupful white sugar; seven tablespoonfuls **Bensdorp's Chocolate;** one tablespoonful corn-starch stirred in the cream; one tablespoonful butter; vanilla flavoring; soda, size of a pea, stirred into cream. Boil all ingredients, except the chocolate and vanilla extract, half an hour, stirring to prevent burning. Reserve half of the cream and wet up the chocolate in it, adding a very little water if necessary. Draw the saucepan to the side of the range, and stir this in well; put back on the fire and boil ten minutes longer, quite fast, stirring constantly. When it makes a hard, glossy coat on the spoon, it is done. Add the vanilla after taking it from the range. Turn into shallow dishes, well buttered. When cold enough to retain the impression of the knife, cut into squares.

Lemon Taffy.—Two cupfuls of white sugar, one cupful of boiling water, one-quarter cupful of vinegar, one-half cupful of butter; flavor with lemon; pour in buttered plates to cool.

Butter Taffy.—One tablespoonful of vinegar, one cupful of sugar, two tablespoonfuls of molasses, and a piece of butter the size of an egg. When done, add a little soda.

Cream Chocolates.—For the *creams*, boil two cupfuls of white sugar and one-half cupful of milk for five minutes; add one teaspoonful of vanilla, then beat until stiff enough to handle and make into drops.

For the *chocolate*, take six ounces of **Bensdorp's Chocolate,** grate and steam over the teakettle. Drop the creams when hard, one at a time, into the hot chocolate, using two forks to take them out quickly; set the drop on one fork on the bottom, using the other fork to scrape the chocolate off the cream; gently slip the drop upon a buttered dish. If, when cool, the drop sticks to the dish, hold it over the steam of the teakettle for an instant.

Chocolate Creams. — *Inside:* Two cupfuls of sugar; one cupful of water; one and a half tablespoonfuls of arrow-root; mix; let them boil from five to eight minutes; stir all the time. After taking from the fire, stir until it comes to a cream. When smooth, add one teaspoonful **Metcalf's Water White Vanilla** and make cream into balls.

Outside: Melt a half pound of **Bensdorp's Chocolate,** but do not add water to it. Roll the cream balls into the chocolate while it is warm.

Cream Walnuts.—Two cupfuls sugar, two-thirds cupful water. Boil without stirring until it will spin a thread; flavor with vanilla. Set off into a dish with a little cold water in it; stir briskly until white and creamy. Have the walnuts shelled; make the cream into small, round cakes with your fingers; press half a walnut on either side, and drop into sifted granulated sugar.

Cream Dates.—For cream dates, take fresh California dates, remove the stones, and fill the centre of dates with the same cream as used in cream walnuts. Drop into sugar.

Peanut Candy.—Boil one scant pint of molasses until it hardens in cold water. Stir in two tablespoonfuls of vanilla, then one teaspoonful of soda, dry. Lastly, the shelled peanuts, taken from four quarts measured before shelling. Turn out into shallow pans well buttered, and press it down smooth with a wooden spoon.

Philadelphia Groundnut Cakes.—Boil two pounds of light brown sugar in a preserving kettle, with enough water to wet it thoroughly and form a sirup. Have ready a quarter of a peck of groundnuts (peanuts). When the sugar begins to boil, throw in the white of an egg to clear it. Skim and try by dropping a little into cold water to see if brittle or done. When it is brittle, remove from the fire, and stir in the nuts. Drop on wet plates, free from grease. The white of egg may be omitted.

Gum Drops.—Dissolve one pound of gum arabic in one and a half pints of water; strain and add one pound of refined sugar; beat until the sugar is entirely dissolved. Flavor to taste, and add coloring if desired. Then evaporate with a slow heat until the mass is thick as honey. Have a shallow box, or dish of fine starch; in this make a series of dents with a rounded stick, the size desired for the gum drops. Into each of these indentations drop from a spout, or a spoon, just enough of the thickened mass to fill the cavity, then set away in a warm place till the drops become sufficiently set to allow handling. This may require several days.

Jujube Paste.—Dissolve gum arabic, and add sugar as for gum drops. Evaporate till very thick, and while still warm flavor and pour out into shallow tin pans to cool.

Fig Paste.—Chop up one pound of figs, and boil in a pint of water till reduced to a soft pulp. Strain through a fine sieve, and add three pounds of sugar. Evaporate over boiling water till the paste becomes stiff, then pour it into a mold of wooden strips tied together. When cool, cut into squares; sugar each well, and put away for use. Flavors may be added to taste, or fresh fruits may be mingled with the paste.

Peppermint Drops.—Mix granulated sugar with enough water to form a paste, and put it to boil in a saucepan having a lip from which the contents can be poured or dropped. Allow it come almost, but not entirely, to a boil. Stir continually. Allow it to cool a little, and flavor to taste with strong essence of peppermint. Then drop the mass on sheets of tin or of white paper. To drop it properly, allow just enough to gather at the lip of the saucepan, and then stroke it off with a piece of stiff wire. They should dry in a warm place.

CHAFING DISH

BLANK PAGE FOR ADDITIONAL RECIPES

XX. — CHAFING DISH.

Oyster Relish. — One cup oysters (drained), one cup bread crumbs, one egg, one cup milk, one teaspoonful salt, dash cayenne. All the ingredients are placed in dish and stirred together, first beating the egg well. Be very careful in stirring not to break oysters, and let mixture stand for a time to swell bread crumbs. Heat a tablespoonful of butter in the chafing-dish, and stir in the mixture and cook until oysters are well curled, then add a little butter.

Cheese Fritters. — Four tablespoonfuls Parmesan cheese, two tablespoonfuls bread crumbs, four eggs, salt and paprika; mix grated cheese with bread crumbs; beat eggs thoroughly and add first mixture; season with salt and paprika; drop from tip of spoon in small cakes on a hot buttered blazer; brown on one side, turn and brown on other side.

Chicken a la Reine. — One cup chicken stock, one cup cooked chicken, one-quarter cup bread crumbs, two tablespoonfuls butter, three eggs, one-quarter cup milk, salt, paprika and celery salt; two tablespoonfuls butter, creamed, and add yolks of three hard-boiled eggs, rubbed to a paste; soak bread crumbs in one-fourth cup milk and add to the egg mixture; pour on gradually one cup hot chicken stock, then add cooked chicken, finely cut; season with salt, paprika and celery salt; serve on toast.

Oysters a la Beleveu. — One-quarter pound butter melted in chafing-dish; add one-half cup finely chopped celery and cook thoroughly; put in one quart cream (or milk) with juice of oysters; allow it to just come to a boil, then add one pint of oysters; add a dash of paprika, salt and pepper, and just before serving add one wineglass madeira wine.

Creamed Oysters. — Melt four tablespoonfuls butter in chafing-dish; then add five tablespoonfuls flour, mixed with one-quarter teaspoonful salt and one-eighth teaspoonful pepper; pour on gradually one pint milk and stir; when sauce thickens, add one pint oysters without liquor; cook until edges curl; serve on buttered toast.

Oyster a la Bechamel. — Drain one pint oysters and save the liquor; for twenty-five oysters add milk to the liquor to make half a pint. Put one tablespoonful butter and one of flour in chafing-dish, then light the lamp; mix thoroughly; add liquor and milk, stir until it reaches the boiling point; add oysters, half a teaspoonful salt, a quarter teaspoonful black pepper, and a dash of red pepper; cover the dish, and when boiling, stir in lastly the yolks of three eggs beaten with two tablespoonfuls of cream; after putting out the light, add a teaspoonful of lemon juice, half a teaspoonful onion juice, and serve on toast.

Lobster a la Newberg. — Remove the meat from a good-sized lobster and cut in small pieces; melt two large spoonfuls butter, add the lobster and cook until thoroughly heated; season with salt and pepper; cook one minute and add one-third cup thin cream and the yolks of two eggs slightly beaten; stir until sauce is thickened, then add two tablespoonfuls sherry wine and one of brandy.

Lobster on Toast. — Remove the meat from a good-sized lobster and cut in small pieces; put in the chafing-dish one-half cup hot water, one tablespoonful vinegar, one-half teaspoonful salt, two tablespoonfuls butter, and a dash of cayenne, and let boil; then add the lobster and simmer for five minutes; serve on buttered toast.

Lobster Stew. — Melt four tablespoonfuls butter, and add three tablespoonfuls flour mixed with one-half teaspoonful salt and one-eighth teaspoonful pepper; pour on one quart rich milk when it reaches the boiling point, add two cups of lobster cut in small pieces; cook one minute and serve.

Lobster a la Somerset. — Melt one-quarter cup butter, add one tablespoonful flour, one-half teaspoonful salt, a few grains cayenne; pour on gradually one cup thin cream, add meat from a good-sized lobster cut in cubes, and when heated add one beaten egg and two table-spoonfuls madeira wine.

Shrimp and Peas. — Melt four tablespoonfuls butter, and add three tablespoonfuls flour mixed with one-half teaspoonful salt and one-eighth teaspoonful pepper; pour on gradually one and one-half cups milk; as soon as sauce thickens, add one cup shrimp broken in pieces and one can of canned peas, drained from their liquor and thoroughly rinsed.

Scalloped Halibut. — Shred one cupful of cold boiled halibut; pour in the food pan one and one-half cups milk and let come to a boil; add butter size of an egg, salt and pepper, then the crumbs of four crackers, and lastly the halibut; let it cook five minutes, then add two hard-boiled eggs chopped fine, and serve on a hot platter with bits of buttered toast.

Welsh Rarebit. — Grate one pint of cheese; sprinkle on it half a teaspoonful of mustard, one-fourth of a teaspoonful of salt, and a speck of cayenne; heap this on slices of buttered toast; put in the hot oven for a few moments, and when the cheese begins to melt, serve at once.—NEW COOK BOOK: *Miss Maria Parloa. Estes & Lauriat, Publishers.*

Welsh Rarebit with Ale. — Put small piece butter in chafing-dish and just melt; add one quart finely chopped new American cheese, melt slowly under light blaze and stir constantly, gradually adding one-half glass ale in small quantities from time to time, stirring in two tablespoonfuls Worcestershire sauce, one tablespoonful French mustard, a dash of paprika, with a little salt; when thoroughly cooked, add one egg previously beaten, allow to cook for a couple of minutes, stirring constantly; serve on toasted bread on hot plates.

Swiss Eggs in Chafing-Dish. — Melt one rounded tablespoonful of butter in the chafing-pan, add one-half cup of milk and cream mixed, or rich new milk if you have no cream; season with walnut catsup or any favorite table sauce; when hot, stir in from one and one-half to two cups of grated cheese, and stir well until it is melted and smooth; then add quickly the slightly beaten eggs, from four to six, and continue the stirring until the egg is set; turn out at once, or serve from the pan, on toast or wafers.—*Mrs. Lincoln.*

INVALID DIET

BLANK PAGE FOR ADDITIONAL RECIPES

XXI.–INVALID DIET.

INVALIDS NEED THE BEST OF DIET; WHAT INVALID DIET SHOULD FURNISH; "SICK-DIET KITCHENS;" HOME COOKING FOR ThÉ SICK. THIRTY RECIPES FOR SICK-ROOM DIET.

WHAT is more disgusting to an invalid than to be served with a liberal supply of food adapted to a laboring man or to a person in robust health? Delicate appetites need to be delicately appealed to with dainty dishes, nicely served. But these dishes must be nourishing and easily digested. In short, the problem in sick-room diet is, how to furnish the patient the most valuable nutrition in the pleasantest form, and with the least tax upon his enfeebled powers.

To meet this need, organized movements have been made in many cities in the line of " Sick-Diet Kitchens." Benevolent contributions and skilled work are the corner-stones of these institutions. The foods are well prepared by competent hands. The sick who choose to purchase delicacies which can be relied on, can find them at these places. Those who are too poor to purchase, but who are deserving, can have them free. Instruction concerning diet for the sick is given also.

But many cannot reach such establishments, and do not care to if they can ; hence the chapter of directions given below. If anywhere in cookery good materials and skillful manipulation are of value it is in cooking for the sick.

RECIPES.

Beef Tea.—One pound of lean beef, cut into small pieces. Put into a jar without a drop of water, cover tightly. set in a pot of cold water. Heat gradually to a boil, and continue this steadily for three or four hours, until the meat is like white rags and the juice all drawn out. Season with salt to taste, and when cold, skim. The patient will often prefer this ice-cold.

Beef Tea, No. 2.—Take lean, juicy beef, chopped very finely; cover with cold water, and set on back of the range for two hours; then draw forward, allowing it to heat gradually; then boil for five minutes. Season and strain.

Mutton Broth.—One pound of lean mutton, cut small; one quart of water, cold; one tablespoonful of rice or barley, soaked in a very little warm water; four tablespoonfuls of milk, salt and pepper, with a little chopped parsley. Boil the meat, unsalted, in the water, keeping it closely covered, until it falls to pieces. Strain it out, add the soaked barley or rice; simmer half an hour, stirring often; stir in the seasoning and the milk, and simmer five minutes after it heats up well, taking care it does not burn. Serve hot, with cream crackers.

Chicken Broth.—Proceed precisely as above, but substitute chicken for mutton.

Chicken Jelly.—Half a raw chicken, pounded with a mallet, bones and meat together; plenty of cold water to cover it well, *about* a quart. Heat slowly in a covered vessel, and let it simmer until the meat is in white rags and the liquid reduced one-half. Strain and press, first through a colander, then through a coarse cloth. Salt to taste, and pepper if you think best; return to the fire, and simmer five minutes longer. Skim when cool. Give to the patient cold— just from the ice—with unleavened wafers. Keep on the ice, or make into sandwiches by putting the jelly between thin slices of bread spread lightly with butter.

Soft Boiled Eggs.—Put in a pan of *boiling* water, and set on a part of the range where they will not boil for several minutes. At the end of that time they will be like jelly, perfectly soft, but beautifully done, and quite digestible by even weak stomachs.

Egg Gruel.—Beat the yelk of one egg with one tablespoonful of sugar; pour one teacupful of boiling water on it; add the white of the egg beaten to a froth, with any seasoning or spice desired. To be taken warm.

Raw Egg.—Break a fresh egg into a glass, beat until very light, sweeten to taste, and add two tablespoonfuls of port wine, then beat again.

Egg Cream.—Beat a raw egg to a stiff froth; add a tablespoonful of white sugar and a half wineglass of good blackberry wine; add half a glass of cream; beat together thoroughly, and use at once.

Indian-meal Gruel.—One tablespoonful of fine Indian-meal, mixed smooth with cold water and a saltspoonful of salt; pour upon this a pint of boiling water and turn into a saucepan to boil gently for half an hour; thin it with boiling water if it thickens too much, and stir frequently; when it is done, a tablespoonful of cream or a little new milk may be put in to cool it after straining, but if the patient's stomach is weak it is best without either. Some persons like it sweetened and a little nutmeg added, but to many it is more palatable plain.

Oatmeal Gruel.—Soak a handful of oatmeal over night in water, in order that the acid gases which oatmeal contains may be withdrawn. Pour off the water, and add a pint of fresh; stir it well, add salt, and boil an hour and a half. This is much used, prepared in this way, by dyspeptics.

Sago.—Soak and wash it well; add a pint of water, a little salt, and boil till clear. Add lemon-juice or wine, if permitted.

Arrow-root Jelly.—Boil a pint of water with a few bits of cinnamon or yellow rind of lemon; stir into it two table-spoonfuls of arrow-root, dissolved in a little water; boil ten minutes; strain, salt, and season with sugar, wine, and nutmeg, if proper.

Arrow-root Broth.—Put half a pint of water into a saucepan; add a little lemon-juice, sugar and nutmeg, and a very little salt. Boil it up, and stir in a teaspoonful of dissolved arrow-root; boil five minutes. It should be taken warm and be very thin.

Cracked Wheat.—To one quart of hot water take one small teacupful of cracked wheat and a little salt; boil slowly for half an hour, stirring occasionally to prevent burning. Serve with sugar and cream or new milk.

Cracker Panada.—Six Boston crackers, split; two table-spoonfuls of white sugar, a good pinch of salt, and a little nutmeg; enough *boiling* water to cover them well. Split the crackers, and pile in a bowl in layers, salt and sugar scattered among them. Cover with boiling water and set on the hearth, with a close top over the bowl, for at least an hour. The crackers should be almost clear and soft as jelly, but not broken. Eat from the bowl with more sugar sprinkled in.

Bread Panada.—Set a little water on the fire in a very clean saucepan; add a glass of wine, if allowed, some sugar, nutmeg, and lemon-peel. The moment it boils up stir in a few crumbs of stale baker's loaf. Let it boil very fast for five minutes. It should be only thick enough to drink.

Chicken Panada.—Boil a chicken; take a few bits of the breast and pound fine in a mortar. Season it with a little salt, a grate of nutmeg, and a bit of lemon-peel; boil gently till a little thick, but so that it can be drank.

Soft Toast.—Some invalids like this very much indeed, and nearly all do when it is nicely made. Toast well, but not too brown, a couple of thin slices of bread; put them on a warm plate and pour over *boiling* water; cover quickly with another plate of the same size, and drain the water off; remove the upper plate, butter the toast, put it in the oven one minute, and then cover again with a hot plate and serve at once.

Milk Porridge.—Two cupfuls of best oatmeal, two cupfuls of water, two cupfuls of milk. Soak the oatmeal over night in the water; strain in the morning, and boil the water half an hour. Put in the milk with a little salt, boil up well, and serve. Eat warm, with or without powdered sugar.

Thickened Milk.—With a little milk, mix smooth a tablespoonful of flour and a pinch of salt. Pour upon it a quart of boiling milk, and when both are thoroughly mingled put all back into the saucepan and boil up once, being careful not to burn, and stirring all the time to keep it perfectly smooth and free from lumps. Serve with slices of dry toast. It is excellent in diarrhœa, and becomes a specific by scorching the flour before mixing with the milk.

Toast Water.—Toast stale bread until quite brown, but do not burn it; put it into a large bowl, and pour over it boiling water; let it stand for an hour or so, strain, and put in a piece of ice before drinking.

Barley Water.—Soak one pint of barley in lukewarm water for a few minutes; then drain off the water. Put the barley in three quarts of cold water and cook slowly until the barley is quite soft, skimming occasionally. This barley water, when cold, flavor with a little jelly or lemonade.

Rice Milk.—Pick and wash the rice carefully; boil it in water until it swells and softens; when the water is partly boiled away, add some milk. It may be boiled entirely in milk, by setting the vessel in which the rice is in boiling water; sweeten with white sugar and season with nutmeg. It also may be thickened with a little flour or beaten egg.

Flaxseed Tea.—One-half pound of flaxseed, one-half pound of rock candy, and three lemons pared and sliced; pour over this two quarts of boiling water; let it stand until very cold; strain before drinking. This is good for a cough.

Appleade.—Cut two large apples in slices, and pour on them one pint of boiling water; strain well and sweeten. Ice it before drinking.

Apple Water.—Roast two large, tart apples until they are soft. Put them in a pitcher, pour a pint of cold water on them, and let them stand in a cool place for an hour. No sweetening is needed. This drink will be found very refreshing if the patient have fever or eruptive diseases.

Roast Apples.—Good-sized, juicy, tart apples are best for roasting. Wipe them clean, and put in a slow oven, allowing an hour for the work of roasting. When entirely done, sift fine, white sugar over them, and serve warm or cold, as desired.

Wine Whey.—Sweeten one pint of milk to taste, and when boiling throw in two wineglassfuls of sherry; when the curd forms, strain the whey through a muslin bag into tumblers

Blackberry Sirup.—One quart of blackberry juice, one pound of sugar, one-half ounce of nutmeg, one-half ounce of cinnamon, one-fourth of an ounce of cloves, one-fourth of an ounce of allspice.

XXII. — HEALTH.

NO attempt will be made in this chapter to give instruction as to the treatment of the sick. When any member of the family is so ill that the experience of the housewife does not indicate the treatment to be adopted, a physician is the only competent instructor.

Two-thirds of the diseases that afflict humanity are preventable, and the occupant of no other station in life has such influence over the well-being of humanity as has the housekeeper. This being so, those who stand in this high position should perfect themselves in the knowledge of the principles of right living.

The essentials to healthful living, while few in number, are too often overlooked or neglec ed. They may be stated, in a general way, as follows, although each is in some measure dependent upon the others: Pure air, water free from pollution, good food, clean surroundings, exercise and recreation, proper clothing. When careful regard for these is maintained, sickness will be a rare visitor.

If, in any way, the human body be deprived of air for only a few minutes, death is the result. Normal out-of-doors air contains a certain percentage of oxygen, and so delicate is the balance of the human system that any decrease in this amount of oxygen in the air, by even a very small amount, quickly causes a serious disturbance of the vital functions.

When the climatic conditions permit of the windows being kept open, the ventilation of the house takes care of itself; but at other times it must be carefully attended to.

The heating of the house is closely connected with the subject of ventilation, and the theory that any kind of a heating apparatus or system is all right if it but keep the house warm, should be abandoned. The heating and ventilating of public halls, theatres, etc., where a few of the family go for a few hours occasionally, is regulated by strict laws enacted in the interest of the public health. How much more important is it that the house we live in, where all of us spend from eight to twelve hours every day, should be properly warmed and ventilated !

While it is true that man can live without water for a longer time than he can without air, impure water is as surely disastrous in its effects upon the human system as impure air. In cities and towns where there is a public water works, the purity of the water from this source can usually be depended upon, in so far as public oversight can guarantee it, and is always to be preferred to water taken from wells or springs within populated districts. Where there is no public water works and the supply is obtained from wells, springs, cisterns or streams, great care should be taken to make sure that no pollution of the supply can have taken place. If there is the slightest doubt as to the purity of the water supply, whatever the source, it should be purified before using by some approved method.

Undoubtedly among all the things that make for the health of the family, none is of greater importance than pure food properly prepared. The well-nourished individual has little to fear from disease, and the selection and preparation of the food for the family may well receive from the housewife the attention that its importance deserves. At the present day, when the housekeeper has such a variety of food supplies, either wholly or partly ready to eat, as well as those which are wholly unprepared, from which to choose, it should be a matter of care and attention only to find the food that will agree with and properly nourish each member of the family.

Clean surroundings.—By this term is meant, not simply clean to the eye, but actually clean. The dirt that is visible to the eye is exposed to the light and air, and is rapidly disinfected by these agents. It is the dirt that hides under carpets and in dark corners, that lodges in the cracks of the wood finish of the sink-room and bath-room, that is a source of constant menace to the health of the family. For this reason closely joined hardwood floors and rugs are to be preferred to carpets, and some wall-finish similar to tile is to be preferred over the usual deep-jointed wood-finish.

Outside the house the surroundings should receive as much attention as is bestowed upon the living rooms, for the air in those rooms cannot be pure if the outside air is polluted with decaying waste products. Kitchen garbage should not be allowed to stand in open tubs near the back door, and all pipes and drains, both within and without the house, should be constructed and maintained in accordance with well-established sanitary practice.

The house should be well screened against flies and mosquitoes, for it is now definitely known that these insects are carriers of disease, and all breeding or swarming places for these insects about the premises should be done away with.

Exercise and recreation.—These are exceedingly important helps in maintaining health, and each member of the family should each day engage for a time in such exercise, game or amusement as will give them a complete change from what they know as work. If this recreation or exercise takes them into the open air, so much the better.

By proper clothing is meant clothing in which one feels neither too warm nor too cold. A person should be so clothed that, as near as possible, the clothing is not thought of. Many people heap clothes upon themselves and their children, creating conditions of too free perspiration, and then wonder why they feel and are subject to the cold.

When, for any cause, sickness comes to any member of the family, accompanied with symptoms which are unfamiliar, or which are known to be grave, consult the physician at once. Nevertheless, for the treatment of those cases with which the housewife has had experience, and for use in emergencies, there are certain supplies and appliances that should be in every home. Approved preparations for the treatment of a simple cold; a cough; indigestion and colic; constipation; diarrhœa. An approved purgative. Some safe preparation to induce sleep. In families where there are children, there should always be remedies for use in cases of croup or convulsions.

In addition to the above, there are certain medical and surgical appliances that should be kept in every home, as they are likely to be needed from time to time, and, when needed, must be had promptly. They include: ᴀ clinical thermometer; a hot-water bag of at least three quarts' capacity; a hand bulb syringe; a hard rubber syringe of about four ounces' capacity; an atomizer; a rubber ice-bag; a glass dropper; a measuring glass; a glass feeding-tube; antiseptic gauze, and some approved disinfectant and germicide for dressing all wounds, burns and sores, however trivial they may appear; a surgeon's scissors; tweezers.

XXIII.—MARKETING.

OPPORTUNITIES vary so in different localities, that general rules about marketing are hard to frame. In rural places the butcher drives to the door, and the customer must be content with what is found in the wagon.

To know the parts of the animals sold in the markets, and to understand their relative value and most economical uses, is the first requisite in successful marketing. Cutting of animals varies somewhat among butchers of different places, but the chart given below will fairly set forth the usual methods of cutting, and the ordinary designations of the several portions.

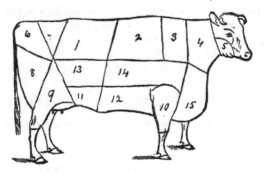

CHART ILLUSTRATING THE CUTTING OF BEEF.

In explanation of the illustration of the cutting of beef the following notes will suffice:

No. 1.—The choice cut of the beef, the *Sirloin*, containing the kidneys and the tenderloin. These are the finest pieces of roasting and steak meat.

No. 2.—The *Standing Rib* piece, also a choice roasting portion, which includes about eleven of the ribs.

No. 3.—The *Chuck Ribs*, also used for roasting, but of a less desirable quality and usually sold at a lower price.

No. 4.—The neck, with considerable bone, used generally for stewing and for pot roast.

No. 5.—The *Cheek*, or jowl, a fleshy part, used for stewing or for boiling.

No. 6.—The *Rump*, sometimes cut differently from the manner shown in the diagram, which is the usual cutting at the East, for domestic purposes. This part has very little bone and is generally used for choice steaks, and the portion next the tail, left from the steak cutting, is a choice piece for corning.

No. 7.—The *Pin-bone*, a choice piece for roasting, being very tender.

No. 8.—The *Round*, which furnishes common steaks, and is the choice cut for dried beef or for corning.

No. 9.—The *Leg*, the choice soup piece.

No. 10.—The *Shin*, also used for soup.

No. 11.—The *Thin flank*, used for boiling and for corning.

No. 12.—The *Brisket*, used for corning.

No. 13.—The *Plate*, used for family boiling and for corning.

No. 14.—The *Plate* (thick end), extending under the shoulder, used for corning and family boiling.

No. 15.—The *Breast*, or butt end of the brisket, also called the "sticking piece." Used for corning and soup-meat.

If the cutting vary materially from this plan, it is still true that the essential parts of the animal continue to exist and are for sale under some name and in some shape. A polite inquiry of any reputable butcher will secure the desired information as to any part. By this means a person may secure intelligent skill in purchasing beef. Some special points concerning beef need a moment's attention.

The *Tongue* is used fresh, salted, or smoked. It is a very

desirable and delicate portion, suitable for table use at almost any time. The *Tail*, which affords some meat and much gelatinous substance, is prized for soups, ox-tail soup especially being founded upon it. The *Heart* and *Liver* are used for food—the former being stuffed and roasted, the latter being fried, usually with onions. The *Tripe*, which is the lining of the large, or receiving stomach of the beef, is used for souse, for pepper-pot, etc. It is a cheap article. The *Kidneys* of beef are sold separate from the sirloin, from which they are cut. They are used for stewing, etc. *Suet*, used for pie-crust, plum-puddings, mince-meat, etc., is the solid, clear fat, which incloses the kidney. When pure it is a very desirable article. The *Feet* are used for jellies, though not so delicate as the calf's foot. The *Head* is refuse. The *Marrow-bones* are those of the shin, leg, and round. Any of the round, hollow bones contain marrow. The other remains of beef are refuse, except as available for manufacturing purposes.

VEAL.

Veal is a favorite meat. Consult the points concerning it made upon page 76. Veal is cut as shown below.

No. 1.—*Loin*, the best end. It is the favorite roasting piece, and furnishes the choice chops. It commands the best price.

No. 2.—*Fillet*, or cutlet piece. This too is a choice part, being excellent for steaks and for roasting and filling. It is also very fine for a cold cut.

CHART ILLUSTRATING THE CUTTING OF VEAL.

No. 3.—The *Leg*, called knuckle also, used chiefly for stewing and for soup.

No. 4.—The *Rack*, used for chops, and for roasting; less

20

desirable and lower priced than the loin, having more bone.

No. 5.—The *Neck*, used for stewing, pies, etc. The best end is quite desirable, that nearer the head being of less value.

No. 6.—*Head.* The brains and tongue are prized by many, the former for frying as a delicacy, the latter for boiling. The head, as a whole, is used in mock turtle and some other fancy soups.

No. 7.—The *Shoulder*, used for roasting, for which it answers a good purpose. It is valuable for a stew also.

No. 8.—The *Breast.* This is the second choice piece for stuffing and roasting. It is too valuable for pies, stews, etc.

No. 9.—The *Shin.* This usually goes with the shoulder, with which it is often roasted. If used separately, it answers fairly well for stewing.

The *Sweetbread*, a very delicate portion, belongs with the breast. It is often sold separately, however. The *Kidneys* are sold with the loin, in the fat of which they are imbedded. The *Heart* and *Liver* are great delicacies for frying, or the heart for stuffing and roasting. The *Feet* are the basis of genuine calves-foot jelly, and are much prized for this purpose. The *Entrails*, cut open and well cleaned, are made into souse by some persons.

MUTTON.

Next to beef, the most profitable and healthful meat is mutton. In all markets this meat is cut substantially in the same manner as shown in the following chart. The names and ordinary uses of the parts are as follows:

No. 1.—The *Loin*, best end. This is the choice piece for filling and roasting and for prime chops. Of course, it commands the best price.

No. 2.—The *Leg*. This joint is nearly always used for roasting and chops, sometimes also for boiling. It has but little bone, as compared with the other parts of the animal, and is, therefore, an economical piece to select, though the price per pound be greater than that of any other cut. It is common to find a good leg weighing from seven to twelve pounds.

No. 3.—The *Loin*, second choice. This furnishes " French

CHART ILLUSTRATING THE CUTTING OF MUTTON.

chops," a favorite dish in eating-houses, and is specially good for a roast.

No. 4.—The *Loin*, rump end. Good for roasting and boiling. It contains considerable bone.

No. 5.—The *Shoulder*, used for boiling and for filling and roasting. It is less in price and nearly as good as the leg, but it has more bone.

No. 6.—The *Breast*, used for stews and for meat pies. A savory, juicy part.

No. 7.—The *Flank*. A continuation of the breast, but somewhat thinner. This with the breast makes a cheap roast, which may be split and filled.

No. 8.—The *Rack*. The best end of the rack is used for second-rate chops. The neck end of the rack is good for stewing only.

No. 9.—The *Neck*. This, with the neck end of the rack, is for stewing only.

No. 10.—The *Head*. The tongue only is used, the re
mainder being refuse.

It is customary to split mutton down the back, and then
to split each half into parts called hind and fore quarters.
The saddle is the middle portion before this quartering is
done. Part of it goes with each quarter.

The hind quarter of mutton, consisting of the leg and
the loin, is the choice quarter. It makes a very superior
large roast, while either of its parts, the leg or the loin, suf·
fices nicely for a small company. A hind quarter from an
animal in good condition will weigh from twenty to thirty
pounds. The *Kidneys* are used as in beef, so also the heart
and liver. The other parts are refuse.

LAMB.

Lamb is cut as mutton, but it is usually dressed with
more care, so as to present a more attractive appearance.
Lamb proper is in market in the spring only. As the season advances older lamb is in market, but what is called
" lamb " in the winter months is usually poor mutton
dressed lamb style. The butcher indulges in a quiet smile
when his customer, in the winter season, asks for and pays
for " lamb." Of course, the superiority and rarity of lamb
demand for it the best
prices. Indeed,"fancy
prices " reign in lamb.
For tests, see p. 82.

CHART ILLUSTRATING THE CUTTING OF
PORK.

PORK.

Fresh pork and salt
pork are much used.
General facts on pork
are given on page 85.
The usual method of cutting for domestic use is shown in
the accompanying cut. For packing a somewhat different
method is pursued.

No. 1.—The *Ham*, the most valuable part of the hog.

When nicely cured it is a very great delicacy. It is a great article of commerce also.

No. 2.—*Sirloin*, furnishing chops and the finest roasting pieces.

No. 3.—*Rack*, used for second-rate chops and roasts, the meat being as sweet, but the bone being greater than in the sirloin.

No. 4.—*Neck*, used for inferior roasting, and for boiling when fresh, and also for corning.

No. 5.—The *Shoulder.* A fair roasting piece, but chiefly used, like the ham, for pickling and curing, though it is greatly inferior to ham in juiciness and flavor. Either fresh or corned it is a fine boiling piece.

No. 6.—The *Jowl.* Useful for smoking. Sometimes cured with the tongues remaining in them.

No. 7.—The *Head.* Used for puddings and head cheese.

No. 8.—The *Belly* or *Flitch.* A good boiling piece either fresh, salted, or smoked.

No. 9.—*Feet.* These are much used for souse and for pickling. They contain so much gelatinous matter that they are exceedingly desirable.

The *Ears* also are used for souse and head cheese. The *Liver*, *Heart*, and *Kidneys* are used for liver pudding. The *Entrails*, nicely cleaned, are used for sausage skins. The *Fat* about the kidneys furnishes leaf lard. The other fat furnishes common lard. The other parts are refuse.

VENISON.

If the marketer desires venison, it is well to remember that buck venison is best from August 1st to November 1st, and that doe venison is best from the latter date to January 1st, after which no deer should be killed. It is quite common, however, to freeze deer meat, and to keep it for months in that state. This adds to the cost, but it also improves the fibre of the meat.

Venison is cut into parts respectively designated haunch,

saddle, leg, loin, fore-quarter, and steaks. The latter should not be cut until ready for use. Venison should be fat. It cannot be too fat. Its flavor is better after hanging a few days, but it should not become rank. To test this, pierce it with a skewer and notice the odor. Shun tough venison.

For roasting, choose the haunch, the saddle, the neck, or the shoulder. Cut steaks from the leg. Stew the shoulder, or any part which is too thin for satisfactory roasting.

POULTRY.

Tests of poultry are given on page 61. But the expedients resorted to in order to mislead purchasers are so numerous that even experts are not wholly safe. Technically, the term *chickens* belongs to fowls under a year old, but actually, the entire tribe is included in the name. *Capons* are young roosters, gelded and carefully fed so as to secure the utmost delicacy of flesh. *Pullets* are young hens.

Turkeys reach their maturity in eight or nine months, and hence young, but well-grown turkeys, are in market about the fall and winter holidays. Young hen turkeys are regarded as best, being fatter and more juicy; but the male turkeys will be larger for the same age. The legs of young turkeys are black; of old ones reddish and rough. Young cocks have small spurs; old ones large spurs and very rough legs. Fat turkeys, with broad, full breasts, are preferable. Soft, pliable feet indicate fresh-killed birds.

Wild turkeys are deemed to be finer in flavor than tame ones. They are in season in November, December, and January. They are usually sold with their feathers on. Small birds have their well-defined seasons, as have other kinds of game, but they admit little choice except as fresh.

VEGETABLES.

Every good marketer will supply his table with a variety of vegetables all the year round. There is hardly a vegetable that cannot be had in our markets at any season, either fresh or canned. Railroads and steamers connect the different climates so closely that one hardly knows whether he is eating fruits and vegetables in or out of their natural season. But it takes a long purse to buy fresh vegetables at the North while the ground is yet frozen. Still, there are so many vegetables that keep through cold weather that if we did not have new ones from the South, there would be, nevertheless, a variety from which to choose. Late in the spring, when the old vegetables begin to shrink and grow rank, we greatly appreciate what comes from the South.

If one has a good, dry cellar, it is wise to procure in the fall vegetables enough for all winter. But if the cellar is warm, vegetables will sprout and decay before half the cold months have passed. Those best adapted for winter keeping are onions, squashes, turnips, beets, carrots, parsnips, cabbages, and potatoes. Squashes and onions should be kept in a very dry room. The others will keep readily in a cool, dry cellar, or bedded in sand beneath the reach of frost.

If vegetables be bought as needed, care must be used to get them in good condition. In season, they should never appear wilted, but should be fresh and crisp. At no time should they be used if suffering from decay. The utmost prudence is needed at this point. A very little waste will more than counterbalance all you save by purchasing large quantities, and by storing for the winter.

The luxuries of the world are spread at the feet of the customer in our markets; still, extravagant expenditure is by no means necessary. Many delicacies are within the reach of all. Those who content themselves with sending to the markets, miss many golden opportunities. Those who go, see for themselves, and embrace many a favoring chance. Personal observation ripens into experience also, and the experienced purchasers command the situation.

These remarks apply with equal force to purchasing of the grocer, the baker, the milkman, and all, in short, who supply us with the necessaries of life. There are reliable dealers and those of doubtful integrity; but in every case the hope of the household is in its provider. Cultivate power in this line.

It is best to deal steadily with persons whom you have tried and found reliable. Do not relinquish your independence, so as to suggest to them the idea that they may impose on you. Be ready to go elsewhere, if the old service falls off; but usually those who are regular dealers at a place get the best attention, and errors or failures can be rectified with ease.

In all marketing and dealing with storekeepers keep your temper. To lose one's temper and scold or threaten, is undignified and worse than useless. State your grievances calmly and plainly. If they are redressed, all right; if not redressed, you can quietly go elsewhere and bestow your patronage. A little suspension of trade with a dealer often works wonders. He does not want to lose customers; but such is the waywardness of human nature, that all of us need reminders to keep us fully up to duty. Let the dealer have these when he needs them, but never at the expense of your own self-possession and courteous dignity.

XXIV.—CARVING.

EVERY person who travels or visits much sees number-
less illustrations of the varied capacities of carvers.
Hotel and restaurant life does not make much display
in this line, as the carving is done out of sight. And yet
even here the marvelous thinness of the slice, which is so
immense in its area, demonstrates that somebody is on hand
who is expert in this line. In private houses the meat and
the poultry are sometimes carved before they come to the
table. By whom done, or with what accompaniments of perspiration and emphatic words, the guests know not. But
meat served thus is chilled and juiceless, and generally dam-
aged. It is worthy of better treatment.

Many amusing and not a few irritating examples of
clumsy carving occur under everybody's eyes. Meat is condemned as tough, knives as dull, dishes as too small, there
is too much gravy, skewers are not drawn, and a thousand
other reasons are blurted out by the clumsy carver, as he
outwardly sweats and inwardly swears at his task. He slops
gravy on to the cloth; he drops part of the meat from the
dish; he cuts himself by an unfortunate slip of the knife;
and sometimes, like a distinguished wit of whom the story
tells, he lands a fowl in the lap of a lady beside him,
though probably, unlike that wit, he will not have the grace
to say, " I will thank you, madam, to return that chicken."

Every housekeeper should learn to carve. Carving should
be done at the table by the gentleman of the house, or, in his

absence, by the lady, unless some other of the family be an expert carver. Unless a guest is known to be an expert, or unless he volunteers for the duty, he should not be expected to carve. He may be a clumsy hand, and the courtesy of hospitality should protect him from exposure at this point.

The carver at a private table should retain his seat while carving and serving. To facilitate this, his chair should be high, so that he can reach readily to his work. The dish should be large enough to prevent soiling the cloth, except by some unusual accident. The centre of a carving-dish for roast meats should be raised nearly as high as the surrounding edge, so that a horizontal movement of the knife in slicing may be made without interference from the edges. No man can slice meat neatly if the meat is in the bottom of a deep dish, into which he must scoop with his knife as best he may. Elevate the meat, but have a surrounding depression between the centre and the edge, where the rich juices of the meat may accumulate, and where they may be served readily.

Not all knives are suitable for carving, nor is any one knife just the thing for all work in this line. For slicing, a long, thin, broad blade is essential. With a fine roast, elevated on the dish, and with a good, sharp slicing knife in hand, a cool-headed man can hardly help doing neat and rapid work.

But such a knife is not the one for poultry or rib carving. For these uses a shorter blade, which is both narrower and stiffer, must be employed. All knives for carving must be sharp. There should be a good steel at hand to touch up the edge—nothing more, for a dull knife should be ground, or whet up on an oil-stone. Any large fork, with a guard to prevent accidents, will do. A rest for the knife and fork when not in use is desirable. The carver's requisites, therefore, are as follows: A high chair, suitable serving plates, two sharp knives, a good fork, and a knife and fork rest. With these he is ready for work. Without them he is at serious disadvantage.

Carving a Turkey.—Nothing delights an expert carver more than the opportunity to cut up a fine roast turkey. Such a man is in doubt whether the eating of the meat even is the greater luxury.

Whether the head of the bird shall lie to the carver's right or left is an open question. Better to the right, as more work is required on the head end, and in this position the knife-hand works less over the hand which holds the fork.

The fork should be inserted astride of the breast-bone, just back of its most promi-nent point. It should be sunk deep enough to pene-trate the encasing bone be-low the white meat. This secures full command of the bird. If the company be small and the bird fairly

TURKEY PROPERLY TRUSSED FOR ROASTING.

large, better do all the cutting from one side, reserving the other in as perfect a form as possible.

Remove all the limbs first unless half the bird is to be reserved. The neat cut is to remove each drum-stick, or lower leg, by a single stroke of the knife, which must ex-actly hit the joint. To remove the thigh, or upper leg joint, make a V-shaped cut, wide enough at the point whence the drum-stick has been cut to include all the meat, but converging at the joint, which can always be distinctly seen near the back. Two strokes of the knife do this work, each of them cutting down to the carcase. A slight outward pressure of the knife-blade, applied between the carcase and the upper point of the thigh joint, will cause it to drop off neatly on the plate. Outside the lines of these cuts, flakes of dark meat will remain adhering to the carcase, which should now be cut off. They help to meet demands for dark meat.

In carving the wings, the neat stroke removes the lower part, which contains the two bones, by cutting at the inner part of the joint, and so turning the blade of the knife as to throw that part off in the direction opposite to its natural movement. The first joint of each wing then follows, the cut being deep enough to fully reach the ball and socket joint. A slight motion of the pinion toward the head of the bird will suffice usually to detach this part. If it does not, the point of the knife may be thrust into the socket of the joint to sever the cartilage. This will free it.

When this dismembering is accomplished, proceed to slice the breast meat in thin, broad slices. Clean off all the white meat, unless part only is needed. Placing your knife close to the front of the breast-bone, and cutting toward the neck, you will dislodge the V-shaped bone, corresponding to the "merrythought" or "pull-bone" of chickens. To dislodge the collar-bones is to many a hard task. But cut the cartilages which bind them to the frame of the bird. These cartilages are in the cavity between the neck and the breast-bone. Through this cavity, thrust your knife outwardly under one of these bones; make a fulcrum of the front part of breast-bone, and a lever of the knife, its edge resting on the fulcrum. You can then easily pry up the troublesome bone and turn it off to the side. This movement takes the bone at the best mechanical advantage. It must come, and come at once, if this movement be made.

Now attend to the other end of the bird. Shave off all superfluous meat from the carcase. Turn the carcase on its side, the back toward you. Insert your knife beside the oil-bag and thrust it forward parallel to the spine. It will cut its way very easily. A slight outward movement of the knife will then throw off these side bones, which are choice pieces, yielding the juiciest of the dark meat. The ribs may now be cut through with ease from front to rear, about midway from breast to back. The breast-bone is incapable of further division, but the back easily divides into six parts. Turn it back up and hold with the fork; separate the oil-bag, about an inch of the spine with it; lift the projecting spine with the knife back and it will break readily, carrying one rib with it. Cut off from each side of the remaining spine the rib parts adherent to it; then divide the remaining spine just back of the neck.

An entire drum-stick, or second joint, need not be served to any one person, but had better be divided among several. A fair-sized turkey divided on the above method will furnish a good supply for twenty people.

BACK OF A FOWL.

[*a, b,* line of easy break-age. *a, c, e,* and *b, d, f,* lines of sepa-ration of side-bones. *a, g, b, h,* rib por-tion.

It will be asked, however, how can one become so expert in hitting these joints? Frequently the carver tries, and tries again, but tries in vain, to strike the right place for his knife. There is one way only to succeed in this art. The anatomy of the turkey or chicken, or any other animal, must be carefully studied. Do it in this way. Whenever a turkey is brought into your house and is made ready for the roasting, place it on its back, as it will lie on the plate when it comes to the table. Carefully manipulate it, and note exactly where every joint lies. Imagine yourself about to carve it. Where would you put the knife to throw off that drum-stick? How would you cut to throw off the thigh bone. Read the preceding directions; apply them in fancy to the bird as you see and handle it; then carry it all out at the table when the bird is cooked.

No surgeon could do his work except he had thus prac-ticed on actual subjects in dissection. He must know by actual trial just what to do and how to do it. So must the carver know. Chickens, ducks, geese, small birds, meat, roasting pigs, every article, in short, which he expects to carve must be understood beforehand; then success will be his.

Carving Roast Chicken.—The same course precisely as has been prescribed for carving turkey must be followed with chickens. The only difference is in the formation of the " pull-bone " or " merrythought," but this makes no difference whatever in the cutting of the bird.

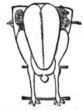

CHICKEN PROPER-
LY TRUSSED FOR
ROASTING.
[Feet may be removed at option.]

Carving Roast Ducks and Geese.—These are more difficult than turkey or chickens, for the reason that they are constitutionally more sinewy in the joints and they have far less flesh proportionately.

GOOSE PROPERLY TRUSSED FOR
ROASTING.

They are barrel-shaped, with thin layers of meat instead of the fine masses of flesh found on the turkey or on fine chickens. The leg joints lie farther to the rear, and higher on the side than in land fowls. They are not so easily reached, therefore

Their anatomy must be studied, however. It is the only way to obtain command of the carcase. In carving, dismember the bird as in other cases. Then cut the meat in long, narrow strips, along the sides and breast of the bird, and use these as the choice cuts. The legs and wings

BREAST OF DUCK
P R O P E R L Y
TRUSSED.
[The lines show the direction of cutting the breast meat.]

BACK OF DUCK
P R O P E R L Y
TRUSSED.
[Feet twisted to lie on the back.]

may be given out if desired or if the supply be short. Duck is but a side dish, however ; it is supposed to be served with other dishes, and so to be served lightly. Goose is some-times the main piece, but not often so at elaborate feasts.

Carving Broiled Chickens.—Chickens for broiling are pre-sumably young and tender. If not, thorough steaming before they are broiled will do something for them. They are trussed in such shape usually that joints are not easily struck. But study the bird when trussed. See where joints do lie and cut them. If the birds are really young and ten-der, however, they may be halved or quartered, cutting through the bones directly and so serving them.

Carving Smaller Birds.—Smaller birds which need carving, may simply be split longitudinally, just beside the breast-bone and the spine. Their bones can be cut easily. This will apply to pigeon, partridge, prairie hen, pheasant, etc.

SMALLER BIRD PROPERLY TRUSSED FOR ROASTING.

Carving Roast Beef.—Pieces of roast beef vary so that no one rule covers all. A safe general direction, however, is to study carefully just what is in the piece before it is cooked. Know your meat before you attempt to carve it. Another general rule, applicable to all meats indeed, is to cut across the grain in all cases. Meat cut with the grain is stringy and fibrous. If cut across the grain, all the longi-tudinal flakes of flesh and the minute sinews are cut so short that any toughness existing in them is wholly con-cealed. The first slice, by this process, will always be a brown, outside cut. Slices should always be thin, but not so as to seem ragged. In carving ribs of beef the knife may be thrust along close to the ribs, so as to separate the meat from them. The cuts then made across the grain will separate the slices with ease and neatness. Never cut beef across the bone. It is the easiest way, but also the poorest.

Carving Roasts of Mutton.—A leg of mutton is carved as a ham, by cutting down to the bone, from the outer edge, making the cuts converge on the bone, so freeing each slice as it is cut.

A shoulder of mutton should be carved as the leg. In each case, when the choice cuts are exhausted, clip off the remaining meat as best you can, always across the grain.

Saddle of mutton is carved in several ways: 1st, in longitudinal slices along the backbone; 2d, by transverse slices, each taking in a rib, which makes thick and clumsy portions; 3d, by oblique slices, not taking in the bones, but forming a slight angle with them. The latter method is deemed preferable by most carvers.

In all roasts which include the ribs the backbone should be well and cleanly cut through by the butcher, between every pair of ribs. Otherwise no satisfactory carving can be done.

Carving Roasts of Lamb.—The cut shows a fore-quarter of lamb with its outer side uppermost. This joint is first to

FORE-QUARTER OF LAMB.

be cut so as to divide the shoulder from the rest of the quarter, which is called the target. For this purpose, put the fork firmly into the shoulder joint, and then cut underneath the blade-bone, beginning at *a*, and continue cutting all around in the direction of the circular line, and pretty close to the under part of the blade-bone. Some cut the shoulder large, while others take off no more meat with it than is barely necessary to remove the blade-bone. It is most convenient to place the shoulder on a separate dish. This is carved in the same way as the shoulder of mutton. When the shoulder is removed, a lemon may be squeezed over that part of the remainder of the joint where the knife has passed ; this gives a flavor to the meat which is generally approved. Then proceed to cut completely through from *b* to *c*, following the line across the bones as cracked by the butcher, and this will divide the ribs (*d*) from the brisket (*e*). Tastes vary in giving preference to the ribs or the brisket.

Other parts of lamb are carved as mutton. The fat is very delicate and should be served to all the guests.

Carving Roasts of Venison.—These resemble roasts of mutton so closely that no different directions for their carving need be given.

Carving Ham.—Boiled or baked ham may be served either side up. The inner edge of the ham, which lay adjacent to the body, is rather more tender than the edge, which lay toward the tail. Slices should be cut directly from the edge to the bone, cutting out the middle portions first. Let the cuts converge upon the bone every time, so that each slice is set free at once. When the choice cuts are gone, trim up the remaining parts neatly as possible, and always across the grain. The knuckle end of a ham furnishes the leaner and drier cuts. Some prefer carving hams with a more slanting cut, rather than a direct, right-angled cut upon the bone, beginning at the thick end, and so continuing throughout. This mode is, however, apt to be very wasteful, unless the carver be careful to take away both fat and lean in due proportion.

Carving Roast Pig.—The cut below represents a pig roasted whole and served in the most approved style. Many, however, separate the head before serving, and garnish the body with the ears, jaw, etc. The head may be severed by a

WHOLE ROAST PIG.

neat cut around the neck, and a little sideward motion, but this is not necessary, as the cheek or jaw can be removed

21

without removing the head.   The shoulder should then be taken off from the body, by passing the knife under it in a circular direction, and the leg separated as shown in the line *d, e, f.*   The ribs may then be divided into two or more parts, helping at the same time an ear or jaw with it, with some of the sauce also.   Pieces may be cut from the legs and shoulders.   Some consider the neck end the finest part, while others give the ribs the preference.

Carving Roast Rabbit.—Begin by cutting longitudinally from head to tail near to the backbone, then make a corresponding cut on the other side of the backbone, leaving the back and the head in one distinct piece.   Cut off the legs at the hip-joint, and take off the wing, or fore leg, nearly as you would the wing of a bird, carrying the knife round in a

circular line.   The ribs are of little importance, as they are bare of meat. Divide the back into three or four equal portions.   The head is then to be cut off, and the lower jaw divided from the upper.   By splitting the upper part of the

RABBIT, OR HARE, PROPERLY TRUSSED
FOR ROASTING.

head in the middle, you have the brains, which are prized by epicures.   The comparative goodness of different parts of a rabbit will depend much on the age, and also upon the cooking.   The back and the legs are always the best parts.

XXV.—SERVING MEALS.

METHODS of serving meals differ widely. The items of conveniences and pecuniary ability always become important elements in the case. Taste, too, enters largely into it.

Square end tables are now the proper style. They should be sufficiently roomy to wholly avoid crowding. A spotlessly white table-cloth should be spread, with padding under it to deaden sound and make a softer appearance. The cloth should not be very stiffly starched, but it should be nicely polished and beautifully glossy. It should hang two feet from the top edge, the corners gathered up, if needs be, to prevent their drooping on the floor. Napkins should be large and heavy. Such texture does not need much starch. The glass and silverware should be perfect in brightness. It may be of inexpensive kind, but it must be scrupulously clean.

Colored table-cloths of ornamental patterns are allowable for luncheon or tea. They are not in place where hot meats are served. Nor are colored napkins. Too often these deep tinted articles are used "to save washing," which means "to conceal dirt." Not unfrequently covers and napkins of this kind are kept in use when their rank odor cries out for the wash-tub, even though their soiled appearance does not. The doily, or D'Oiley, as some will have it from the proper name of its first reputed maker, is a small, colored napkin used with fruits and wines. Stains will not show so readily upon these, but they must always be scrupulously fresh and clean. To conceal filth under rich coloring is sacrilege of the worst sort, but to bring it to the table, and ask guests to wipe their lips with it, is a crime.

A great variety of ornaments and adornments are admissible on a table, but nothing is so pure and so appropriate as a handsome display of ferns or flowers. The flowers should not be just such as ladies wear so profusely and so beautifully in their belts and on their dresses. Larger blooms are preferable for the table, especially those of the pure white and fine texture belonging to the lily family.

It is quite the proper and beautiful thing to place a neat bouquet beside each plate, in tasteful bouquet-holders. For gentlemen the little bunching suitable for the button-hole is desirable. For ladies the belt bouquet will meet the case. The floral centre-piece may be composed of small bouquets, which at the end of the meal may be distributed.

Fruit pieces and handsome confectionery pieces may be disposed to advantage in ornamenting the table. Tasty folding of spotless napkins is so important a decoration that the subject will be treated fully farther on. These may be perched in polished goblets, while bouquets, or small rolls of bread nestle amid their snowy folds. Little arts like these embellish a table, and delight the guests.

But these embellishments must not be overdone. What will be correct for a large table will be too much for a small one, and what will be just right for a small table will look thin and meagre on a large one. Study the proprieties of every occasion. What suits once does not suit forever.

Embellishments may be liberally bestowed upon the dining-room itself. In addition to its permanent decorations, flowers are always admissible. At the great ball on March 20th, 1883, at the Vanderbilt Mansion in New York, the decorations of the supper-room were absolutely regal. The walls were completely hidden with palms and ferns, from which a countless number of orchids were suspended. Two large fountains were introduced into the far corners of the room. The doors of the main entrance to the supper-room were in an open position and were completely covered with roses and lilies of the valley. In the centre of the room a large palm towered almost to the ceiling, and about it from the dome was suspended an immense Bougen Villa vine, the tendrils of which drooped in bunches from the branches of the palm. Throughout the room there were many stands and vases filled with flowers, the entire effect more resembling fairyland than an earthly home. Few can rival such a display, of course, but all enjoy at least a pen-peep upon such princely splendor.

No ornament should be so large as to obscure to any great extent a view of the entire table, or to conceal any of its guests. As many knives, forks, and spoons as will be needed for the various courses may be placed at each plate, though, to avoid the display of so much cutlery, a better style is to supply these accessories as needed. Goblets and wine-glasses, if the latter be used, should be on the table at the start. Large spoons, with salt and pepper casters, should be on the table also. The dessert-plates, finger-bowls, etc., should stand ready on the sideboard, awaiting the time when they shall be needed. The hot closet should be well stocked with dishes needing to be used warm.

Finger-bowls should be half filled with water. In Paris they are served with warm water scented with peppermint. A slice of lemon in cold water answers the purpose entirely, as it removes any grease from fingers or lips. A geranium leaf may float in the water. Its fragrance on the fingers, if it be pressed, will be agreeable. It is customary to place a fruit napkin, or doily, on the dish on which the finger-bowl rests, to avoid the rattle of the bowl, and to protect the dish from injury if it be highly ornamented. Little openworked mats will, however, answer better. Do not summon your company to dinner by a bell. Country hotels and cheap boarding-houses may do that, but not a refined home, especially when guests are present.

Soup is dished by the lady of the house at a home dinner.

Meat is cut and dished by the gentleman of the house. Vegetables, bread, butter, water, etc., are served by the waiter, dessert by the hostess, except in the case of melons, requiring to be cut at the table, which is the work of the host.

Home meals should all be sufficiently ceremonious to dispense with haste and confusion. On the other hand, they should not run into stiffness and frigidity. Bright, cheery, pleasant chat should enliven every meal. If the leading dish be nothing but hash, let it be served in good style and amid a profusion of genial, social sunshine.

WHAT TO AVOID.

1st.—Never use table-linen which is open to the suspicion of being soiled. The napkin-ring business is of questionable propriety. Why not, as at hotels, furnish a clean napkin to each person at every meal?

2d.—Crockery with an abundance of nicks and splints and cracks is not unsightly merely, but, where the glazing is broken, the porous material absorbs grease and dish water, making these spots dense with unsavory and unwholesome matter.

3d.—Partly emptied dishes become unsightly, and sometimes positively repulsive. They look like refuse and scraps. At the great State dinners at the Tuileries, no guest saw a partly emptied dish. A full, beautifully garnished dish was presented for his approval, upon expressing which, his personal plate was taken to a side table and supplied from another serving dish.

4th.—An overloaded table or plate satiates appetite rather than stimulates it. A gracious expectancy of what is to come is a great help at the table.

5th.—A stinted supply is very discouraging. To the apprehension of a lack of food, the moral sense of mortification is added in this case.

6th.—Beware of ill-assorted dinners or tea-parties. An occasion intended to be a pleasure is often a pest for lack of care in this regard. This caution applies to the selection of guests, and more strongly to the disposition of guests at the table. Secure fitness both in the viands presented and in the parties present.

7th.—Do not inaugurate new features at a dinner party, unless you are sure you have the mastery of them, and that when done in a masterly way they will certainly prove agreeable.

8th.—Beware of the delusion that hospitality is expressed by the weight of its beef and mutton, and the multitude and rarity of its viands.

9th.—Have no meddlesome, noisy, or slovenly service. Waiters should be attired neatly, and should wear light shoes or slippers. They should take no part in the social proceedings, not so much, indeed, as to smile at the best things. On formal occasions the man-servant should wear a dress-coat, white vest, and white necktie. The maid-servant should be attired in a neat, inconspicuous dress, with spotless white apron.

10th.—Both haste and slowness should be shunned. At the finished French dinners, the courses will not average more than five minutes each. French waiters are marvel-ously expert, however, in removing and replacing dishes.

GARNISHES.

Much of the attractiveness of a table depends on the *garnishes*, which are added to certain dishes to embellish or beautify them. A few hints on this subject will be of value.

Parsley is the almost universal garnish to all kinds of cold meat, poultry, fish, butter, cheese, etc.

Horse-radish is the garnish for roast beef, and for fish in general; for the latter, slices of lemon are sometimes laid alternately with heaps of horse-radish.

Slices of lemon for boiled fowl, turkey, and fish, and for roast veal and calf's head.

Carrot in slices for boiled beef, hot or cold. They may be cut into ornamental forms if desired.

Barberries, fresh or preserved, for game.

Fried smelts for turbot.

Red beet-root sliced for cold meat, boiled beef, and salt fish.

Fried sausages or force-meat balls for roast turkey, capon, or fowl.

Fennel for mackerel and salmon, whether fresh or pickled.

Lobster coral and parsley for boiled fish.

Currant jelly for game, also for custard or bread-pudding.

Seville oranges in slices for wild ducks, widgeons, teal, and such game.

Mint, either with or without parsley, for roast lamb, whether hot or cold.

Pickled gerkins, capers, or onions, for some boiled meats, stews, etc.

A red pepper, or small red apple, for the mouth of a roast pig.

Spots of red and black pepper alternated on the fat side of a boiled ham, which side should lie uppermost on the serving dish.

Sliced eggs, showing the white and yellow parts, for chicken salad.

Sprays of celery top for salads, cold meats, etc.

Modern Embroidery

Linen and Lace Centerpiece
No. B-149, 23 inches.   On Linen 35 cents.
Lace Materials to Work, $1.25

Send 10 cents for illustrated and instructive Catalogue and Guide to Fancy Work.

A beautiful display of Pillow Tops, Linen and Lace Centerpiece, Doilies, Collars, Handkerchiefs, Bound Goods, etc.   All Embroidery Materials.

WALTER P. WEBBER
73-75 Harwood Street   ::   ::   Lynn, Mass.

INSEPARABLE

from the charm of the turkey is the dressing thereof. It is difficult, however, to make a perfect dressing. It is sometimes too tame, sometimes too strong, again it contains too much of one kind of herb, not enough of another.

BELL'S SPICED SEASONING

overcomes the difficulty. It gives the effect of a dozen different varieties. Made from pure sweet herbs and choice selected spices, it is pure, economical, rich, yet delicate. It makes a perfect dressing every time, appetizing, delicious.

For meats, game and fish; in croquettes, scalloped dishes and soups the housekeeper finds Bell's Seasoning invaluable. It saves time and bother.

Get Bell's from your grocer. Be sure and get Bell's. There are always imitations of a good thing. Ask for our dainty booklet of receipts, every one tested. Sent by mail to any address.

If your grocer cannot supply you, send 10 cents in stamps for a sample can containing enough to flavor the dressing for 100 lbs. of meat or poultry. Please mention where you saw this advertisement.

The WILLIAM G. BELL COMPANY

SOLE PROPRIETORS

50-54 Commercial St., Boston, Mass.